FAMOUS
SEA BATTLES

Above A French and Genoese expedition to Barbary, from a fifteenth-century manuscript.

Endpapers HMS Superb leads the Mediterranean Fleet, 1918, by F. Mason.

Overleaf The Spanish Armada by Henrik Vroom.

LITTLE, BROWN AND COMPANY
Boston Toronto

FAMOUS
SEA BATTLES
DAVID HOWARTH

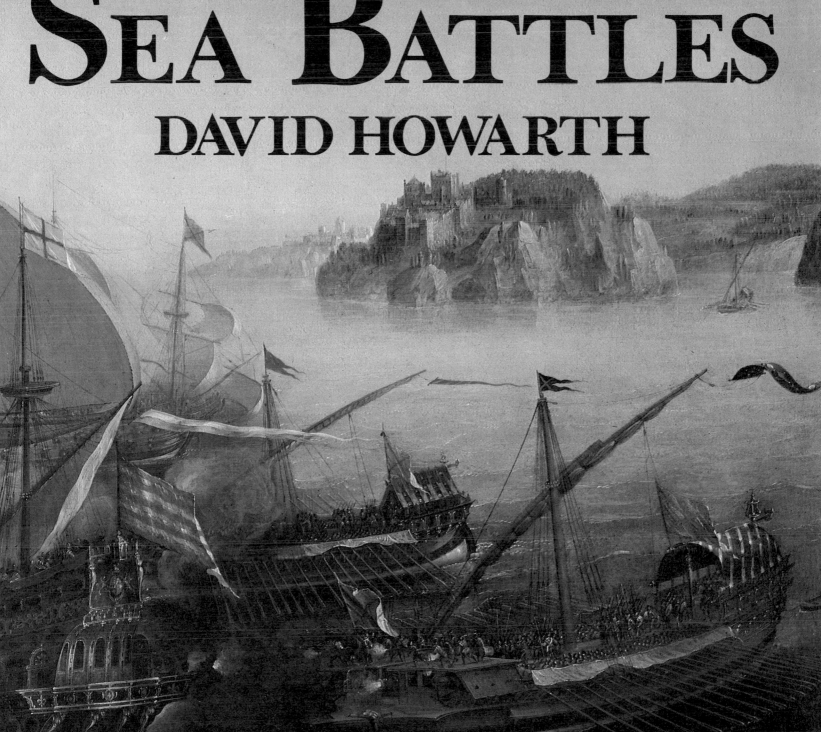

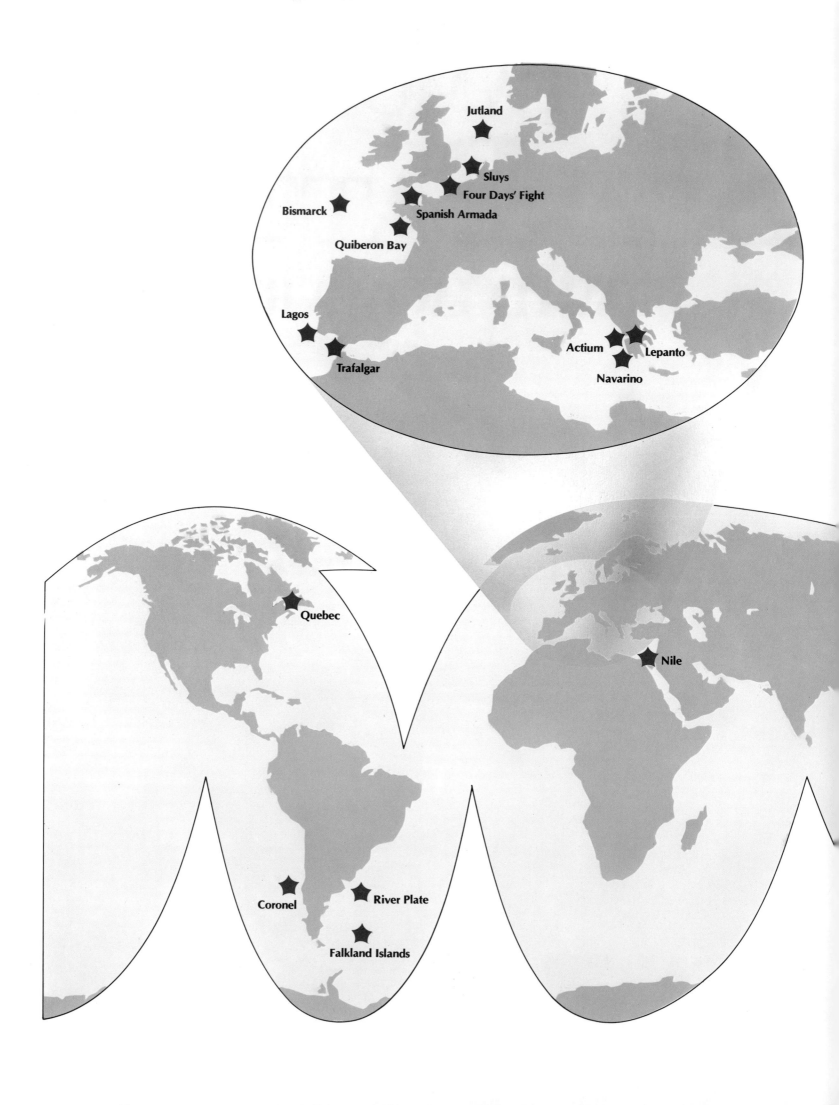

Contents

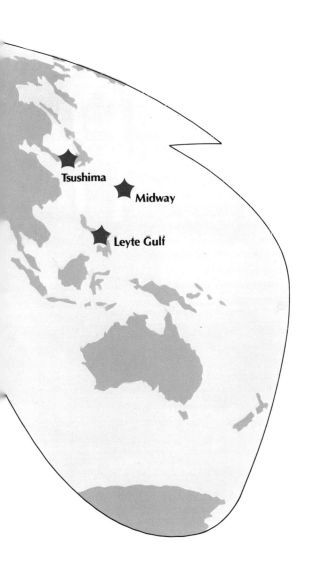

ISBN 0-316-37480-6

FIRST AMERICAN EDITION

PRINTED IN ITALY

Early Battles
31BC – AD1571

FIGHTING IS ALWAYS foolish. But fighting at sea has one advantage over fighting on land: soldiers fight against men, but sailors fight against ships. Of course in a naval battle men get hurt and killed, but that is never the object of the battle: the object is to sink the enemy's ship, and if you succeed your next immediate duty is to rescue the survivors of the enemy's crew. So there is still room in naval warfare for compassion, and the ancient fraternity of sailors. There is seldom any furious enmity: all sailors, of all nations, have a common enemy, the sea.

This duty, to save the lives of one's enemies rather than kill them, has been recognized with very few exceptions for the past four hundred years. It was in the sixteenth century, about the time of the Spanish Armada, that battles at sea were first fought by sailors. Before that, they were fought by soldiers, and sailors were regarded as inferior people whose sole function was to take the soldiers to the scene of battle and put them in an advantageous position for winning it. Sea battles in those early days were therefore just as bloodthirsty as battles on land. Luckily, they very seldom happened. In the 1,600 years from 31 BC to AD 1571, while battles on land decided the fate of nations, not more than half a dozen battles of any importance were fought at sea.

All through that enormous span of time, sea-fighting evolved in two quite separate ways, with different techniques and different ships. In the Mediterranean, battles were fought in galleys built for the purpose, propelled by oars and rowed by slaves or convicts. In northern seas they were fought in the sailing ships that were normally used for trade. There was only a single occasion when Mediterranean and northern ships and sailors met and fought each other. That was off Acre during the Crusades in 1191. The period began and ended with galley battles of the Mediterranean type, the Battle of Actium in 31 BC and the Battle of Lepanto in AD 1571 – two battles which, far apart in time, were by a strange coincidence fought within a few miles of each other off the coast of Greece.

Britain, who was to dominate sea power for so long, was a late starter: most of the maritime races of Europe had had their times of leadership before the British began. Within 170 years, starting with the Spanish Armada and ending with three victories in 1759, Britain defeated all her rivals. Nelson's battles confirmed her supremacy. But her greatest achievement was not to have won her battles, but that having won them she kept the peace at sea for a century, a hundred years in which only one great sea battle was fought – and that one, at Navarino, to put an end to a war on land.

The Battle of Actium in 31 BC was mainly distinguished by the fame of its commanders: on one side Gaius Octavius, the future Roman Emperor Augustus, and on the other Antony and Cleopatra. It was the first and only time in history that a fleet in battle was commanded by a pair of lovers. Since then, indeed, there has only been one woman admiral, the formidable lady called Bubulina in the Greek War of Independence in the 1820s.

Octavius and Antony, or Antonius, had been rivals for Roman power since the murder of Julius Caesar in 44 BC, rivals also because Antony had been married to Octavius's sister and had divorced her for the charms of Cleopatra, Queen of Egypt.

In 31 BC Antony and Cleopatra had collected enormous forces by land and sea on the western coast of Greece. Headquarters for their fleet were in the Gulf of Ambracia, now called Amvrakikós Kólpos, some 50 miles (80 km) south of Corfu. It is a large gulf with a very narrow entrance, and most of their army was encamped on the southern shore

Previous pages A medieval manuscript illustration of a contemporary sea battle.

The bow of a Roman fighting galley. The Egyptian crocodile suggests this was one of Antony's ships at Actium.

of the narrows, opposite the modern town of Préveza. On that shore was a temple called Actium which gave its name to the battle.

Octavius embarked his troops on the opposite side of the Adriatic, in ports from Taranto to Brindisi, sailed or rowed across to Greece, took Corfu and the island of Levkás, and finished up on the other side of the narrows, pitching camp somewhere on the hills behind Préveza. So the two armies, each eighty to a hundred thousand strong, faced each other across the narrow sound, while the fleet of Antony was inside the Gulf and the fleet of Octavius outside it.

Not very much is known about these fleets. Both consisted of galleys, which were rowed by slaves in battle but also carried sails for longer voyages. The ships of Antony, of Greek or Egyptian build, were said to have been much bigger than the Roman galleys. On the other hand, they were clumsy and slower than the Romans', and their oarsmen were less expert. There had been sickness and desertion, and the ships' captains had had to round up local peasants to make up their crews.

Some of these big ships of Antony were said to have ten banks of oars. Whatever that meant, it is unbelievable that they really did have ten levels of oars, one above another. They might have been triremes, which had three banks on three separate decks, with long oars at the top and short ones at the bottom. A big trireme might have been 130 feet (39 m) long, with 170 oars and perhaps 500 oarsmen, and have had a speed of eight or nine knots for short distances, until the rowers were exhausted. In later centuries, their main armament was a long iron ram, but rams are not specifically mentioned at Actium.

It is said – though by Roman historians – that

Cleopatra was so alarmed by the arrival of Octavius in Greece that she decided to retreat to Egypt, and that Antony was so discouraged by desertions of his leaders that he agreed. While they occupied the narrows of Actium with their ships their fleet was impregnable, but they could not get out without a battle. So he prepared for both: for battle by embarking his men-at-arms, and for retreat by loading on board his treasures and the sails which were usually put ashore when battle was imminent.

By the end of August in 31 BC both sides were ready for a trial of strength, but a gale blew up and lasted four days. 2 September was calm, and Antony put to sea while Cleopatra, in the most suitably magnificent ship, waited offshore for the outcome.

For most of the day, it was an equal fight, watched in breathless suspense by enormous audiences of soldiers on the shores. Antony probably put well out to sea, because the water inshore is very shallow except for a narrow channel – though of course the depth may have changed in two thousand years. The Roman galleys, drawing less water, would have had more freedom of movement without the risk of running aground, but they were unable to board the monsters, which were protected by baulks of timber along their sides. Instead, they manoeuvred quickly round and round them in groups of three or four, and darted in under cover of flights of arrows to slice off the enemy oars with their bows. The Antonians threw rocks from the tops of wooden turrets, and also threw grappling irons. All these were techniques of sea-fighting which lasted over a thousand years.

At noon, a breeze came up, and Cleopatra, commanding her purple sails to be hoisted above her gilded decks, sailed out through the mass of combatants, followed by sixty Egyptian ships of her

Above left Model of a Mediterranean merchant ship of the Middle Ages. It is mainly distinguished from a northern ship by its lateen sail.

Below William the Conqueror's ship *Mora*, from the Bayeux tapestry. In contrast to the oared Roman galley, these ships of the Viking type relied mainly on their single square sail.

Ships of Richard II in 1399, from a fifteenth-century manuscript.

Stem post of a Viking ship of about 800 AD, found in the River Scheldt in Belgium.

entourage. Antony, seeing her go, jumped into a small fast boat and followed her. His fighting crews saw their leaders were deserting them. Some of them in rage and shame tore down their turrets and threw them overboard to lighten their ships for escape. When Antony caught up with Cleopatra he was so ashamed that he refused to speak to her for three days; this at any rate is the story of the Roman historians, who were glad enough to ascribe the result of the battle to a woman's cowardice but could not bring themselves to say that a Roman commander was a coward.

However, the battle was not yet over. Many, perhaps most of the galleys of Antony were too badly damaged to escape. But they were still too big and strong to be sunk or carried by boarding. Octavius sent ashore for torches. These, and burning javelins, were thrown from a distance onto the enemy ships, and 'piles of combustibles' were floated against them – perhaps the first use of fire-ships, which remained in use as a naval weapon longer than all the rest. One by one, the Antonian ships caught fire. Then the Octavians tried to save them, not from any humanitarian motive but for the sake of the treasures they were supposed to contain. But it was too late. The fire spread from ship to ship, and most of the fleet went down in the shallow sea.

Antony and Cleopatra both reached Egypt safely, but their power never recovered from Actium, and within a year they had both killed themselves.

It was many centuries after Actium before anyone in northern seas was organized enough to fight a battle. The first were the Vikings. They fought each other in their own home waters, and built special ships for the purpose, the famous long ships; but for a very long time they never fought anyone else, simply because they met no opposition. The first man who fought them at sea was King Alfred, and the first sea battles in northern waters were during his reign. In the year 885 the King sent a fleet of ships across the estuary of the Thames from Kent to East Anglia. There is a very brief description of what happened in the *Anglo-Saxon Chronicle*. In the mouth of the River Stour, where the town of Harwich now stands, 'they met sixteen ships of pirates' – that is, of Danish Vikings – 'and they fought against them and captured all the ships and slew the crews. When they were on their way home with the booty, they met a great fleet of pirates, and fought against them the same day, and the Danes were victorious.'

That is all that is known about the affair. It was a chance encounter, but evidently it was a real sea battle, fought in open waters, and it ended with slaughter all round and honours on both sides. Probably both fleets lowered their single square sails and rowed into the fight, as Mediterranean galleys did, because ships were more manoeuvrable under oars than under sail; and certainly they fought by the only method known in northern seas – by steering their ships alongside each other and fighting hand to hand with the weapons they used on shore, the sword and battle-axe.

During the next ten years, King Alfred built ships especially for war, the first in English history. They were very large for that era, twice as long as an ordinary ship, faster and more seaworthy, some with sixty oars and some with more. The *Anglo-Saxon Chronicle* says they were not built after the Viking design, 'but in the way the King thought would be most effective'; and since he had been to Rome when he was a boy, his ships' design may have been based on what he had seen of Mediterranean ships, a northern version of a Mediterranean galley.

But their only recorded battle, in the year 896, was something of a farce. There were nine of them, and they caught six Danish Viking ships in a harbour near the Isle of Wight: it may have been what is now Poole Harbour. Three of the Danes were drawn up on the beach and the crews had gone off marauding inland. The other three sailed out to meet the English. Two of them were defeated, but the third escaped because all nine of the English ships ran aground, three on one side of the Channel and six on the other. Then the Danes who had been ashore came back, and a bloody battle was fought, not in the ships, which were high and dry, but on the sandbanks. Sixty-two men were killed on the English side, and a hundred and twenty of the Danes. 'But the tide came first to the Danish ships', the Chronicle says, 'before the Christians could push off their own, and so they rowed away to sea. They were so sorely crippled they could not row farther than Sussex, where the sea cast two of the ships ashore. The men were taken to the King at Winchester, and he had them hanged there.'

King Alfred has sometimes been called the father of the British navy, because he was the first to build ships of war. But if he was, one has to admit the embarrassing fact that in its first battle the British navy ran the whole of its fleet ashore on a falling tide, the most ignominious mistake a sailor can commit.

One has to move on for three more centuries – centuries in which innumerable battles were fought on land – before finding another sea battle of any note. There are two reasons why sea battles were so rare in those days. The first is that fleets of mediaeval ships could only sail downwind. A single ship, with its one square sail, could make progress with the wind on the beam, or even perhaps, with a skilful crew, make a point or so to windward. But a whole fleet of ships could not. The Vikings solved the problem by rowing when the wind was against them, because every Norseman had learned to row as a child; but no other northern race had that skill. If a French or English king wanted to transport his army by sea – across the English Channel for example – he therefore waited for a fair wind. When the wind was fair for one side, ships on the other side would be stuck in harbour, and consequently rival fleets scarcely ever met at sea.

The second reason is that nobody in authority wanted to fight at sea. The aristocracy of northern Europe after the Viking era was imbued with ideas

Fourteenth-century French fleet, with fore- and after castles, and fighting tops at the mastheads.

Crusaders in a fortified harbour, from the Froissart Chronicle, first published about 1500.

of chivalry, which was a mixture of mysticism and horsemanship. Chivalric knights were trained from their boyhood, in an elaborate education, to fight in armour on horseback with sword and lance. They were therefore miserable in ships, where their horses were useless and they could not wear their armour (or if they did, they must have known they would sink like a stone if they fell or were pushed overboard). They knew that in battles at sea they could not use their skill; so they avoided them. All through the age of chivalry, from say the eleventh

to the fourteenth centuries, if armies had to put to sea, in order to fight a battle on the other side, their one idea was to get ashore again as quickly as they could.

But the longest and most adventurous voyages that northern seamen made in that period were made in the ultimate cause of chivalry, the Crusades. It was on one of those voyages that the next notable battle was fought – one of the strangest battles in history, and the first in which northern seamen and Mediterranean seamen met. It hap-

χοχριω|τοιϲεραμπόιϲ · καιτωαι φυζλωκαταπληξαμγοι · πολλατεμραντλιδρωϲεϲχν
πύρρικων. Ηγαϲδεκαιτωοκλαπιπρποολοωπρι ·

τολϲερωιωζ πυρπολ ω ΤΟΝΤΩΝΕΝΗΛΝΤΙΦΟΛΟΝ ·

pened on Richard Coeur de Lion's Crusade in 1191. King Richard, having vowed to fight the infidels in the Holy Land, set forth to march across Europe with his knights and his army, and he sent a fleet of ships to sail there, with orders to meet him at Messina in Sicily. These were the same small ships, with a single mast and sail, that had been in use in the north for centuries, the kind of ship the Vikings used not for war but for transport and trade. They made the long voyage successfully, met the army in Messina and wintered there. Probably not one of the sailors, who were Englishmen and Flemings, had ever been so far from home before, and in spite of their holy intention they behaved very badly in Messina, quarrelling with the local people and finally sacking the place and slaughtering its leading citizens. There for the first time they saw Mediterranean ships, which were very much larger and more sophisticated than their own, with two or three masts and elaborate rigging. The King saw them too, and he bought or chartered a fleet of them for the onward voyage to carry his army to the Holy Land. So in the following spring the mixed fleet set sail from Messina, English and Mediterranean ships together, all manned by Englishmen and Flemings. Among them was a number of Mediterranean fighting galleys. After many adventures they sighted the coast of the Holy Land near the town of Acre – and offshore the biggest ship that any of them had ever seen, with towering sides and three tall masts.

King Richard sent a galley to ask who commanded this enormous vessel, and its crew said it belonged to Philip II, King of France. The King of France was King Richard's ally in the Crusade, and at that moment was besieging Acre. But it looked suspicious: it was not flying any Christian

flag. A second galley was sent, and this time the crew said they were Genoese. As a test, the King told the galley to row past it without giving any salute, and at that the crew of the ship gave up pretending and began to throw darts and shoot arrows at the galley. In fact, it was a Saracen ship under the orders of Saladin.

The English had rowed or sailed their galleys all the way from Sicily, but nobody seems to have told them how a galley was intended to fight: it had an iron-shod prow or beak below the waterline to ram the enemy. But the only idea the English had was to try to board the Saracen ship, because that was the only way battles had ever been fought in northern waters. They rowed round and round it, looking for a way to climb its sides. But whenever any of them managed to scramble up, their heads and hands were chopped off when they reached the gunwales. Discouraged, they drew off; but Richard was urging them on. Some tried to climb its anchor cables; some swam underneath it and lashed up its rudder with ropes so that it could not sail. At last, the King thought of ramming, or somebody reminded him. He gave the order. The galleys drew back, turned and rowed full speed at the ship; the beaks pierced through its planking and it immediately started to sink. They may have wondered why he had not thought of it before, but any regret they felt was forgotten in victory; for it turned out that the ship was on its way to relieve the siege of Acre. The chronicler who told the story said there were seven admirals on board the ship, with a hundred camel-loads of slings, bows, darts and arrows, a large quantity of Greek fire in bottles, which was a kind of self-igniting oil, and two hundred deadly serpents for the destruction of the Christian armies.

A thirteenth-century Byzantine manuscript shows Greek Fire, a self-igniting liquid, being thrown at an enemy ship. Northern sailors in the crusades learned how to make it, but thought it too dangerous to use.

The seal of Winchelsea shows a ship of Viking type with fighting castles built on it fore and aft.

13

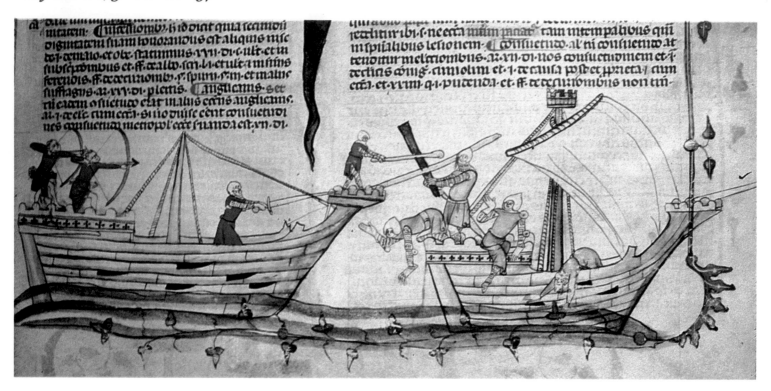

Fourteenth century; these ships are Hanseatic cogs, which superseded the ships of the Viking type and spread all over northern Europe.

After King Alfred, all northern kings had a few ships of their own, but never anything like enough to transport their armies. When they wanted to make a military expedition, they chartered or requisitioned the ordinary trading ships of their subjects. In England, ships chartered by the king were usually taken first to the Tower of London, and the words '*de la Tour*' – in the Norman French which was the language of the Court – were added to their names. In 1340, for example, King Edward III used a ship with the English name of *Thomas*; and while he was using it it was known as *Thomas de la Tour*.

At about the time of Richard's Crusade, and perhaps as a result of what they had seen in the Mediterranean, northern knights began to demand that fighting castles should be built on the ships they embarked in. These castles, the fore- and after-castles, were added at the Tower, and they can be seen in the mediaeval pictures of fighting-ships, which are often on the seals of coastal towns. Nowadays, they seem ludicrous structures, like toy replicas of castles on land. Most of them have model battlements, some have gothic windows, and some have brickwork painted on. They must have been lightly built, or they would have upset the stability of the ships, so they cannot have given much real protection; one feels their main use must have been to make the knights feel more at home when they had to go to sea. But they did at least give the advantage of height for throwing missiles, mostly rocks, at the enemy. For the same purpose, some ships were given fighting-tops, which were like large buckets men could stand in at the tops of the masts. Some pictures show a basket on a rope, in which the rocks were hauled up to the tops; and with luck a rock that was thrown down from there would go through the decks of the enemy and out through the bottom of his ship.

It is not only the castles that seem rather

ludicrous: battles themselves in those early days often have a comic air. Even contemporary chroniclers write about them with a sense of amusement, as if battles at sea were not to be taken as seriously as battles on land. It is partly perhaps because weapons invented for ships were so elementary. The beaks on the galleys were the most effective, but they were never used in northern battles. Greek fire also, of which the English learned the formula from the Saracens, was never

popular in the north, probably because a fire in the enemy's ship was so likely to spread to one's own. Experiments were made with the unpleasant practice of throwing quicklime at the enemy's eyes. One weapon in particular seems more like a practical joke than a serious means of making war. This was to throw triboli and soft soap on the enemy's deck. Triboli were small iron objects with four spikes, so designed that they always fell with one spike pointing upwards. The theory was that the enemy on his rolling deck would slip on the soap and sit down on the triboli. Another tactic that sometimes succeeded was for one brave man to jump aboard the enemy's ship as soon as it was near enough and cut the halyard with his sword, so that the sail fell on top of the enemy crew. With luck, before they disentangled themselves, the ship could be taken.

A sea battle with this element of absurdity was fought by King Edward III of England in 1350. He was with his ships in Dover, and a Spanish fleet – the Castilian ships, commanded by Admiral Charles de la Cerda – was sighted coming down the Channel on a north-easterly wind. This was one of the rare situations when two mediaeval fleets could come to grips if both sides were willing, and the name of the fight shows how unusual it was. It was not called, like most sea battles, after the nearest point of land, but became known as the Battle of *Les Espagnols sur mer*, The Spaniards at Sea.

Edward put to sea in his ship, and of course had to sail downwind to the westward. The Spanish ships were larger and faster than his, and they could have escaped; but they altered course slightly towards him, and the fleets converged, both with the wind behind them, until they met, about thirty miles west of Dover somewhere off Winchelsea.

The King had no galleys, but he decided to ram a Spaniard. It was a rash thing to do, but perhaps the only way to bring a faster fleet to battle. He hit it so hard that its mast collapsed and went overboard with the men in its fighting-top, and its sail of course went too. But English ships were not built for ramming. His own ship was split so badly that even his knights had to get to work with buckets to keep it afloat. His son Edward, the Black Prince, in another ship, copied his tactics and rammed another Spaniard with even more dire results: his own ship sank. But both of the English crews succeeded in boarding their enemies and slaughtering them, or throwing them overboard. In a third ship, one man boarded a Spaniard, cut its halyard and brought down its sail; so that Spaniard was also taken.

Excepting fights against pirates, this was the first true battle at sea for hundreds of years, and it was claimed as an English victory. But ten years before, in June 1340, King Edward III had fought and won a far more serious battle in his ships – the Battle of Sluys. Strictly speaking, it was not a sea battle because it was fought in harbour; but it was fought between huge rival fleets of ships, and it was by far the bloodiest and most important northern ship-battle of the Middle Ages.

Like the great land battles of Crécy and Agincourt, the Battle of Sluys was an episode in the Hundred Years War that England waged against France. In history, it has always been difficult to say why that war was fought; after all, a war that lasts for four generations cannot have a single factual cause. It was partly that England under King and Parliament had evolved to a state of

The Battle of Sluys. This illustration for a fourteenth-century French manuscript shows steering oars and fighting tops, and the gory slaughter of a hand-to-hand fight in ships.

de filio za) uvotem de marito
erunt ualde illu i tali articulo fuisse
r timuit filio excomunicato

Angue z pirata nequimin. etii cu re depnemun
cognouitseo: optuut p uitra fua z menbut iestimabi
lem pecunie quantitate. zqo de ceto ili rege anglorum

p: exut en obuia i fuf coi
tozib; of epi qi ibi erat eu
militia z poplo. facf ioinn

re prodicone. hic accestic q iuadiam epat fuu y secenit in ...
fil. Ehu accestic camcestic ... ut pucatet stipendiauos.

ne sellegm
ti occutye

vexilla Rohm ... de etemu ... z aliozu ... magn ... atu fucie

uestib; z eeib;
zuexilt ea
tautet sei
leuut
din col
t iauda
Eustachii agondech stigne

Above A sea fight on St Bartholomew's Day, 1217.

Opposite The Battle of Lepanto, 1571, the last great battle fought by oared Mediterranean galleys.

internal peace; partly that Englishmen were experts with the most devastating weapon of the age, the longbow. To make an expedition across the Channel and come home with booty and exciting stories to boast about was an outlet for adventurous spirits, an Englishman's idea of fun. They went on doing it year after year for no specific reason except that they enjoyed it.

Normally they used ships only to transport their armies across the Channel and land them on the other side. But in 1340 King Edward III was fighting this interminable war in Flanders, and was so deeply in debt that he had had to pledge his golden crown. He came home to England to raise more money. While he was away, King Philip VI of France sent a very large fleet up the Channel and into the harbour of Sluys, on the estuary of the river Scheldt – thinking no doubt to cut off King Edward from his army and attack it from the rear. Sluys silted up long ago, and now it is several miles inland; but then it was a major commercial port. With the French came a notorious Flemish pirate called Lanisius Spoudevisch, who had twenty-four ships of his own, and a Genoese adventurer called Barbarveria, who had a fleet of Mediterranean galleys.

King Edward's own fleet was assembled at Ipswich on the River Orwell, and he sent out a summons, as was the custom, for all merchant ships in the district to join him, with crews and men-at-arms. Within a fortnight, hundreds of ships had collected, miscellaneous merchantmen of all sizes, and, it was said, twenty thousand men. On 20 June, the King himself embarked with his nobles and ordered the fleet to sail. He left the Black Prince in England as Regent, and the best account of what happened is in a bloodcurdling letter he wrote to the boy, who was then just over ten years old:

My dearest son, We are sure you will want to hear good news of us, and all that has happened since we left England. So we must tell you that on Thursday, after we left the port of Orwell, we sailed all day and all the following night, and on Friday about noon we reached the coast of Flanders off Blankenberghe, where we sighted our enemy's fleet all packed together in the harbour of Sluys; and because we had missed the tide we anchored off for the night. On Saturday, St John's Day, soon after noon on the tide, in the name of God and trusting in our just cause, we sailed into the harbour upon our enemies, who had drawn up their ships in a very strong array and offered a noble defence all that day and the night after; but God, through His miraculous power, gave us victory, for which we devoutly thank Him. And we must tell you that the ships, galleys and great barges of the enemy numbered 910, all of which were taken except 24; and the number of gentlemen-at-arms and other armed men amounted to 35 thousand, of whom only five thousand escaped, and we have heard from some who were taken alive that the bodies are scattered all over the coast of Flanders. ... Dearest son, may God be your guardian.

Other chroniclers make it clear that both sides fought this battle, as nearly as they could, with the tactics they used on land. The French drew up their ships in ranks like an army, and the first rank was actually chained together so that they could not move. King Edward made a headlong attack like a cavalry charge. He had stationed his men-at-arms in every third ship, with their usual weapons, the sword and lance; the other two ships in every three were full of archers. He waited for the flood-tide to make his attack; luckily, it came at a time of day when the French, who used the cross-bow, had the sun in their eyes. Before the ships met, the arrows of the expert English longbow men were wreaking havoc, and Frenchmen were jumping overboard to escape them. When at last the hulls crashed

Don Juan of Austria who commanded the international fleet of the Holy Alliance which defeated the Turks at Lepanto.

together, the men-at-arms jumped across and hand-to-hand fights began.

Of course the King's statement that 30,000 French were killed is incredible, but certainly the slaughter was terrible. Flemings, who were lining the shore to watch, finished off the French who managed to swim to land. An abbot said that if God had given speech to fishes, they would have ended up speaking French after all the bodies they had eaten. Most of the ships that escaped seem to have been those of the pirate Spoudevisch, who knew when to make a tactical retreat. And Barbarveria the Genoese, whose profession was fighting at sea, withdrew his galleys in protest at the landlubberly method of defence, saying that the French Admiral Quiéret knew more about book-keeping than battles – which may well have been true. Both sides fought fiercely, but neither side showed the least understanding of how to fight at sea.

The end of sea-fighting in the Middle Ages is marked by another Mediterranean battle: the Battle of Lepanto on 7 October 1571. In many ways, four hours on the afternoon of that day were a turning point: for Lepanto was the last great battle fought between fleets of galleys, and the first in which gunpowder was important. It was also a climax in the long confrontation across the Mediterranean Sea between the forces of Christendom on the northern shores and Islam in the south.

On one side was a Turkish fleet of 273 galleys, and on the other Holy Alliance fleet organized by Pope Pius V, about 200 galleys from Spain, Naples and Sicily, and the states of Venice and Genoa.

Lepanto is a misleading name for the battle. The tiny, beautiful and ancient harbour of Lepanto is still there, just inside the narrow entrance of the Gulf of Corinth. Now it is called Návpaktos. But there could never have been room for more than half a dozen galleys in it. The rest must have anchored outside; and the battle itself was fought 50 miles (80 km) to the west of it, off the rocky island of Oxia and the shallow marshy northern shore of the Gulf of Patras – by a coincidence, close to the site of the Battle of Actium, fought sixteen hundred years earlier.

MESSANAE PORTVM VICTRIX
CLASIS INGREDITVR REMVLC
RAHENS CXXX TRIREMES
CAPTAS ALIIS FRACTIS ET
SVBMERSIS IN PRELIO

The winning ships approach the Port of Messina after the Battle of Lepanto.

Here the two fleets sighted each other, the Moslems advancing from Lepanto and the Christians from Messina, where King Richard had assembled his fleet in 1191. The Moslems were commanded by Ali Pasha; the Christians by Don Juan of Austria, the illegitimate younger brother of King Philip II of Spain, who was only twenty-four years old but already had a high reputation as a general. Both fleets, as ever, were drawn up like armies in lines abreast. Both were in three divisions, with the commander-in-chief in the centre. It is said each line was 3 miles long and each fleet had 80,000 men in it, of whom more than half were slaves, with a proportion of volunteers, who manned the oars.

The Moslems still relied mainly on the sword for close fighting and the bow and arrow as a kind of artillery; but the Christians had three innovations. Their soldiers were armed with muskets or arquebuses, and their galleys had a gun mounted in the bows – this, however, could only be aimed by turning the whole ship. They also had six Venetian galleasses, an entirely new kind of ship, much bigger and more heavily armed than the galleys. These were propelled by banks of 50-foot (15-m) oars, each worked by half a dozen or more oarsmen, some pulling and some pushing. Over the oarsmen they had a deck for the fighting-men. They had swivel-guns, and sharp, armoured stems which, with so much weight behind them, were expected to cut in half any galley that got in the way. These big ships were stationed in front of the fleet. It was hoped they would be impregnable and would break up the enemy forces as they approached. But it seems that on this first appearance they had to be towed into battle. Perhaps there had not been time to collect the huge number of rowers they needed.

The Holy Alliance, as one might expect with such a mixture of nationalities, had formed a thoroughly quarrelsome fleet, and the councils of war its leaders held often ended in angry arguments. But Don Juan, a very handsome and attractive man, was a popular leader, and in spite of his youth a genius at patching up the quarrels of older men. He also had an original view of tactics. Before the battle he had the rams removed from the galleys. With a gun in the bows and musketeers on board, the rams were obsolete and probably an encumbrance. He intended to fight more in the northern manner, by boarding and close combat. He is said to have given the gruesome order that everyone was to hold his fire until he was 'near enough to be splashed by the blood of an enemy'. Ali Pasha, on the other side, is said to have promised his thousands of Christian galley-slaves their freedom if he won; if he lost, then God would have given it to them. The position of a galley-slave, chained to his bench and quite unable to defend himself, must have been as unpleasant as any man has ever had to endure in battle.

When the Christian fleet was drawn up – Venetians on the left, very close to the shore, Genoese and Papal galleys on the right, and Spaniards in the centre – Don Juan sailed along it in a fast boat to cheer and be cheered by his men. Then battle was joined. Cervantes, creator of *Don Quixote*, was amongst the Spanish soldiers that day and lost the use of his left hand in the battle.

The galleasses seem to have done no good at all, in spite of their swivel-guns. The aim of a gun in that era was so unsure that it needed more luck than skill to hit a target beyond a few yards' range. The Turks did not attack them; they simply rowed past them, but in doing so their line was spread out and they lost their close formation.

On the Christian left, close to the shore, things went badly at first. The Turks, who had been a long time in the neighbourhood, probably knew that coast and the Venetians did not. It is a tricky place. The shore of the island of Oxia is steep and one can sail right up to the rocks; but off the marshy point of the mainland the sea is so shallow that one can see the bottom, in the clear Mediterranean water, over a mile offshore. The Turks ventured even closer inshore than the Venetians, turning their flank and surrounding them. Both lines broke up into a horrible mêlée: galleys crashing into each other and entangling their oars; musket balls and arrows

A painting in commemoration of the Battle of Lepanto.

flying everywhere; and men swarming aboard the enemy ships wherever they could get a grip. Early on, the Venetian admiral, Barbarigo, was killed by an arrow. His flagship was captured and re-captured twice. Then the Turkish flagship was sunk, and their admiral, Mahomet Sirocco, wounded, fell in the water. He was dragged out and instantly beheaded; and all around, with religious fervour, the slaughter was merciless and terrible.

On the right of the Christian line also, the advantage went first to the Turks. To avoid being outflanked, the Genoese admiral, Andrea Doria, ordered his ships to stand out to seaward; but that left a gap between him and Don Juan in the centre. The Turks under Uluch Ali saw their chance and rowed through the gap to attack Don Juan's flank. That part of the line was occupied by ships of the Knights of Malta, commanded by Giustiniani, a prior of the Order of St John. He fell dead, hit by five arrows, and his flagship was captured and taken in tow.

But Don Juan had a reserve of twenty-five galleys behind his line, commanded by the most distinguished of Spanish admirals, the Marquis of Santa Cruz. He came up and counter-attacked, forcing the Turks to give up their prize and retreat.

The battle was decided in the centre, where the two commanders-in-chief in person met prow to prow. There, gunfire and musketry won over bows and ramming. Don Juan's bow-gun holed Ali Pasha's flagship and his musketeers made havoc in its crew. He gave the order to board. At first, his boarders were unsuccessful: twice they were driven off. But at a third attempt some of them stormed the Turkish poop. There, they found Ali Pasha already wounded by a musket ball, and a soldier killed him and hacked off his head. He stuck it on a pike and

held it up in the bow of the Turkish ship. Somebody hauled down the sacred Turkish standard (it is still in the Doge's palace in Venice). The loss of a standard in those days and the death of a commander-in-chief were usually accepted as signals of defeat, and the remnants of the Turks began to flee back to the fortified shelter of Lepanto. On the Christian right, however, it was a fighting retreat, and an isolated battle was started there, after the rest had ended, which was the goriest of all. Five hundred Christians were caught in it; only fifty survived unharmed.

When it came to counting the cost, it was reckoned that 8,000 Christians had been killed and twice as many wounded. The Christians could not possibly know how many Turks had died, but they reckoned three times as many, 24,000. A slightly more reliable figure was that 12,000 Christian galley-slaves were freed. All in all, in those four hours there had been one of the bloodiest sea battles in history. Both sides had fought with ghastly determination, and the Christians had won because with their guns and muskets they were one short step ahead in the evolution of sea-fighting.

Yet the whole technique of fighting in galleys was archaic, and was very near its end. Things had not changed very much since Actium, sixteen hundred years earlier. But it was only seventeen years after Lepanto that the Spanish Armada sailed from Lisbon. Many men fought in both. But the Armada sailed into a different world.

'Portuguese carracks off a rocky coast', attributed to Cornelis Anthoniszoon.

The Spanish Armada

1588

independence: it would be a sailor's weapon, not merely a floating fort for soldiers. Getting rid of the soldiers meant one could also get rid of their unseamanlike castles. The result was called a race-built ship, because its castles had been razed, and it was faster, quicker on the helm, and much better in sailing to windward than anything before it.

While the Elizabethans were building these revolutionary ships in the 1580s, King Philip of Spain was collecting his Armada in Lisbon for the invasion of England, and his soldiers were insisting that ever-higher fighting castles should be built on his ships. Although it was called an Armada, which simply means a fighting fleet, not all of it was composed of fighting ships – far from it. It was the largest sailing fleet that had ever been assembled, 130 ships in all, manned by 8,000 sailors and some 22,000 soldiers and other landsmen. But only twenty-five of the ships had really been built for war: twenty-one galleons, which were strong ships, heavily armed, designed to protect Spain's trans-atlantic trade; and four galleasses from Naples, which had evolved from the Lepanto galleasses, big ships designed to be either sailed or rowed. The rest were small pinnaces, mainly used for carrying messages, and large merchantmen from the Mediterranean and the Baltic, converted by building castles on them and fitting more and bigger guns.

King Philip's plan was that the Armada should sail up the English Channel to Margate. It would destroy or drive away whatever English ships it met, and clear the seas for his army under the Duke of Parma which was fighting rebellious Dutch in the Spanish Netherlands. The army would come across in boats, and the combined forces would make landings on both sides of the Thames.

His aim in invading England was to set the English free from their heretic Protestant Queen, to convert them to the Catholic Church and take the

Previous pages The Armada by Henrik Vroom. In the left foreground is the ponderous bulk of a Portuguese galleon, probably the *San Martin*, and astern of her the slenderer lines of an English race-built ship, probably the *Ark*.

Above Sir Francis Drake, Vice-Admiral of the English fleet, and the greatest strategic expert of his time.

Right Sir John Hawkins who, with Drake, created a new kind of fighting ship and a new technique of gunnery.

WHEN THE ARMADA sailed in 1588, the technique of sea-fighting was halfway through a revolution. The English had determined to put their faith in guns, and try to destroy their enemies from a distance by gunnery alone. The Spaniards still clung to the ancient idea of grappling and boarding and fighting hand to hand, and thought of gunnery only as a means of damaging the rigging of an enemy ship and slowing it down, so that they could come alongside it and fight in the old-fashioned way. The English also had another innovation: their ships were commanded by sea-captains, but Spanish ships were still commanded by soldiers, as they had been since the time of mediaeval knights.

The new English idea of gun-fighting, perhaps the most daring innovation ever made in fighting at sea, has been attributed mainly to Francis Drake and John Hawkins. It was Drake who first insisted, on his voyage round the world in the *Golden Hinde*, that a ship at sea and everyone in it should be under the captain's command, whatever his social status. Hawkins, as treasurer of Queen Elizabeth's navy, was the leader in the design of a new kind of ship, which would make use of the sea-captain's new

crown for himself or his daughter, the Infanta Isabella. All of this he regarded as the will of God; but God's cause and his own worldly ambition were inextricably muddled in his mind.

The plan, which he had made all alone in his palace of the Escorial, was also a muddle. He never allowed his separate commanders, the Duke of Parma in the Spanish Netherlands and the Duke of Medina Sidonia who led the Armada, to discuss it either with him or with each other; when at the last moment they received his orders, both of them saw it could not possibly work as he expected – but it was too late to say so.

The first defect of the Armada showed as soon as it left the river in Lisbon at the end of May. The merchant ships were very slow. They had not been designed to sail to windward – in their usual trade, if the wind was against them, they simply waited for it to change, with the patience of the ages of sail – and building castles on them had made them worse. The Armada indeed, like a mediaeval fleet, could only progress downwind. It took three weeks to cover the 270 miles (435 km) from Lisbon to Corunna in the north of Spain, and at one time it was driven 100 miles (160 km) in the opposite direction. Off Corunna it was scattered by a storm, and had to wait there another month for the ships to reassemble.

The year 1588 not only brought a new kind of tactics to fighting at sea, it also showed the beginning of naval strategy. Strategy at sea can only exist with a certain confidence in seamanship, a feeling that one can command the sea itself whatever weather comes. Drake had that confidence to a greater degree than anyone before him. When the Armada threatened, he was vice-admiral of the major part of the English fleet, at Plymouth under the Queen's Lord High Admiral, Lord Howard of Effingham. Drake passionately insisted that the proper place for the defence of England

Lord Howard of Effingham, Lord High Admiral of England.

Plymouth in the sixteenth century was impregnable against a sea attack.

was not off the shores of England but off the shores of Spain – the same strategy, based on the same confidence, that led to the great blockade of the ports of France before Trafalgar. Lord Howard came round to the idea when he understood it; but Queen Elizabeth and her Council never understood it fully, and Drake was thwarted time and again by contrary orders.

In June he was even more certain he was right. The Armada was known to have sailed from Lisbon over a month before. It had not arrived. Therefore, he argued, it must have been damaged by storm and be sheltering, vulnerable, in the northern ports of Spain. At last the Queen's permission came, and the fleet put out from Plymouth. Off Ushant it was headed by a south-westerly gale. Not even the race-built ships, like his own *Revenge* or Howard's *Ark Royal*, could do much against a gale, and by no means all the fleet were race-built ships. For ten days they held on in the teeth of the wind, and then it changed to north-east – fair for Spain.

Howard still hesitated. To go on was a daunting risk. The Armada might have come out with the south-west gale behind it. If it had, there was every chance they would miss it somewhere in the Bay of Biscay; and England behind them was guarded only by a small fleet under Lord Henry Seymour in the Thames. Moreover, Howard's ships were very short of food.

A council of war was held on board the *Ark Royal*. Present, beside Howard and Drake, were Martin Frobisher, an old-fashioned and illiterate captain who detested Drake, and Thomas Fenner, who was a member of a large seafaring family from Southampton and one of Drake's faithful followers. It was a long and probably angry discussion, but Drake's forceful arguments won the day. Howard gave the order, and the whole English fleet stood south for Spain.

It was probably the greatest gamble ever taken with the fate of England at stake, and it failed. Drake was right: the Armada was still in Corunna. But 60 miles short of the Spanish coast the wind fell calm, and then went back to the south: it was a foul wind for the English, fair for the Armada. They were just too far from Corunna to be sure of intercepting the Armada if it came out. There was nothing for it but to turn and go back to Plymouth.

That was on 20 June.* On that very day, the commander-in-chief of the Armada, the Duke of Medina Sidonia, was also holding a council of war. The Armada too was desperately short of food. It had started from Lisbon with immense supplies, enough for a six months' voyage; but the build-up

---

*SIX YEARS before the Armada, Pope Gregory learned that the ancient Julian calendar had lagged ten days behind the seasons. He decreed that ten days should be omitted from the year 1582, and so founded the Gregorian calendar which is still in use. But Protestant England rejected the decree, and for many years English dates remained ten days behind. Most modern historians of the Armada campaign use the new-style Gregorian dates, because they correspond with our own knowledge of the seasons; but they differ by ten days from the dates in earlier English histories.

of the fleet had been delayed again and again, and the food had been on board too long: most of it had rotted in the casks, and the water had turned green and slimy. Thousands of men had already suffered from food poisoning, in addition to the usual shipboard diseases of typhus, dysentery, influenza and unidentified fevers. The Duke had desperately appealed to Philip II of Spain for fresh supplies, but very little had come. Privately, he had even advised the King to abandon the whole project; but Philip II seldom listened to anyone's advice. The council was therefore riddled with doubt, about the food, the suitability of its ships, and the feasibility of the royal plans. But the King was adamant, and the council decided to sail against the better judgement of many of its senior officers.

Some nineteenth-century historians, writing at the peak of British imperial pride, turned the defeat of the Armada into a national heroic tale, and made much of a legend that the Spanish commanders were fools, especially their commander-in-chief. But that was not how it seemed to the men who fought the Armada. They ascribed their victory much more to the winds of God than to any efforts of their own. They also admired the skill and courage of the Spaniards. After all, it was the Spaniards who needed most courage: the English fought to defend their own shores, but the Spaniards ventured into unknown seas. The faults of the Armada were technical and were caused by the King's mistakes. His plans were impossible and his ships were unsuitable. But once it had sailed, his commanders and men made no mistakes at all.

It is part of the legend that the Spaniards had bigger ships and bigger guns than the English, which gave a David-and-Goliath air to the story. But it was not so. The Spanish method of calculating the tonnage of a ship was different from the English method. Both of them were vague, but all experts agree that the Spanish method gave figures that were twenty-five to forty-five per cent higher. So, although lists of the Spanish ships recorded tonnages up to 1,200 (Spanish) tons, Martin Frobisher's *Triumph*, an old-fashioned galleon of 1,100 (English) tons, was the largest ship in either fleet. And since race-built ships were more slender in their lines and were therefore longer in proportion to their tonnage, Lord Howard's *Ark Royal* of 800 tons was probably the longest of all. The average size was just about the same.

As for the guns, it is true the Spaniards had more of the largest size, the cannon which fired a 50-pound (23-kg) shot. But cannon were comparatively short-range guns, and the English had deliberately armed themselves with more culverins and smaller guns, which fired shots of only 17 pounds (8 kg) or less but had a longer range. The English plan was to fight beyond the range of Spanish cannon, and beat them with long-range shots from their culverins.

However, the best known of all the legends of the Armada is probably true: Drake's game of bowls. It was on Friday 29 July (new-style dates) that the pinnace *Golden Hinde*, captained by Thomas Flemyng, came sailing up Plymouth Sound with the news that the Armada was sighted off the

Alexander Farnese, Duke of Parma, appointed to command the invasion of England.

The game of bowls on Plymouth Hoe: a nineteenth-century version of this legendary scene.

Lizard. The story that Drake was playing bowls on Plymouth Hoe has been traced back to a pamphlet of 1624, well within living memory of the event. The story of what he said – 'Plenty of time to finish the game and beat the Spaniards after' – is a later addition: it does not appear in print until 1736. One can only say it is just the sort of thing he would have said, if people around him were getting over-excited. After all, he was expecting the Armada, and he was not the kind of man to let anyone think he was taken by surprise.

Besides, there really was plenty of time. It seems likely the *Golden Hinde* came in in the afternoon, and low water in Plymouth that day was at three o'clock. The English fleet was loading stores, and probably many ships were aground in the mud alongside the quays. They could not possibly get out of harbour against the flood tide. So there was nothing much anyone could do before high water at nine o'clock that evening.

It has often been said the English fleet, caught in harbour, was vulnerable to the kind of attack Drake had made on Cadiz the year before, and planned to make on Corunna. But Plymouth harbour with its strong tides, its 3-mile (5-km) approach up Plymouth Sound and its narrow entrances, is nothing like the harbour of Cadiz or Corunna, and the Armada was nothing like the highly mobile fleet that Drake commanded. If the Armada intended to enter Plymouth, it could only do it with a following wind and a rising tide. The wind was fair enough, but the next rising tide was not going to start before dawn. At worst, therefore, they could not attack before the following evening: and by then the English had every intention of being outside to stop them.

It is very doubtful that the English, knowing Plymouth as they did, ever expected a seaborne attack. In fact, an attack was discussed at a council in the Armada as it sailed up from the Lizard. But the whole council agreed it could not sail into the harbour, and what they talked about was probably a land attack, putting their army ashore outside Plymouth Sound. However, Medina Sidonia had to veto it: the King had given emphatic orders that they were not to land, or pause for any reason, until they had made the rendezvous with Parma.

Some of the English ships probably beat out of the Sound in the dark that night, against a west-south-west wind: they were reported to the *San Martin*, the Spanish flagship, by a crew of fishermen who were captured, to be waiting in the lee of Rame Head, the south-westerly point of the Sound. Most of them waited in harbour for the morning ebb. It was hard work to get out in a contrary wind, but by three o'clock that afternoon, 30 July, Howard and Drake with fifty-four sail were off the Eddystone Rock. Against the wind, with the help of the tide, they had made 13 miles (21 km) in four hours. It was not perhaps a remarkable achievement, but it was something the Armada could not possibly have done. There, through squalls of rain, they had their first glimpse of the Armada to the westward. They were sighted too: 'a number of ships,' Medina Sidonia wrote in his diary, 'but as the weather was thick and rainy they could not be counted'.

One tactic – and only one – had already been established for fighting under sail: to win the weather gauge, to get to windward of the enemy. From that position, with the wind behind him, an admiral or captain could choose his moment to attack. That night, with the wind veering to westerly, both commanders competed for the weather gauge. The only thing Medina Sidonia could do was to anchor, because he could not sail to windward. Howard, however, made long tacks all night, and by dawn he was upwind of the Armada, 5 miles (8 km) to the west of the Eddystone. Frobisher, with ten more ships, had come later out of the Sound: he commanded the *Triumph*, which still had the old high castles, and he probably had more of a struggle against the wind. But he also beat to windward on the opposite side of the Spanish fleet and joined Howard early in the day.

Both sides, seeing each other for the first time, had a shock. The Spaniards were shocked by the skill of the English in sailing to windward, and the speed and handiness of their ships. The English were shocked by the sheer size of the Armada, and its formidable compact formation.

That formation was described by the English as a crescent moon, and the best-known charts of the Armada's progress show it always in a tidy moon; but naval historians are sceptical, because it would be impossible for any fleet – let alone a sailing fleet – to keep station in a curve. The commanders of the Armada never said what their formation was, but a much more likely description was published in Rome while they were at sea. This looks more like a bird than a moon. The main body of storeships and transports was in the middle, with Medina Sidonia in the vanguard ahead and a rearguard astern, and on each side there was a defensive wing of galleons and converted merchant ships. This might have looked like a moon to the thousands of landlubbers who watched from the clifftops of southern England, or indeed to a seaman following behind.

Accounts of the battles up the Channel in the

following week are totally confused. It is not surprising. By the end, some 260 ships were involved, all moving – though very slowly – and nobody in any one of them could see what all the rest were doing. Spanish accounts are much more detailed than English accounts but equally difficult to sort out and put together. Many attempts have been made to analyse them and trace deliberate tactics through them, but at best these efforts involve a lot of guesswork, and some of the classic versions are plainly wrong.

But the general effect is perfectly clear, and very surprising. Here were the two most powerful fleets that had ever been assembled, both equally intent on fighting the other, and – until the very last day – with no possible means of joining battle. The fleets had quite different plans for fighting, and neither of them was going to work. The Spaniards with their tens of thousands of soldiers wanted to grapple and board, but whenever they tried, the nimbler English ships altered course and slipped away to windward. The English wanted to fight at a distance with gunnery, but the Spanish formation was so large and compact that their longest shots could only reach the nearest edges of it, leaving the rest unscathed. All the way up the Channel, both

One of the set of charts of the Armada's progress designed by Robert Adams. They were probably wrong in showing the Armada's formation in the shape of a moon.

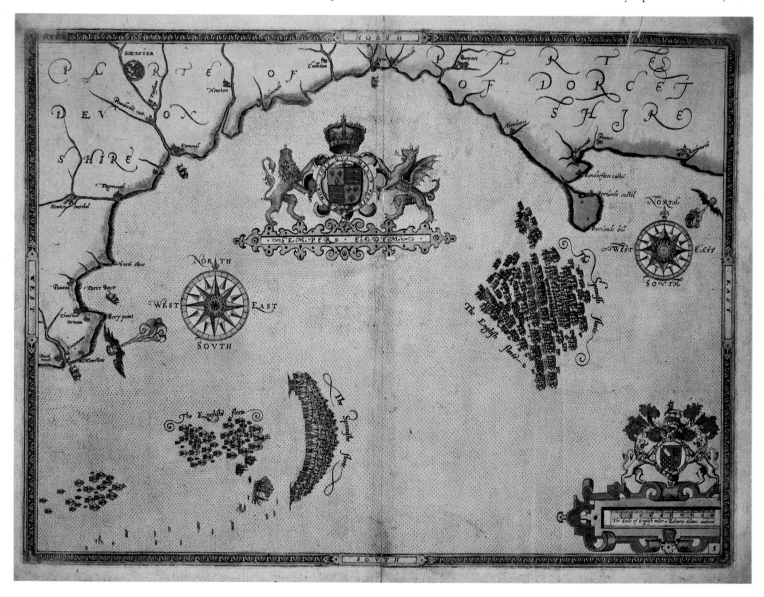

sides did their utmost, shooting off enormous quantities of ammunition, but all to no effect. No serious damage was done to anyone.

The first day's fight, 31 July, off Plymouth, was typical. There are at least six accounts of it, and they might all be describing different battles. Medina Sidonia himself wrote two, one in his diary and the other in a letter, and they are quite different. Howard wrote, very briefly, 'at nine of the clock we gave them fight. In this fight we made some of them bear room to stop their leaks.' But even that was a guess: he could not know if his shots had made the Spaniards leak, and in fact it is extremely unlikely. Drake wrote, even more laconically, 'There hath passed some cannon shot between some of our fleet and some of them, and as far as we perceive they are determined to sell their lives with blows.' That was true enough, but he went no further. The only certain thing is that one Spanish ship, the *San Juan*, had a damaged mast, and a few Spaniards – but not a single Englishman – were wounded.

That afternoon, however, the Spaniards had two accidents. One galleon in their close formation, the *Nuestra Senora del Rosario*, fell foul of two other

ships and carried away her own bowsprit, which made the foremast fall against the mainmast. She took in all sail to make repairs, and consequently fell astern. For some hours Medina Sidonia in his flagship *San Martin* and other ships stood by her, but for some unexplained reason she made no attempt at repairs and set no sail on her remaining masts. When night fell they lost touch with her and left her in the dark.

While this was happening, there was a great explosion in the Spanish fleet. The gunpowder store of the merchantman *San Salvador* had gone up and blown off her poop deck and most of her stern. She was taken in tow, and pinnaces laboured all night to put out the fire and take off survivors.

For that night Howard had appointed Drake to lead the fleet in the *Revenge*: the rest were to follow his stern lantern. But in the darkness he extinguished the lantern and veered off course to seaward. Afterwards he said he had seen some suspicious ships which turned out to be German merchantmen. But nobody else had seen them and probably nobody believed him; for he was well known to have a nose for a possible prize, and at dawn he found himself – purely by chance, he said –

Contemporary pictures of the Armada are accurate enough in the details of the ships, but highly imaginative in showing the fighting. This design for tapestry shows an oared galleass in the foreground (the Armada had four of them), an English ship astern of her and a Spanish ship ahead.

close to the damaged *Nuestra Senora del Rosario*. He called her to surrender, and she did. He took off her commander, Don Pedro de Valdes, and senior officers, and sent a pinnace to take her into port.

As a result of this escapade, there was no fighting at all the following day. The fleet, excepting Howard himself and two or three ships with him, had shortened sail when they lost Drake's light, not knowing whom or what to follow. At dawn Howard and his few companions found themselves close to the Armada, with the rest of the fleet hull down or out of sight astern. The fleet took all day to catch up, and the Armada was left to make its stately progress undisturbed along the coast of Dorset. But encumbered by its merchant ships, it went remarkably slowly. Its average speed all the way up the Channel was barely two knots. A man ashore on horseback, or even on foot, could easily keep up with it.

But during that day, Medina Sidonia received a report that the *San Salvador* was sinking. He gave orders to take everyone off and scuttle her. But the order was not carried out, probably because there were some fifty men still on board who were too badly burned or wounded to be moved. She was left to drift astern.

There was a story afterwards that the explosion had been set off deliberately by a German or Flemish gunner, who was angry because he had been beaten by an army captain. One version said the captain had made advances to the gunner's wife, who happened to be on board. Historians scorned this story for centuries, because the strictest orders had been issued in Lisbon that no women were to be kept in the Armada, and it seemed impossible that a gunner could have hidden his wife for all those weeks in Corunna and at sea. But there was a curious sequel to the story. When the English came up with the derelict ship they towed her into

Launching of the Fireships, by an unknown artist. Again, the battle details are vague: the fireships in fact were launched in the middle of the night, when all other ships were at anchor.

Weymouth. The mayor of the town took charge of her, and some weeks later he made an inventory of her stores. Sending the list to London, he wrote that only twenty survivors were still alive. Among them was a German woman. So perhaps the old story was true.

As the English fleet proceeded along the coast it was joined by more ships from every port it passed, full of enthusiastic volunteers who came to see the fun. Before he was half way up the Channel, Howard had over a hundred ships. But only a small proportion did any good. As in the Armada, the great majority of the English ships were merchantmen; some were hastily fitted with extra guns but many had only the little guns they carried in case of pirates. The Queen only possessed about twenty-five ships and about ten pinnaces, and only a dozen or so were the new race-built sort. But they were the ships which led the fleet and did almost all the fighting, aided by a few privately owned warships and a few of the more robust merchantmen. The rest, according to Howard, were no use except to put on a show – 'to make a brag' was the phrase he used. They fired an immense amount of shot at impossible ranges.

On the third day, 2 August, when the fleets were off Portland, a major battle was fought. Early that morning, the wind went round to the north-east, and suddenly gave the Spaniards the weather gauge. The result, in an English report, was 'a wonderful sharp conflict. There was never seen a more terrible value of great shot, nor more hot fight than this was . . . The great ordnance came so thick that a man would have judged it to have been a hot skirmish of small shot.'

Individual accounts are again in almost hopeless confusion. When the battle began, there was no sort of organization among the English fleet, nothing to match the Spaniards' fleet formation. But there was

one incident during the day that can be identified as the same in English and Spanish stories; and it seems to show the English were learning. It gives the first glimpse of deliberate battle tactics.

The English report says, 'His Lordship called unto certain of Her Majesty's ships then near at hand and charged them straitly to follow him, and to set freshly upon the Spaniards, and to go within musket shot of the enemy before they should discharge any one piece of ordnance.' Then it lists seven ships which followed him in order into the fight: the *Elizabeth Jonas*, the *Galleon of Leicester*, the *Golden Lion*, *Victory*, *Mary Rose*, *Dreadnought* and *Swallow*. Medina Sidonia's diary says, 'When our flagship saw the enemy's flagship leading towards her, she lowered her top sails; and the enemy's flagship passed, followed by the whole of his fleet, each ship firing at our flagship as it passed.'

There was not much result from this manoeuvre: the Spaniards said the English fired at least 500 shots at their flagship *San Martin*, and 'carried away her flagstaff and one of the stays of her mainmast'. The English admitted no damage at all. But it does look as if Howard had invented the line ahead, which in later years became the whole basis of naval tactics and remained so until the Battle of Jutland.

It also seems that some of the English that day began to venture in to shorter range and found they could do it in safety – partly because the Spaniards' gunnery was slower and more erratic than their own, and partly because they were learning to choose positions where the Spanish guns could not be brought to bear. But again, in spite of the 'terrible value of shot', they did no serious damage whatever to the Armada; while the Spaniards discovered that even with the wind behind them, they could not board a single English ship. In the early afternoon the wind fell calm and the battle ended.

By the end of that day the Duke of Medina Sidonia was faced by an awful dilemma. He knew he was going to fail in carrying out King Philip's primary order. He could not hope to beat the English and clear the seas for the Duke of Parma to bring his army across from the Netherlands in boats. The Armada, the weapon he had been given, was unfit to do it, because its ships were so slow and so bad to windward that they could never catch an English ship and board it. Worse still, he had had no word from Parma. He had repeatedly sent fast pinnaces ahead to Dunkirk, with letters asking whether Parma was ready, where he was and where and when they should meet; but no answer whatever had come. It was inviting disaster to sail on into the Narrow Seas, the Straits of Dover, without knowing what he would find there. Yet he could not turn back unless he got a steady easterly wind. Nor could he anchor in the open sea, because everyone knew a fleet at anchor was vulnerable to the most dangerous weapon of that era – fire-ships which could be floated down on it with the tide. His only hope – though it defied the King's orders – was to enter the Solent and fortify himself on the Isle of Wight. That was also what the English guessed he meant to do.

The next day, Wednesday 3 August, was calm. The Armada drifted very slowly past St Alban's Head. The English were close astern, but Howard made no attack. He was almost out of ammunition. From the beginning he had been sending urgent requests ashore for more, but it was only on this day that small ships began to bring it out from the ports. The two captured Spanish ships had been lucky windfalls. In harbour, the shot was taken out of them and sent after him in the fastest boats that could be found; and meanwhile all the southern ports of England prepared to send what shot they had as soon as the Armada had passed them.

Thursday was a day of crisis. At dawn the Armada was off the southern point of the Isle of Wight, within a dozen miles of the entrance to Spithead and Portsmouth and the spacious anchorage of the Solent. But there was not a breath of wind. That morning, the tide was right for entering Spithead. It was due to change and start running out at midday. If a southerly wind came up before then, there was every chance the Armada would be in the Solent before that afternoon.

Knowing he must do something, Howard had his leading ships towed into battle by rowing boats until they were well within musket range. Another gunnery battle was fought between ships which could scarcely move. At one time, the Spaniards' hopes were high that they were going to grapple an English flagship – it was probably Frobisher's *Triumph*. But at the crucial moment a breeze came up. A Spaniard wrote sadly that the two fastest ships in the Armada gave chase, but compared with the Englishman they seemed to be standing still.

The breeze was not south, it was south-west. The course into the Solent is first north-west and then west. The Spanish galleons might have made it, but the merchant ships could not; and after the morning calm there was not even time to try before the tide turned. Medina Sidonia perforce had to sail on to the eastward. Howard followed at a distance. He had resolved to wait and see what the Armada meant to do.

On 6 August it came to anchor off Calais, and the English anchored a mile away, still to windward.

Miniature of Sir Francis Drake by Nicholas Hilliard.

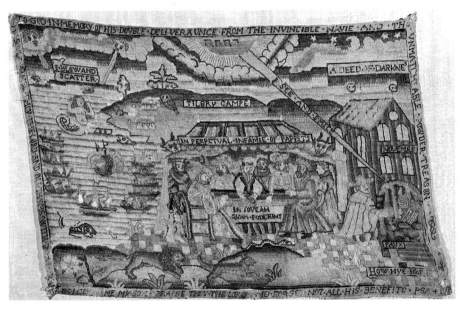

Prayer Book cushion worked to commemorate the defeat of the Armada in 1588 and the discovery of the Gunpowder Plot in 1605.

For 150 years this spirited picture by an unknown artist has been entitled The Battle of Gravelines. But with its off-shore wind, and the figure of Queen Elizabeth symbolically watching from the shore, it would seem more like the battle off Portland several days before.

But Calais was French, and 20 miles (32 km) short of Dunkirk, which was the principal port held by Parma. At the last moment, Medina Sidonia's pilots had told him that was as near as they could go. Off Dunkirk, sandbanks extend 10 miles (16 km) out to sea, and the approach was too shallow for the big Armada ships.

That evening and on Sunday morning, messengers came out to Medina Sidonia to tell him that Parma was not ready. For the crossing, he had collected a fleet of river barges and rafts, which had not a chance of reaching England unless the weather was exactly right, and moreover were quite unable to protect themselves. Parma was not prepared to move until the Armada had done its job and cleared the English off the seas. There was a total misunderstanding between the two commanders, which was due to the secretive way King Philip had organized the expedition. Anchored where they were, the commanders of the Armada knew they were sitting ducks for fire-ships, but there was nowhere else they could go.

The English knew it too. That same day, 7 August, they were joined by Lord Henry Seymour's fleet from the Thames, which was fully stocked with ammunition and included two more of the newest race-built ships, the *Rainbow* and the *Vanguard*. They had made no preparations for a fire-ship attack, but they filled eight old ships with anything that would burn, and soon after midnight they launched them with wind and tide against the Armada.

Seeing them approaching and bursting into flames, there was nothing the Armada could do but cut its anchor cables to escape. At dawn its close formation was gone and it was scattered 10 miles downwind, as far as the village of Gravelines, which gave its name to the battle that began that day, 8 August.

Howard ordered a charge (that was the word

they used, as for cavalry) but he himself was tempted by a prize, as Drake had been off the coast of Devon: the galleass *San Lorenzo* with a broken rudder was being rowed very close inshore, making for Calais. Howard turned the *Ark Royal* aside to attack it, and left Drake in the *Revenge* to lead the charge. Medina Sidonia had only three or four galleons with him, but he bravely stood his ground and prepared to defend his fleet alone.

Again, there was a semblance of line ahead. Drake fired his bow-guns, turned and fired his broadside, then passed on while other ships came in astern of him and did the same. Slowly, the forces

The approximate track of the Armada on a contemporary English chart.

on both sides built up in a general mêlée – but nothing like all of them. 260 ships were present that day, but a far smaller number took any part in the fighting – at the most, perhaps thirty Spaniards and forty English.

This battle was quite different from those that had gone before. It was still disorganized. Captains received no orders unless they came within shouting distance of a senior officer, and each of them, obscured in the gun-smoke, did whatever seemed best to him. But the English had learnt that their range had been far too long. Now, against a scattered fleet, they ventured to within a few yards – yet still never gave the Spaniards a chance to board. At that range, their shots began to penetrate the Spanish hulls and cause dreadful havoc on the gun-decks. Two Spanish galleons were entirely crippled, full of holes, half their men dead or dying, and they drifted to leeward, ran aground and were captured by their Dutch enemies. One other, the *Maria Juan*, sank that evening, and by then every ship that had taken an active part was leaking through shot holes on the waterline. The *San Martin*, in the thick of it all the time, was hit by 107 shot. One 50-pounder went right through both sides of the hull.

Yet – and this is the mystery of Gravelines – not a single English ship had a single shot hole in her hull: there were plenty in the upperworks, which were lightly built, but none in the hulls. Several explanations have been suggested for this extraordinary fact. The Spanish gunners were admittedly slower in loading and firing than the English, which would have meant that they did less damage. They may have slowed down, or even stopped firing, disorganized and appalled by the carnage all round them. Some may have run out of ammunition: they were all short of it before the battle began. But at that range, they could not have

missed. Some shots must have hit the English hulls. The fact was that none of them went through.

The only plausible explanation has been given by underwater archaeology in the last decade or so. Divers have salvaged hundreds of shot from the wrecks of Spanish ships, and some have been analysed. They were all badly made. The Spaniards and Portuguese were notoriously backward as iron founders, and the iron of their shot was full of impurities. It also had concentric rings in it, which showed it was quenched while it was still red hot. Both of those faults would have made it brittle, and possibly, unknown to their gunners, their shot was breaking into fragments when they fired it, or when it hit an enemy hull. This may have been the ultimate reason why the Armada was beaten.

Beaten it was: but only by the folly of King Philip's plan and the technical defects of the fleet – the clumsiness of its ships and perhaps the brittleness of its shot. Nobody can question the courage of its men. The Englishmen who fought it made no claim of victory. They were disappointed at Gravelines: it did not seem to them a successful battle. Their only achievement, in their own eyes, was to have driven the Armada to the leeward of Parma's ports. But that was enough. In the prevailing south-westerly wind, a fleet which could not sail to windward had no chance of coming back. The English followed it most of the way up the North Sea, but they did not fight it again, because they had no ammunition left, or not enough to risk provoking a battle. In the latitude of Newcastle they left it, sending only two frigates ahead which shadowed it to the Orkney Islands; and then they put back to the Thames to stock up with food and shot in case a change of wind brought it back again.

But it never came back. Its only way of escape was round the north of Scotland and Ireland; and it was there, not in battle, that it met its final disaster. Most of its ships, built for coastal trading, were too weak for Atlantic weather in September, and some were further weakened by the stress of battle. They began to break up. Sinking ships with diseased and starving crews were driven in to the western coasts of Ireland, Scotland, England and France. They had all lost their principal anchors on the night of the fire-ships, and nearly a half of them drove ashore or foundered at sea.

Both sides ascribed the defeat of the Armada to the intervention of God. The English would have been happy to claim they had a superior fleet, but it was more important to claim that God had aided the Protestant side. The famous inscription on the medal that Queen Elizabeth ordered to be cast expressed a sincere belief: '*Flavit Jehovah et Dissipati Sunt*', (God Breathed and They are Scattered). As for the Spaniards, it was easier to admit defeat at the hands of God than those of a human enemy, and it was not for them, they believed, to question the wisdom of God's designs. Nevertheless, the doom of the Armada was seen all over the rest of Europe as the first defeat of Spanish military might, and it marked the beginning of the downfall of the Spanish empire.

The Four Days' Fight
1666

A GUNNERY BATTLE under sail was certainly a terrible experience: terrible, yet for most men intensely exciting, like a dangerous sport. At least, as they went into battle, they hid whatever fear they had and showed their elation. In the Four Days' Fight they attacked, one eyewitness said, 'with trumpets sounding, and drums beating in every ship, the seamen waving in defiance their hats, and the officers their plumed beavers'.

To a modern imagination, the scene on the gun-decks must have been hellish: a hell of noise, with the shouts and cheers and screams of agony, and the concussion of the guns which sometimes deafened men for life; a hell of vision too, in the smoke and half-darkness lit by gun-flashes, when the enemy shot began to come through, and the surgeon's men shoved mangled corpses out through the gun-ports and carried the wounded below, and the blood ran back and forth as the ship rolled, making curious patterns on the deck, and little boys ran through the shambles each carrying powder to his gun.

On the upper decks the dangers were different: from falling masts and spars and the shot that flew everywhere – everything from musketry to the cannon-balls that could smash a man to pieces.

But here the excitement perhaps was stronger. Success could be seen to depend on skill, the skill of the captain's judgement and the crew in the handling of the ship. The best seamanship won, and battles were full of quick decisions: to spot an enemy who might be cut off from the rest; to set a course that would bring your own guns to bear where his would not; to come to close range without being boarded. Approaching, could you luff up a little more to cross his bows without losing too much way, or should you pay off and tempt him to fire his broadside at too long a range, then cross his stern before he could reload? And what was he going to do, and what was everyone else doing? Would your manoeuvre put you in peril from another enemy? It had all the elements of sport – and the best sports have an element of danger. There cannot be any doubt that many men enjoyed it.

But perhaps it was just as well that battles at sea were normally very short. In general, they began with a sighting at dawn and an approach which lasted all morning. They were fought in the afternoon, and were finished before the evening. Trafalgar, the most consequential of them all, only lasted four hours. But the Four Days' Fight in 1666 did literally last four days, and both sides spent the whole of each night repairing their damage. It could only have happened between two fleets that were equally determined. The rivals were English and Dutch.

In the second half of that century, starting in 1652 when England was under the rule of Oliver Cromwell, the English fought three wars against the Dutch, who had been their allies against Spain; and those wars were unique because they were fought entirely at sea. No armies took part in them on either side.

They were singularly pointless wars. There was no religious dispute to divide the two countries, and

no real enmity between their peoples. The nominal cause was that both Dutch and English were building empires, and were rivals in far-flung trade. One major bone of contention, for example, was a small island in the East Indies called Pulo Run. Very few people had heard of it before, or have heard of it since: but it was the only place in the world that could produce a crop of nutmegs, and the merchants of both nations wanted its monopoly.

However, men seldom fight to the death for merchants' profits, and one cannot help feeling the real cause of the war was different: both nations had built new fighting fleets, with ships of new design, and both were itching to try them against a worthy enemy. So they did, with immense enthusiasm, in dozens of battles. Sometimes the English won and sometimes the Dutch, and each war ended as soon as the navies grew tired of it. In terms of politics and power the results of the wars were negligible.

The English had started to build their new fleet in 1610. In that year a warship was launched at Woolwich on the Thames and named the *Prince Royal*. She had the same lines as the Elizabethan race-built ships, but she was half as big again: she carried sixty-four guns and needed a crew of five hundred men. By the 1660s, however, she was merely a ship of average strength. By then the major English ships had eighty-two guns and a crew of eight hundred; and the Dutch ships were almost identical.

The quantity of ships was also enormous. Both nations could send to sea fleets of over a hundred ships; and these, unlike Queen Elizabeth's fleet or the Armada, did not include converted merchantmen but only warships built for the purpose of fighting. Both nations had also studied the technique of fire-ships. They no longer relied on improvising that weapon, but took with them ships designed to be set on fire, ready-filled with combustibles and provided with cunning arrangements of chimneys to make a forced draught.

With these new weapons both sides had evolved simple systems of signalling with guns and flags, which enabled admirals to control their fleets as a whole and order a limited number of manoeuvres. Both sides had accepted the virtues of the line ahead, where the ships followed in single file, which gave the best field of fire for broadside guns and the least risk of hitting one's friends. Battles, which hitherto had been mêlées, took on the curiously formal air they presented for the next two hundred years: both the opposing fleets formed lines which slowly converged, until each ship could fight an artillery duel with the one opposite. A hundred ships, of course, made a line that was many miles long. The first diagram of this formation – or at least, the first that has survived – was drawn by an eye-witness, an English surgeon, at a battle in July 1666; and with the flagships of admirals, vice-admirals and rear-admirals interspersed along the line it still gives a clear impression of the size and length of seventeenth-century fighting-fleets.

The English fleet in 1666 was under the joint

The *Royal Prince* surrenders,
stranded on the Galloper
Shoal, by William van de
Velde the Younger.

command of Prince Rupert and George Monck,
newly created Duke of Albemarle, both veterans of
the Civil War. They sailed together from the
Medway in the flagship *Royal Charles* of eighty-two
guns, with a fleet of eighty men-of-war. The Dutch
were commanded by Michel de Ruyter, who was
certainly the greatest seaman of the age. The
English knew he was ready for sea with eighty-five
ships. They took station in the Downs, the
customary anchorage between the coast of Kent
and the Goodwin sands. They expected day by day
to see the Dutch masts above the horizon to the
east, and they were eager, as usual, to give battle.

At that moment the Dutch had an ally: the
French had joined them, and declared war on
England. Louis xiv had a fleet, but it was not in the

same class as the Dutch and English, and it
succeeded nimbly in keeping out of their battles.
But it did cause a false alarm. While the fleet
waited, a ship came in to the west of England and
sent a report to Charles ii that a French fleet of
thirty-six sail was entering the Channel from the
west. To meet that threat, the King decided to
divide his fleet. He told Prince Rupert to go down
the Channel in the *Royal James*, seventy-eight guns,
taking one third of the fleet and leaving Albemarle
in the *Royal Charles* to face the Dutch with what
remained.

This was a classic mistake, the sort of thing that
happens when kings take part in strategy. Instead
of one powerful fleet, the English now had two,
which were both outnumbered. And the report

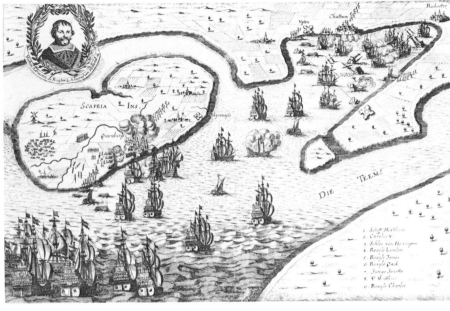

A Dutch map of the Medway: it would, however, have misled anyone who tried to use it. It shows the river at high tide, when most of its area is only a few feet deep.

itself was mistaken. The fleet that had been sighted turned out to be not French but Spanish, and it was not coming up the Channel but was minding its own business on the coast of Portugal. A message was sent to recall Prince Rupert, but through yet another mistake it was not sent by relays of horsemen but by the ordinary mail coach, and it took a week to reach him off the Isle of Wight.

Meanwhile de Ruyter in *Zeven Provincien* had come out with an easterly wind, but as he approached across the North Sea the wind changed to a strong south-wester and the weather grew thick with rain: so he came to anchor. Albemarle sighted him downwind. He called a council, and ran up the signal to form the line of battle. He had only forty-six ships against de Ruyter's eighty-five, but he

attacked at once. De Ruyter cut his anchor cables and stood away, also in line ahead, to the south-east, keeping the wind abeam. Albermarle followed him round, into the new conventional position of converging lines.

The English then discovered a disadvantage in holding the weather gauge which nobody seems to have foreseen. In line ahead, with a strong beam wind and a choppy sea, all the ships of the fleet that was to windward were heeled towards the enemy. Consequently, they could not open their lower gun-ports on that side. The fleet downwind, of course, was heeled away from the enemy. It shut its lower ports on the side that was disengaged, but could open them all on the side that was in action. Thus Albemarle was into a running fight against the foreward half of de Ruyter's fleet, with only his smaller upper-deck guns in action.

All the same, he gave as good as he got. But at length the coast of Flanders came in sight and the sea grew shallow. De Ruyter, either by luck or foresight, had driven the English into a corner. They had to change course, and with the coast ahead and the enemy to leeward the only new course they could make was back in the direction they had come. Albemarle had to order his fleet to tack together. That way, they had to pass the whole rearward half of the Dutch who had hitherto not been engaged. Again, he had to shut his lower gun-ports on the side that mattered, and as the fleets passed, now in opposite directions, the English were badly battered. Three or four with damaged masts and rigging fell astern and were surrounded by the Dutch. Two of them sank and one was captured; but one, the 65-gun *Henry*, refused to do either.

The *Henry* was the flagship of Rear-Admiral Sir John Harman. She was partly dismasted and completely disabled by gunfire. The Dutch sent in a fire-ship to finish her off. It grappled her and its crew put off in their boat, but a lieutenant from the *Henry* boarded it, cut or cast off its grapnels and jumped back aboard unhurt. The Dutch sent another, on her other side, which set her remaining sails on fire. That caused the beginning of a panic, and about fifty of her crew jumped overboard; the first, Pepys wrote in his diary, was the parson. The Admiral drew his sword and threatened to kill the next man who tried to desert the ship. Put to shame, they started to fight the fire, but before they succeeded a rope burnt through and a yard fell down and broke the Admiral's ankle. A Dutch flagship hailed him to surrender, but he shouted back 'No, it has not come to that yet', and fired a broadside which killed the Dutch commander, Evertzoon.

The Dutch then left him alone, believing perhaps that he was harmless. But the seamen of that era were amazingly resourceful: on long voyages, they had to be able to repair any part of their ship. They could do it in battle too, and the *Henry*'s crew rigged jury masts and sails, and took their ship 60 miles across the wind into Harwich, where they landed their wounded and set to work to make her ready to fight again. By the next evening she was fit, and Harman, despite his broken ankle, sailed her out to follow the sound of the guns and find the fleet.

At the end of that first day, Albemarle had only forty-four ships in action. He called a council and made a most memorable speech: 'If we had dreaded the number of the enemy, we should have fled: but though we are inferior to them in ships, we are in all things else superior. Let the enemy feel that though our fleet be divided, our spirit is entire. At the worst it will be more honourable to die bravely here on our own element than be made

The *Royal James*, 78-guns, flagship of Prince Rupert in the Four Days Fight by William van de Velde the Younger.

spectacles to the Dutch. To be overcome is the fortune of war, but to fly is the fashion of cowards.' Next morning, therefore, now outnumbered about two to one, they began the battle again.

In those extraordinary wars, each side admired the other and was willing to say so. Of that decision to fight, the Dutch statesman Johan de Witt said afterwards: 'Our own fleet could never have been brought on after the first day's fighting, and I believe that none but theirs could; all the Dutch discovered was that Englishmen might be killed and English ships be burnt, but that English courage was invincible.'

That second day, against such awful odds, many more English ships were crippled, though none of them sank: it was still very difficult to sink a wooden ship by gunfire, and even fire-ships were hard to use against ships that could move at all. By the evening, Albemarle had only sixteen ships that were fit to fight. The Dutch still had nearly eighty, but many of them were badly damaged too. De Ruyter

himself was lagging astern with his main yard and main topmast gone; and his vice-admiral Cornelis Tromp (the son of the famous admiral, Marten Tromp) had had to shift his flag to another ship when his own was put out of action.

During that day, Albemarle began to retreat towards the Thames. But it was a fighting retreat, well organized. The ships most damaged were sent ahead, and the sixteen that were fit formed a rearguard to protect them. The Dutch followed closely, and tried again and again to force a way through the rearguard, but they failed. The retreat continued, very slowly as the wind fell away, all through the morning of the third day. Day and night, the crews of the damaged ships were working not only to keep them afloat and moving, but to make them fit to fight again.

Early that afternoon, another fleet was sighted, coming up the Channel past Dover. Was it Prince Rupert coming back, or was it the French? Nobody knew, and for hours the battle proceeded in

dreadful suspense. Just before dusk, their flags could be distinguished. They were English.

This was the first battle ever described by an ordinary seaman. He was Edward Barlow, who had run away to sea as a boy and kept an amusing and vivid journal all his seafaring life, illustrated with paintings. He was present all through the Four Days' Fight, and he wrote of the meeting with Prince Rupert and a subsequent disaster:

We began to edge towards them; and being near to a sand which is called the Galloper through the unskilfulness of the pilots, thinking they had been farther off, we ran just upon it, the *Royal Charles* striking upon it, and some other great ships. And the *Royal Prince*, being the biggest ship and drawing the most water, stuck fast upon it, all the rest of the fleet sailing away and leaving her all alone: they durst not stay to help her for fear of running more of the Great Ships on the ground.

This was a serious loss. The *Royal Prince*, as Barlow called her, was the first and oldest of the big ships, the one that was christened *Prince Royal* in

The successful Dutch attack on the English fleet in harbour at Chatham on the Medway: a composite picture of the fighting by van Soest.

41

The Four Days' Fight, 1666

This panoramic view of the Medway's winding course shows Chatham in the distance, Sheerness in the left foreground, and Upnor Castle on the far right. In the centre is the useless barrage of sunken ships which failed to stop or even hinder the Dutch ships. By W. Schellincks.

1610. She now carried ninety guns instead of the sixty-four she had been built for, and she was commanded by Sir George Ayscue, who was second only to Albemarle. The Dutch surrounded her, and there was nothing anyone could do to help her. To save the lives of his crew, Ayscue surrendered to Cornelis Tromp. Tromp believed he could get her off the sands and take her home as a prize, but de Ruyter refused to wait, since the battle was still raging. He insisted she should be burnt, and she was. Tromp was exceedingly annoyed with his commander-in-chief.

By the time Prince Rupert joined, seventeen of Albemarle's damaged ships had been repaired at

sea, and another three had put out from the Medway to help. Between them they therefore had sixty – better odds than when they had started; and Prince Rupert and his men were annoyed and ashamed to have wasted time on the fool's errand down the Channel. Albemarle went on board Prince Rupert's *Royal James* to confer. He was exhausted, and so were his crews, after three days of fighting and two nights busy in repairs. But Prince Rupert's fleet was fresh, and they agreed to fight again next day. Edward Barlow, at the opposite end of the scale of rank, understood and approved the decision:

They concluded to set upon the Holland fleet again the

42

fashioned mêlée with shot flying everywhere. Barlow was wounded in the leg by a spent shot which came through the side of the ship, and he spent the day limping about, not much use to anyone. But he was very unwilling to admit defeat, and when at last the fleet retreated towards the Thames, his grammar deserted him in a list of excuses:

The fight continuing very hard until four of the clock in the afternoon, and few or none but were much disabled in one thing or another, being engaged with so much odds that some of our ships began to retreat towards our own coast, and it being almost night and a mist arising, our General made the sign to retreat, the mist increasing and it beginning to be dark; but the Hollands fleet made no great haste to follow us, being willing to leave off, having their bellies full as well as we.

That mist was fortunate. Both sides had fought until they were too exhausted to fight any more. They both needed a reason to stop without loss of honour and the mist gave it to them. On the whole, the Dutch could claim a victory. Once again, the number of ships that were sunk was remarkably small: four of the eighty or so on each side, with another six English captured. But the human casualties were enormous: on each side some 2,500 men killed or wounded, and 2,000 English taken prisoner. Yet nobody despaired or was even apparently discouraged. Two months later, all the ships were mended and the fleets were at it again; and this time, the victory went to the English.

But the wars were coming to an end. In early September the fleet returning to port met the news of the Fire of London, which had caused damage amounting to more than the cost of the first two wars. King Charles could find no more money. The navy was bankrupt, its sailors unpaid and mutinous. The King sued for peace; but next summer, while negotiations were going on, de Ruyter inflicted the most disgraceful defeat a British navy ever suffered, when he sailed up the River Medway and burnt the ships at their moorings in Chatham dockyard.

Yet at the end of it all, these strange wars decided nothing. Nobody won, and nobody lost – except the thousands of men who lost their lives. The Dutch stayed in Pulo Run, but it was six months' voyage away and nobody could be bothered to go and turn them out. Elsewhere, two territories were exchanged. The English conceded a Dutch claim to Surinam in South America, and the Dutch conceded an English claim to the island of Manhattan, and both sides seemed happy with the bargain. The fact was that both had won what they wanted from the wars experience. They had learnt how to build the most efficient warships, and how to handle them in battle.

It ended with a typically graceful gesture. De Ruyter's son Engels was then eighteen and already a frigate captain. The Dutch sent him to London to bring a diplomat home, and while he was there he was received with the greatest honour by the admirals his father had defeated, and was knighted by Charles II.

next day to see what fortune would befall them, being very loath that the groat-headed Flemings should go home victorious, though their fleet were still twice the number that we were. By sunrising the Hollands ships bore up to us, and the fighting began anew, very fiercely on both sides, Prince Rupert and his Vice-Admiral being engaged very hot, venturing into the midst of them and running into much danger, whereby in a small time they were very much disabled, losing a great many men.

The fleets began again to fight in line of battle. But the wind had increased, most of the ships were more or less damaged, and most of the men on both sides were tired out. They soon lost their close formation, and the battle degenerated into an old-

Quebec, Lagos
and Quiberon Bay
1759

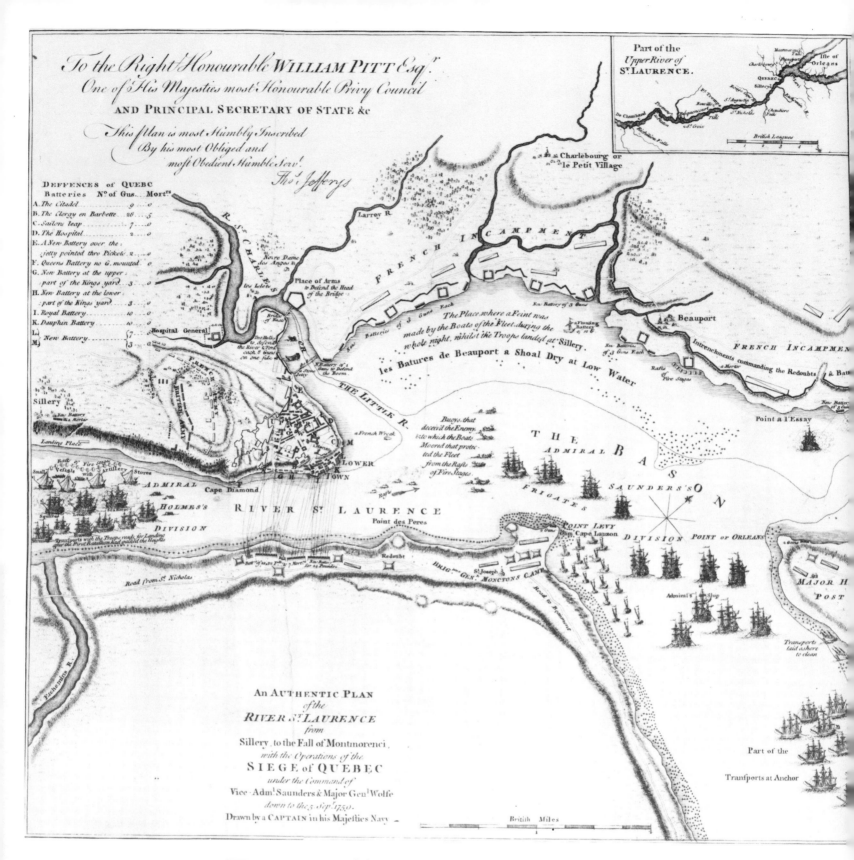

Previous pages French fire-rafts float down river against the British fleet at Quebec, by S. Scott.

Above Contemporary map of Quebec, drawn from the surveys of the attacking army.

IN THE TWO remaining centuries of fighting under sail, very little changed in ships or guns. Indeed, if wooden ships had been sufficiently durable the major ships the Dutch and English used could have taken a place in Nelson's line at Trafalgar. One of them almost did. She was built as the *Prince* (a successor to the *Prince Royal*) in 1670, fought in the last Dutch war, was still fighting at Quebec in 1759, and was afloat, though not in first-line service, in 1805. In those centuries, tactics also remained substantially the same. The only thing that evolved was signalling. By the 1750s, flag-signals were much more elaborate, and admirals could therefore control their fleets more exactly.

But politically everything had changed by then. The Dutch had fallen out of the competition for supremacy at sea, the Spaniards' power was waning, and the only threatening rivals of the English – or to be more exact, the British – during King George II's reign, were the French. Within four months of the summer and autumn of 1759, the English beat the French navies of Louis XV in three widely separated battles, at Quebec in

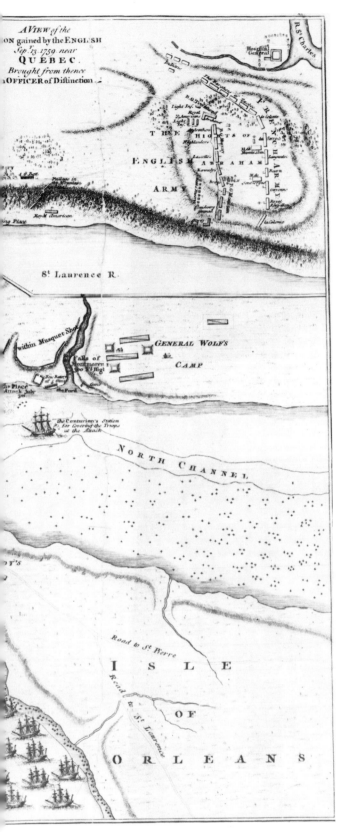

A VIEW of the
...ON gained by the ENGLISH
Sep.r 13. 1759. near
QUEBEC.
Brought from thence
...OFFICER of Distinction...

St. Laurence R.

GENERAL WOLF'S CAMP

NORTH CHANNEL

ISLE OF ORLEANS

Road to St. Pierre

Seven Years' War, to seize control of Canada from the French and prevent the junction of their forces in the north and on the Mississippi, which would have hemmed in the British colonists and stopped their expansion to the west.

It really began with the taking of Louisburg on Cape Breton Island the year before. That was a strange achievement in itself. There had been five French ships of the line in the harbour, but one had blown up – as wooden warships did from time to time – and set two more on fire. The remaining two, the *Prudent*, 72-guns, and the *Bienfaisons*, 64-guns, were annoying the British army with their fire, and the army was unable to stop them. Nor could the navy enter harbour with its ships; so the admiral put 600 sailors in rowing boats, and sent them in at night. They were fiercely attacked by fortresses ashore, and by the ships themselves, but they boarded them both – an astonishing feat from rowing-boats – forced their crews to surrender, and cut their cables. One drifted ashore, so they set her on fire. With their boats, they towed the other away and took her as a prize. Relieved of their fire, the army took the town.

The capture of Louisburg opened the way to the mouth of the St Lawrence, the route to Quebec. But nothing bigger than a frigate had ever navigated the river. The French had removed the buoys and beacons, and were free to man and fortify the banks. The only charts were French and unreliable. Yet Charles Saunders, the admiral in command, who was flying his flag in the *Neptune*, seems never to have doubted that his captains and crews could reach the city; or at least, he did not hesitate to try.

He waited all winter, when the river was frozen, and as soon as the ice began to break up in the spring of 1759 he sent his ships' masters in boats up the river to survey it. Among them was Mr James Cook, who had joined the navy as a seaman and had only recently been promoted – and who survived to become the greatest of all navigators. Marine surveying at the best of times needed infinite patience: to correct whatever maps existed, to sail or row across the river again and again, taking soundings with the lead at proper intervals, observing the boat's position, allowing for stream and tide and methodically writing down the depths. This survey, in water that still had lumps of ice in it, was made entirely under the enemy's observation: much of it had to be done at night. But between them the masters made perfectly adequate charts, and Cook in particular founded his reputation as a cartographer.

With that preparation, the whole of the battle fleet entered the river in June and anchored 100 miles (160 km) from the open sea and 60 miles (97 km) below Quebec: twenty-two ships of the line, twenty-seven frigates and smaller warships, and the transports to carry over 9,000 soldiers commanded by General James Wolfe. This was already much farther than Wolfe had expected the ships to escort him, and also much farther than the French had thought a fleet could come. Above that point, the river narrowed to its most dangerous passage. Saunders shifted his flag from the *Neptune*,

Below Vice-Admiral Charles Saunders, by Joshua Reynolds.

Canada, Lagos in Portugal, and Quiberon Bay in France. Those four months, after the centuries of struggle, put the British firmly in the lead.

Quebec was not strictly a sea battle, because it happened 160 miles up the St Lawrence River, and a great deal farther than that from the open ocean. It was a combined operation: the navy was again in its mediaeval role of transporting an army. But it was a triumph of pilotage, and could not have happened at all without naval skill.

It was part of the great strategic plan, in the

Above A magnetic ship's compass set in a wooden bowl dated about 1750.

Above right A reflecting quadrant of the mid-eighteenth century. This recent invention gave a new accuracy to charts and maps, and a new freedom to explorers.

Right Major General James Wolfe, killed at Quebec at the age of 23.

90-guns, to the smaller *Stirling Castle*, 60-guns, then left the largest ships there and proceeded with four ships of the line, the frigates and transports.

Below the narrows, one English ship had lured some local French pilots on board by showing false colours, and they were distributed among the other ships. But any patriotic Frenchman might have been expected to run his ship aground, so nobody took any notice of what they said.

Not one of the ships ran aground. Boats were sent ahead and moored on the edges of the channel, with port and starboard flags. Some masters conned their ships from the forecastle, watching the ripples and eddies and shouting their orders to the helmsmen with their megaphones. The fleet passed through the narrows without mishap, and came to anchor again while the army began to reconnoitre the defences of the city. At midnight, seven fire-ships and two burning rafts came down the river, a sight that might have appalled the crew of any wooden ship; but men went out in boats with confidence, threw grappling irons aboard the flaming ships and towed them clear. Next day, a little over a week after entering the river, the first of the ships were anchored in sight of Quebec.

There they remained throughout the two-month siege that followed. In the narrow confines of the river, and always in sight of the enemy, it was a strange kind of battle for a navy. Of course the ships bombarded the city, but the navy's main activity was in rowing boats, finding the possible landing-places and putting the troops ashore on them in the strong current at night – work mainly for junior officers which needed a skill and precision of its own. In the final famous assault on the cliff that led up to the plains behind the city, the soldiers were embarked 14 miles (23 km) up-river. The boats

A View of the Taking of QUEBEC September 13th 1759

Showing the manner of debarking the English Forces, & of the resolute scrambling of the light Infantry, up a Woody Precipice to dislodge the Captains post, which defended a small entrenched path, through which the Troops were to pass. Also a view of the signal Victory obtained over the French regulars, Canadians and Indians, which produced the surrender of Quebec.

Vüe de la Prise de QUEBEC le 13 Septembre 1759.

Qui Represente le débarquement des Troupes Angloises, & L'Intrepidité de L'Infanterie Legere en Escaladant un Precipice Boiseux P. pour déloger le poste du Capitaine qui défend un Sentier retranché par où les Troupes devoient passer & Ausi P la vüe de la Victoire Signa. Remporté Sur les Francois, Canadiens & Indiens qui obligeai la Ville à Capituler.

came down in the dark with a six-knot tide and current behind them, and yet they put the men ashore at exactly the chosen spot, the only one where a path led up the cliff. It was a kind of seamanship not often needed in battle. 'Considering the Darkness of the Night,' Saunders wrote afterwards, 'and the rapidity of the Current, this was a very critical Operation, and very properly and successfully conducted.' Anyone who has used small boats will recognize that as a naval understatement.

After putting the army ashore, it was the navy who hauled the first guns up the cliff, ready for the battle next morning when General Wolfe was killed, but the French were defeated and the city fell.

The voyage up to Quebec was certainly a great feat of ship-handling. It must have needed not only an admiral who would try it, but also captains, masters and men right through the ranks who knew without exception what they were doing. It was an early example of an attitude of mind that came to distinguish the British navy, or perhaps all navies: a will not only to do what the army or anyone else expected, but to go one better, and astonish landlubbers by doing something they thought was

impossible – and then, of course, to make light of it.

While the fighting was going on in Canada, the French at home were preparing an invasion of England, as they often did, and the other two battles of that year were fought to prevent it. The moves and countermoves at sea were so like Napoleon's and Nelson's, forty-five years later, that they look like a dress rehearsal. The main French fleets were at Toulon in the Mediterranean under Admiral de la Clue and at Brest in Brittany under Admiral de Bonpart. They were meant to combine and escort an invading army. But both ports were blockaded by the British navy, as they were in Nelson's time. The fleet off Toulon, like Nelson's, had no base that was nearer than Gibraltar, 800 miles (1,290 km) away; and the fleet off Brest, standing off and on in the open Atlantic and among the rocks and tides of Ushant, was driven off its station from time to time by westerly gales.

The Mediterranean fleet was commanded in 1759 by Admiral Boscawen, who had also commanded at Louisburg the year before. He was a Cornishman with a long and adventurous naval career: he could claim, in this series of wars, to have defeated and captured the same French captain,

Hand-coloured engraving of the taking of Quebec.

whose name was Hocquart, three times in eleven years. Off Toulon he did his best – again like Nelson – to lure the French out of port, but they would not come, and in July he had to put back to Gibraltar for food and repairs. The French took the chance, hoping to pass Gibraltar unseen. But a frigate sighted them. The British were re-rigging and the flagship *Namur*, 90-guns, had not a single sail bent; but they got out of harbour in two hours and Boscawen hoisted the most exciting signal of all: General Chase – which meant that each ship should carry all the sail she could and make her best speed, irrespective of order, to overhaul the enemy.

In that chase, there was a strangely patchy wind. The first morning, 18 August, the British had a following breeze while the French were becalmed. By afternoon, the British caught up with them but then fell into the calm themselves. A gunnery battle began between ships that were almost motionless – like the Armada off the Isle of Wight. But by now naval gunnery was much more effective, not through improvements in the guns or shot, but in the skill and training of the men. The sternmost French ship was quickly crippled and forced to surrender, and Boscawen's flagship lost her mizzenmast and both her topsail yards. At the height of the battle, Boscawen ordered his barge to take him to an undamaged ship, the *Newark*, 80-guns. On the way, the barge was holed by a shot, and the

Right Admiral Edward Boscawen, after Reynolds. He commanded the capture of Louisburg, and in the following year won the Battle of Lagos.

Below HMS Warspite in pursuit of the French at Lagos.

Admiral, with splendid presence of mind, snatched off his wig, stuffed it into the hole and stopped the leak. At nightfall a breeze sprang up, and two French ships escaped unseen to Cadiz. In the dawn, the remaining four were 3 miles (5 km) ahead, on a course for the coast of Portugal. They ran for the Bay of Lagos; and there, as she entered the bay, the French flagship *Océan* ran aground with the breeze behind her and all her sails set, so that all three masts in an awful tangle of rigging and canvas fell over her bows. She and another damaged ship were boarded and burned, while the other two were taken as prizes. One of them had a name that won fame in the British navy: *Temeraire*.

Boscawen's comment on the battle was essentially naval: 'It is well, but it might have been a great deal better.' Only three prizes, he might have said, out of seven major ships; for all navies, and the British in particular, measured their success not from the ships they damaged, but from those they brought home in prize. The government, which paid them miserable wages, paid enormous sums for prizes which could be added to the British fleet. A few hours' fight, with luck, could make an admiral or captain a wealthy man for life; and though the seamen's share of a prize was minute in comparison, it was enough to provide a memorable party – like the one in Portsmouth when the seamen celebrated by buying gold watches and frying them. The British always planned their battles and fought with this in mind.

Three months later, the other fleet, which was blockading Brest, won a greater and far more dramatic victory – but one which brought them only a single prize. The most memorable thing

his mind and bore away towards Quiberon Bay, the nearest shelter to leeward. By midday it was blowing a gale straight on shore, with very heavy gusts, and the sea was rough. Quiberon Bay is notoriously dangerous, full of small islands, shoals and rocks, and the French admiral may have thought Hawke in that kind of weather would keep clear of a lee shore for which he had no pilot. But the Brest blockade had given Hawke and his fleet total confidence in their seamanship. They set far more sail than the French thought it safe to carry, and as the French entered the bay, rounding the outer island of Belle-Ile and the dangerous rocks called the Cardinals, the British were overhauling them and engaging them as they passed. The flagship *Formidable* of the French rear-admiral was wrecked by gunfire and surrendered after an awful loss of life. A 74-gun ship, *Thésée*, overturned and foundered because she had her lower gunports open in the heavy sea, and only 20 of her crew of 800 men were saved. Another, *Héros*, sank after broadsides had holed her between wind and water.

As dusk was falling, Hawke himself entered the inner bay and met the French flagship *Soleil Royal*, desperately trying to beat her way out again, and in spite of his master's protest he ordered his ship to be laid alongside the enemy and then drove her down to leeward, towards the eastern shore which has other hidden groups of rocks and shoals. As

Left Admiral Sir Edward Hawke, by F. Cotes.

Below Hawke's flagship at Quiberon Bay, *HMS Royal George*, by Dominic Serres.

about Lagos was perhaps the Admiral's wig; but the next battle was a classic scene of apocalyptic horror.

That other fleet was commanded by Admiral Hawke in the *Royal George*. It was November, and an Atlantic gale had driven him to leave his dangerous post off Brest and run 150 miles (240 km) across the Channel to shelter in Torbay on the coast of Devon, knowing the gale would imprison the French in harbour. But on the day it began to moderate, the French put to sea. On the same day, Hawke got under way from Torbay, sending the fastest frigates ahead. Off Ushant, one of them told him the French had left port and set course to the southward – the same frigate, as it happened, that had sighted the fleet off Gibraltar. Hawke followed, but headwinds drove him off to the westward. He still had frigates out ahead. At dawn on 20 November the wind came westerly and began to grow in force, and he sent his fastest ship of the line ahead too, to make the coast and fix the fleet's position. It was probably no coincidence that this was a ship that had been captured from the French, the *Magnamine*; for the English generally admired French ships as faster than their own. Her captain was Lord Howe, who was then thirty-three years old and later became one of England's most famous admirals.

Early that morning, a frigate signalled she had sighted a fleet, and a little later the *Magnamine* reported it was the enemy's. Hawke signalled line of battle and set all possible sail. The French also began to form line and seemed to be willing to accept battle, which gave Hawke a chance to catch up with them. But then – perhaps because of the rising wind – the French Admiral, Conflans, changed

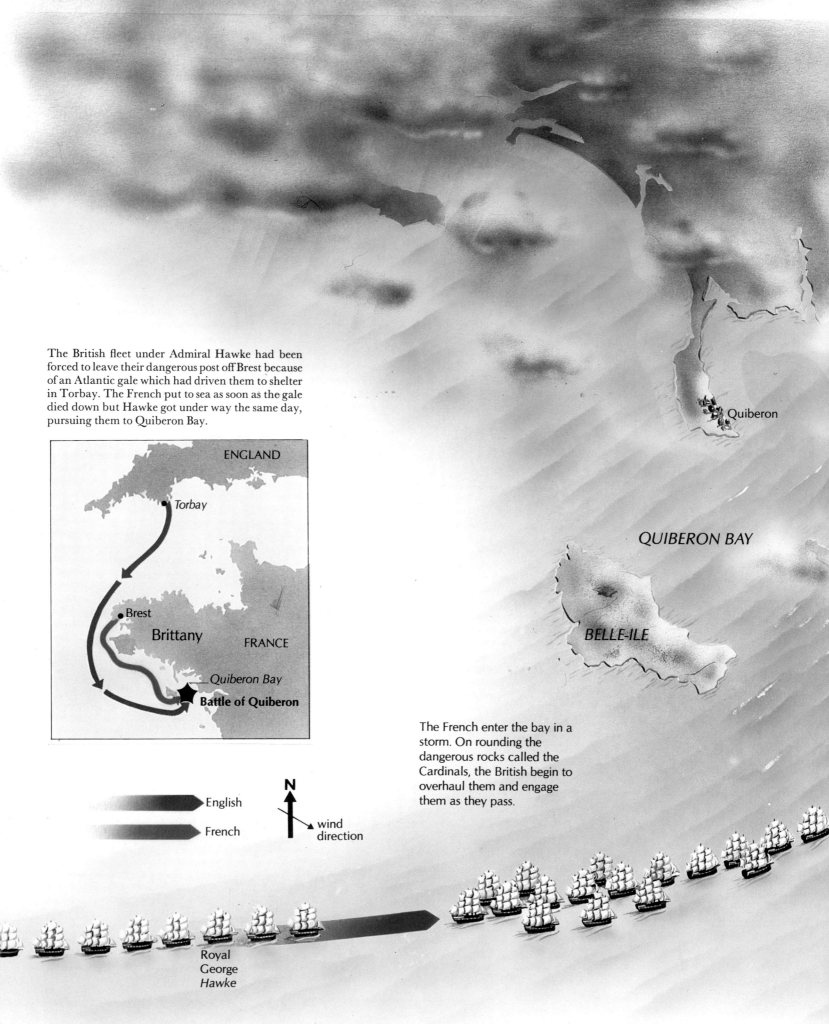

The British fleet under Admiral Hawke had been forced to leave their dangerous post off Brest because of an Atlantic gale which had driven them to shelter in Torbay. The French put to sea as soon as the gale died down but Hawke got under way the same day, pursuing them to Quiberon Bay.

ENGLAND

• Torbay

Brittany

• Brest

FRANCE

Quiberon Bay

★ **Battle of Quiberon**

English

French

N

wind direction

Quiberon

QUIBERON BAY

BELLE-ILE

The French enter the bay in a storm. On rounding the dangerous rocks called the Cardinals, the British begin to overhaul them and engage them as they pass.

Royal
George
Hawke

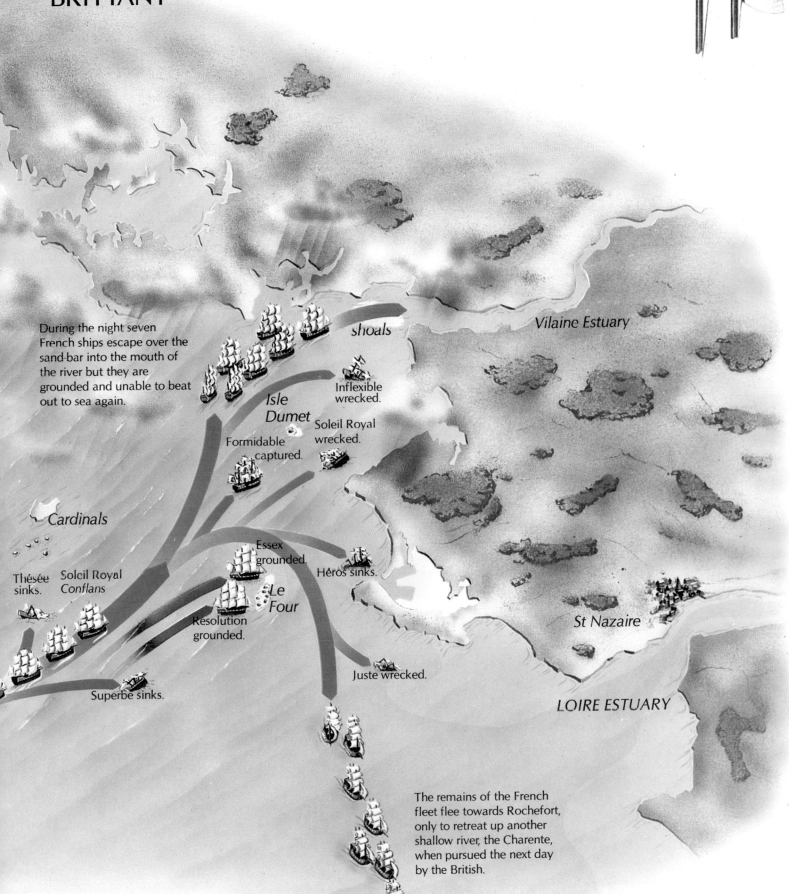

The Battle of Quiberon Bay
20–21 November 1759

BRITTANY

During the night seven French ships escape over the sand-bar into the mouth of the river but they are grounded and unable to beat out to sea again.

shoals

Vilaine Estuary

Inflexible wrecked.

Isle Dumet

Soleil Royal wrecked.

Formidable captured.

Cardinals

Essex grounded.

Héros sinks.

Thésée sinks.

Soleil Royal Conflans

Le Four

Resolution grounded.

St Nazaire

Juste wrecked.

Superbe sinks.

LOIRE ESTUARY

The remains of the French fleet flee towards Rochefort, only to retreat up another shallow river, the Charente, when pursued the next day by the British.

Opposite The stormy Battle of Quiberon Bay, by R. Paton.

Left Daybreak at Quiberon Bay. In the foreground are *HMS Resolution* and *Essex*, both wrecked, on a shoal; beyond them the French flagship *Soleil Royal* and the *Héros*, also aground.

darkness fell, he made the signal to the fleet to anchor. But that signal, in the still primitive book of those days, was simply the firing of two guns. The bay was full of gunfire and the thunder of breakers on the rocks all round; and a good many ships did not hear the signal, but continued to tack around in the confines of the bay on a pitch black night. One, the *Resolution*, ran ashore on a shoal and was wrecked.

It was a night of raging gales. Reports and flashes of guns, fired as signals of distress, could be heard and seen from every part of the bay, like thunder and lightning in the storm. The shouts of ship-wrecked men adrift in boats or on wreckage were heard and then snatched away by the wind. Ships in deep water and over a rocky bottom helplessly dragged their anchors. Others loomed out of the darkness a few yards away and vanished again. The fleets were mixed up together, and nobody was safe.

At dawn, the *Soleil Royal* was found to have anchored in the middle of the British fleet. She cut her cable, ran herself ashore, and her crew set her on fire. This happened to another ship which had surrendered the night before. The British *Essex*, sent to engage them, ran on the same reef as the *Resolution*. Seven French ships, driven as far to the east as they could go, were embayed in the mouth of the river Vilaine and could not beat out again. To escape from British attack, they jettisoned their guns and provisions and managed to cross the bar, but four of them grounded in shallow water and broke their backs.

A few days later Hawke, outside the bay again, sent a squadron in to find what French ships were left. There were only seven, and they retreated up another shallow river, the Charente. Probably none of them ever escaped to sea again. 'Only glory and honour was saved,' a French historian wrote, and perhaps indeed there may be glory and honour in defeat. But while the British only lost two ships that hit the rocks, an entire French fleet of twenty-one ships of the line and four frigates had met its doom.

The immediate effect of these three victories was that French possessions fell like ninepins in the West Indies and in India. And since France had dragged Spain into the war, the British took Havana and Manila, the keys to Spanish wealth in the west and east. But Britain could not absorb and administer this sudden empire, and perhaps did not want to try. When peace was signed in 1763, she gave back most of the places she had conquered to the nations who had owned them before. But she kept Canada.

The victories, coming in such quick succession, irrevocably changed the balance of power at sea. The British had won supremacy. Henceforth, even through the great age of Napoleon, it was always the British who sought a fight at sea, because they were sure they would win, while the French and Spanish knew in their hearts they would lose.

The Nile
1798

Previous pages Nelson's fleet enters Aboukir Bay to attack the French line at anchor, by T. Whitcombe.

Right Lord Nelson: the portrait by Lemuel Abbot painted after the Battle of the Nile.

Below A papier mâché box commemorating the Battle of the Nile.

Opposite: above The middle deck of a man-of-war.

Opposite: below 'A First-rate taking in Stores', by J. M. W. Turner.

I T IS SAID that success breeds success, and it is certainly true of the British navy in the last decades of the eighteenth century. Their victories gave them unbounded confidence which led to further victories. They also led to an astonishing generation of brilliant admirals: Hawke, Howe, Jervis, Hood, Barham, and a little later – because he was a little younger – Nelson.

Nelson brought many qualities to the navy: personal courage (he really enjoyed danger), tactical genius, and – most strangely in a fighting service – kindness and love. Nobody at second hand has ever quite defined the reasons why his fellow men were so devoted to him. In letters that other men wrote, one can read of his numberless acts of kindness and thoughtfulness, great and small; one can see that however busy he was, tired by responsibility, worry and ill-health, he never neglected old friendships or failed by some instinctive touch to make new ones. Nor can one hope to recall his irresistible charm: one can only

imagine it from the way that hard-bitten sailors of every rank wrote more or less laboriously of their love for him – and love, not respect or admiration, was the word that all of them used. Yet history has to take account of this intangible fact; for ships and fleets under Nelson's command had a loyalty, pride and efficiency no other had ever achieved.

In 1795, the British were forced to abandon the Mediterranean, because the advance of Napoleon's armies on land made all its northern ports untenable. Nelson was the last man out, bringing the remnants of British troops and stores from Corsica and Italy.

In May 1798 he was the first man in again. As Rear-Admiral with his flag in the *Vanguard* (there had been *Vanguards* in the navy ever since the time of the Armada) with two other ships of the line and three frigates in company, he re-entered that hostile sea. He was sent because the British had heard Napoleon was assembling an enormous fleet of warships and transports, and nobody knew where it

Middle-Deck of the "Hector", Man of War.

Nelson's successive flagships: *Agamemnon, Vanguard, Elephant* and *Victory*, by N. Pocock.

The battle begins soon after 6 pm when daylight is already failing. *Goliath, Zealous, Orion, Theseus* and *Audacious* sail round the head of the French line and down the inshore side of it, where the French are least prepared for them.

was bound for. It was destined in fact to conquer Egypt and open a route for Napoleon to India.

Nelson's voyage began badly with a gale off the main French port of Toulon, in which the *Vanguard* was dismasted on a lee shore and only rescued by Captain Ball of the *Alexander*, who took her in tow. The three frigates lost touch, and returned to Gibraltar, believing the *Vanguard* would have to go there for repairs; but the *Alexander* towed her to Sardinia, and the fleet carpenters repaired her in four days. Nelson was left without the scouting frigates, which he called 'the eyes of the fleet'. He went back to Toulon, and heard that the French fleet had gone.

In early June a large reinforcement joined him, eleven ships of the line with captains whom the Commander-in-Chief Lord St Vincent described as 'a few choice fellows'. For the first time, Nelson was in charge of a large independent fleet, and he began at once his miracle of command. Very soon he referred to himself and his captains as 'a band of brothers', and it was a just description.

Whenever Nelson was aware of a job well done, he said so at once, and ungrudgingly. There was an example soon after the Battle of the Nile. On a dark and stormy night the 36-gun frigate *Penelope*, Captain Blackwood, intercepted the 80-gun flag-

After searching the Mediterranean for the French fleet Nelson, arriving from Syracuse in Sicily, sighted it in Aboukir Bay.

GREECE
TURKEY
CRETE
CYPRUS
MEDITERRANEAN SEA
Battle of the Nile
Alexandria
EGYPT

ship *Guillaume Tell*, and fought her single-handed until the morning. Blackwood, as it happened, had never met Nelson. He had a right to expect some formal praise from his admiral, but what he got was a letter: 'My dear Blackwood, Is there a sympathy which ties men together in the bonds of friendship without having a personal knowledge of each other? If so, (and I believe it was so to you) I was your friend and acquaintance before I saw you. Your conduct stamps your fame beyond the reach of envy: it was like yourself – it was like the *Penelope*. Thanks; and say everything kind for me to your brave officers and men.' Needless to say, Blackwood became another of Nelson's devoted friends.

Whenever the weather was fine, Nelson invited his captains to dine with him. His dinner parties

The Battle of the Nile

1–2 August 1798
The approach at about 6 pm

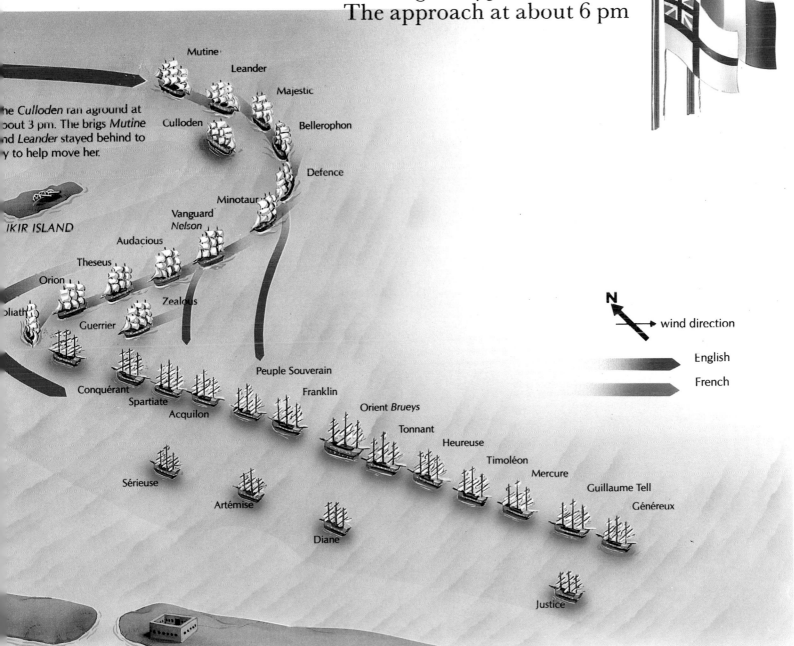

Mutine

Leander

Majestic

he *Culloden* ran aground at
bout 3 pm. The brigs *Mutine*
nd *Leander* stayed behind to
y to help move her.

Culloden

Bellerophon

Defence

Minotaur

Vanguard
Nelson

IKIR ISLAND

Audacious

Theseus

Orion

Zealous

oliath

Guerrier

N

→ wind direction

English

French

Peuple Souverain

Franklin

Conquérant

Spartiate

Acquilon

Orient *Brueys*

Tonnant

Heureuse

Timoléon

Mercure

Guillaume Tell

Généreux

Sérieuse

Artémise

Diane

Justice

were always cheerful. He made use of them to
explain exactly what he meant to do when they
found the French, whatever the situation they
found them in, and he showed the captains he had
perfect confidence in them to use their own
discretion in doing it. The food on these occasions
was simple, but the wine and conversation were
good; and after them each captain was rowed back
to his ship determined to live up to the Admiral's
trust. The same confidence, reinforced by constant
battle practice, spread down through all ranks in
the fleet until the smallest boy knew what Nelson
expected of him, and felt sure he would achieve it.

It was a long search: Genoa, Corsica, Naples and
Sicily, always with the French a few days ahead
and no means of knowing where they were going:

the Admiralty's guesses had extended from the
Black Sea to Ireland. The first firm information was
at Messina in Sicily, where he heard the French had
captured Malta. Half way to Malta, a passing ship
said the French had left again with a north-west
wind. That, for the first time, suggested Alexandria
in Egypt, and Nelson stood down there under all
sail. But when he arrived there was nobody in the
harbour.

Back he went to Syracuse in Sicily for supplies;
then east again, this time by way of Greece where
he had a report that the French had been seen four
weeks before, sailing south-east. South-east he went
again, with a fresh wind astern, and in the morning
of 1 August sighted the minarets of Alexandria for
the second time. The harbour was packed with

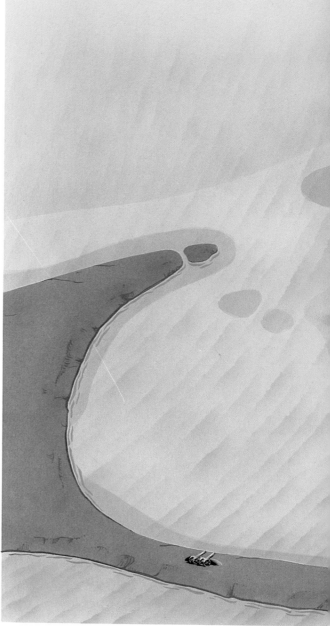

Above A detail from a painting of the Battle of the Nile, by Mather Brown.

Right Admiral François Paul Brueys, killed at the Nile.

shipping. The time before, he had outsailed the French and arrived there too soon, and on the way back he had passed them again on a dirty night. It was all for lack of frigates.

But there were no warships in the harbour. It was not until one o'clock that afternoon that the French fleet was discovered, thirteen ships and four frigates anchored in line in the Bay of Aboukir, a dozen miles to the east. Nelson hoisted the signal 'Prepare for Action', ordered dinner and prophesied for himself, before the next day, 'a Peerage or Westminster Abbey', the latter being the place where heroes were buried.

It was said the French Admiral, Brueys, believed he was safe where he was, protected by shoals and shore batteries, and that Nelson could not attack

The Battle of the Nile

1–2 August 1798
The mêlée at about 9 pm

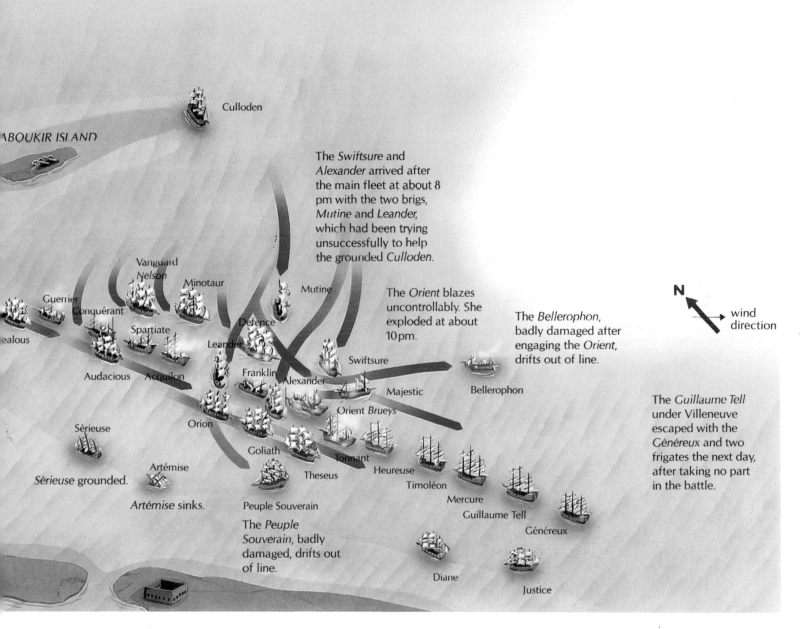

Culloden

ABOUKIR ISLAND

The *Swiftsure* and *Alexander* arrived after the main fleet at about 8 pm with the two brigs, *Mutine* and *Leander*, which had been trying unsuccessfully to help the grounded *Culloden*.

Vanguard *Nelson*

Minotaur

Mutine

The *Orient* blazes uncontrollably. She exploded at about 10 pm.

The *Bellerophon*, badly damaged after engaging the *Orient*, drifts out of line.

Guerrier

Conquérant

Défence

N

wind direction

ealous

Spartiate

Leander

Swiftsure

Audacious   Acquilon

Franklin

Alexander

Majestic

Bellerophon

Orient *Brueys*

The *Guillaume Tell* under Villeneuve escaped with the *Généreux* and two frigates the next day, after taking no part in the battle.

Sérieuse

Orion

Goliath

Tonnant

Artémise

Theseus

Heureuse

Sérieuse grounded.

Timoléon

Mercure

Artémise sinks.

Peuple Souverain

Guillaume Tell

Généreux

The *Peuple Souverain*, badly damaged, drifts out of line.

Diane

Justice

that evening or night because he had no charts. It was true the French had the only reliable charts of the bay that existed, but Nelson simply reckoned that where the French could anchor, he could anchor too; and so did every captain. So complete was the understanding of the captains that Nelson gave them no further orders, and did not pause to form a line of battle: it did not matter which captain led his line. Even in the falling dusk, he wrote afterwards, 'I was sure each would feel for a French ship'. Later, he put it that he was sure 'each would find a hole to creep in at'.

He made only one more signal, and that was technical: to prepare to anchor by the stern. It needed no explanation. Going in with the wind behind them, if the ships anchored by the bows in the usual way, they would swing to the wind and would be vulnerable while they did so. In each ship, they therefore made a cable fast to the mizzen mast, took the end out through one of the stern ports and along the outside of the hull to an anchor. When that anchor was let go with its own cable slack, the ship would bring up by the stern cable and would not swing; and afterwards, by slackening one cable and hauling in the other, they could turn her to bring her broadside to bear on any target.

As darkness fell, each captain did find a hole. Two of the leading ships, *Audacious* and *Zealous*, dropped their anchors in line with the French, and three others, *Theseus*, *Orion* and *Goliath*, sailed round the head of the French line and down the inshore side of it, each choosing an opponent

63

The night battle lit by flames from the French flagship *Orient*, by T. Whitcombe.

and anchoring close alongside it. Nelson in the *Vanguard*, sixth in the line, anchored very close indeed on the outside of the French, at 80 yards. So did the five ships astern of him. Thomas Troubridge in the *Culloden* had the mortification of running on a shoal in the mouth of the bay, where he stuck and could act only as a warning to the others astern of him.

So, when it was quite dark, the head and centre of the French line was brought under concentrated fire at very short range on both sides, which was exactly the plan that Nelson had propounded to the captains for a fleet that was found at anchor.

The cannonading and slaughter went on all night, the flashes and thunder of about 2,000 guns in an area scarcely a mile along and 200 yards across. Nelson's tactics had caught the French in an impossible position, but they fought with astonishing bravery and many heroic stories were created. The French Admiral Brueys, for example, who suffered a ghastly wound – his third – insisted on staying on deck saying, when they tried to take him below, 'A French Admiral should die on his quarterdeck.' The captain of the *Tonnant* whose right arm was shot off, then his left arm, then one of his legs, had himself put in a tub of bran, from which he continued to give his orders – one of them being to nail the flag to the mast – until he died from loss of blood.

Brueys' flag captain, Comte de Casa Bianca, was mortally wounded soon after the Admiral's death, and his son, who was ten, achieved an immortality of his own in the poem which begins, 'The boy stood on the burning deck'. For by then the flagship *Orient* was uncontrollably on fire. Foreseeing disaster, all the ships close to her drew away, or closed their ports and hatches, removed am-

munition from the upper deck and stationed men with buckets. At about ten o'clock, her magazine exploded and blew her to bits with such a devastating concussion that the battle ceased entirely for several minutes. Blazing wreckage shot into the sky and fell all round, starting fires in at least three other ships, where the crews, forewarned, were able to put them out.

After midnight the firing began to die down, because so few French ships were left in action, and at dawn it ceased. Daylight showed the British *Bellerophon* with all her three masts gone, and the *Majestic* with only her foremast. These two ships and Nelson's *Vanguard* had been badly damaged in their hulls and suffered the highest casualties. All the rest were knocked about, but were still capable of getting under way with reduced canvas.

Of the thirteen French, two were burned, and nine, which were more or less wrecked, surrendered. Only the last two in the line were able to put to sea, with two frigates, and escape in the early dawn; and the British were too battered and exhausted to chase them. All four of them were taken in the next few months, but Rear-Admiral Villeneuve, who commanded them, survived to be Nelson's opponent at Trafalgar. Meanwhile, he was thought in the French navy to have disgraced himself: left unmolested in the rear of the line, he could have set sail in the night and taken a long tack to the north-east to join in the battle. Three of the nine prizes were burned in the bay as useless, one was taken to Gibraltar and left there as a guardship, and the other five, *Conquérant*, *Spartiate*, *Acquilon*, *Franklin* and *Tonnant*, were brought in triumph back to Plymouth and added to the Royal Navy.

What? our Fleet capture & destroyd, by the Slaves of Britain? —
by my Sword & by holy Mahomet I swear, eternal Vengeance! — yes, —
when I have subjected Egypt, subdued the Arabs, the Druses & the Maronites;
become master of Syria, turn'd the great River Euphrates, & sail'd upon it through
the sandy Deserts; compell'd to my assistance, the Bedouins, Tuscomans, Kurds,
Armenians, & Persians; form'd a Million of Cavalry, & pass'd them upon Rafts,
six or seven Hundred Miles over the Bosphorus, I shall enter Constantinople —
Now I enter the Theatre of Europe, I establish the Republic of Greece,
I raise Poland from its ruins, I make Prussia bend y.ͤ knee to France;
I chain up the Russian Bear; I cut the Head from y.ͤ Imperial Eagle;
I drive the ferocious English from the Archipelago, I hunt them
from the Mediterranean, — & blot them out from the catalogue of
Nations! — Then shall the conquer'd Earth sue for Peace,
& an Obelisk be erected at Constantinople, inscribed,
"To Buonaparte, Conqueror of the World,
& extirpater of the
ENGLISH NATION".

BUONAPARTE hearing of Nelson's Victory, swears by his Sword, to Extirpate the English from off the Earth.
See. Buonaparte's Speech to the French Army at Cairo: publish'd by authority of the Directory, in Volney's Letters.

A contemporary caricature of Napoleon raging at the English after hearing of Nelson's victory.

The Battle of the Nile was unusual, probably unique until modern times, in that it was fought entirely in the dark. It has been called a masterpiece of tactics, and so it was, but it should rather be remembered as a masterpiece of command. The tactics, of enveloping a fleet at anchor from both sides, were original but simple. It was Nelson's technique of command, his trust in his captains, which enabled them to do it without hesitation as dusk was falling, and to do it so quickly that the French could not escape.

It was probably also unique in the gifts and honours showered on the victor: pensions of £3,000 a year, an award of £10,000 from the East India Company, and numberless other orders and rewards from foreign potentates. For the battle could be plainly seen as a check to Napoleon's ambitions. Napoleon himself escaped from Egypt in a fast Venetian ship, but he abandoned most of the army he had landed there, and his plans for eastern expansion were thwarted for ever.

I N MAY 1803 Nelson hoisted his flag in the most famous of his ships, the *Victory*, captained by Thomas Hardy, bound again for the Mediterranean.

The navy's task at that moment was easy to define but difficult to achieve. Napoleon's armies were ready at Boulogne for the invasion of England which was his greatest ambition. But they could not cross the Channel unless his fleet could win command of it, if only for a few days. The fleet was scattered in the ports of France and Spain, from Toulon in the Mediterranean to Brest on the Bay of Biscay; and the navy's job was to keep them in port, or fight them if they tried to come out.

The long blockade of all Napoleon's ports in the years before Trafalgar was the greatest sustained and communal feat of seamanship there has ever been or ever will be. The watch on Brest, under Admiral Cornwallis, was perhaps the hardest of all: it was a notoriously dangerous shore which lay to leeward in the prevailing winds, exposed to seas with a fetch of thousands of miles. No modern mariner would dare to explain exactly how the navy was able to stand off and on that coast, estimating the tidal streams and currents, constantly solving the problems of navigation and ship-handling – and not merely in one ship, but a whole fleet of them. The achievement astonished the French, who looked out every morning and saw the sails still there, and it is just as astonishing now. So is the toughness of the crews, who lived in wind and rain and spray, with neither shelter on deck nor warmth below.

Nelson's watch was on Toulon, where the problems were different. He did not try to keep the French in harbour: his burning wish was to lure them out and beat them. All the neighbouring coasts were hostile, with the exception of Sardinia, which was neutral but primitive. The nearest ports under British control were Malta and Gibraltar,

each over 600 miles (1,000 km) away. So his fleet had to cure its own sick, repair its own ships and find its own provisions where it could. He took infinite pains to keep his crews healthy and as happy as they could be. From the time he joined the *Victory*, Nelson was two years on board without setting foot ashore, and it was the same for almost every one of her 850 men.

In 1805 Napoleon issued grandiose orders to his admirals. All the fleets were to escape the blockade and assemble in Martinique in the West Indies. Thence they would return, forty French ships, perhaps twenty or thirty Spaniards and at least a dozen frigates. They would take the English by surprise and sail up the Channel to defend his invasion force. The plan broke down at once because the fleet in Brest could not possibly escape. But the Toulon fleet under Admiral Villeneuve broke out, evaded Nelson, and sailed to the Indies. Nelson pursued it across the Atlantic and back again. It finished up in Cadiz, and the British fleet assembled to keep it there.

Nelson was not with them: the *Victory* had been ordered back to Portsmouth, and he was at the house at Merton in Surrey which he shared with Lady Hamilton, enjoying a taste of the happy home life all sailors dream of. The fleet off Cadiz was commanded by Admiral Collingwood, a man with many fine qualities but without Nelson's inspiration. Morale was low. The blockade had been deadly boring, and captains and men could hardly bear the idea of another winter of it.

Nelson wanted never to go to sea again. Only one thing could have dragged him back: the chance of a final fight. When news came that the French and Spanish fleets were trapped, he drove to Ports-

Previous pages Deck of the *Victory* at the moment which Nelson fell, by Denis Dighton.

Above right Emma Hamilton, by Schmidt: Nelson's favourite portrait, which hung and still hangs in his cabin on board the *Victory*.

Right Admiral Pierre Villeneuve, French Commander-in-Chief at Trafalgar.

mouth to rejoin the *Victory*. The crowds were so dense that he embarked far down the shore, but they followed him and people knelt down to bless him as he passed; for the English looked to him as the man who would save them from invasion.

When the *Victory* was sighted off Cadiz, the fleet was transformed. In those last weeks Nelson showed all the qualities his reputation had grown on: the clear thinking and bravery, the warmth, understanding and tact, and the sudden unpremeditated kindnesses. He asked all the captains to dinner, half one night and the other half the next. The first evening was his birthday – he was forty-seven – and it turned into a birthday party. He had taken the trouble in England to collect messages and letters from his colleagues' wives, news of how their children were getting on. He listened to their worries and patiently soothed any ruffled feelings. And he told them exactly how they were going to beat the enemy. He rebuilt their pride and confidence and re-awoke their affection, and those feelings spread at once throughout the fleet.

It was a revolutionary tactical plan that he described at those dinner parties. Nelson had a large fleet, the enemy even larger. No day was long enough, he said, to form so many in the usual line of battle. Therefore they would attack in two separate smaller lines, with a third in reserve. He would lead one, to cut through the enemy line at its centre, and

Admiral Collingwood, now second in command of the fleet, would lead the other to overwhelm the rearguard. So two separate battles would be fought, each with a superiority of numbers; and both would be won, he believed, before the enemy's van could turn in formation to take any part.

He wrote in the memorandum which confirmed what he had said: 'Something must be left to chance, nothing is sure in a Sea Fight beyond all others. Shot will carry away the masts and yards of friends as well as foes; but I look with confidence to a Victory before the Van of the Enemy could

Top Nelson by Lemuel Abbott.

Left Admiral Cuthbert Collingwood who commanded Nelson's second line of battle: portrait by H. Howard.

Above At each of two dinner parties in his cabin, Nelson explained to his captains his revolutionary plan of attack.

Above The *Victory* and *Royal Sovereign* cut the line, by N. Pocock.

Right Having chased Villeneuve across the Atlantic to the West Indies Nelson lost the French fleet and returned to England leaving most of his fleet with Admiral Cornwallis at Brest. In August he heard news of Villeneuve's presence in Cadiz and he sailed from Portsmouth to join the rest of his fleet at Cadiz on 28 September.

Below A papier mâché box commemorating the Battle of Trafalgar.

succour their rear. ... No captain can do very wrong if he places his ship alongside that of an enemy.'

This tactical plan was entirely new, and two of its novelties were surprising. First, it had been the hope of every tactician for centuries to 'cross the T' of the enemy's line, in other words to lead his own line across the head of it; because in that position he could bring his own broadsides to bear on the enemy's leading ships, while they could hardly reply at all. Nelson's plan to get into action quickly gave this advantage to the enemy: his own leading ships would be endangered. Also, it was going back to the old idea of grappling the enemy at close quarters, which the English had discarded before the Armada. There were perhaps two reasons for this. One was unbounded confidence. The other was that warships of this era were built with a big 'tumble home': they were wider on the waterline than at upper deck level, so that even when they were touching and grinding together, there would still be a gap of 15 feet or so between their decks, which boarders could only cross with difficulty.

The first problem was to tempt the enemy out of Cadiz. He stationed the fleet 50 miles (80 km) offshore, out of sight, with frigates to watch the port and a line of ships to repeat their signals to him.

But it was Napoleon who drove the French and Spanish fleets to sea. After those years of blockade, the navy lying in Cadiz was already beaten. For lack of sea training, it was incompetent to sail in formation, let alone to fight; its more intelligent officers knew that if it met the British at sea, it was doomed to destruction. But Napoleon in those last

weeks had had to give up his invasion of England because his fleets were unable to protect it; and he was so furious with his navy that he no longer cared what happened to it. He ordered it to sail, on a useless voyage back to the Mediterranean. His final order said: 'His Majesty's wish is that his admirals, captains, officers and men should not hesitate to attack equal or superior forces in battles of

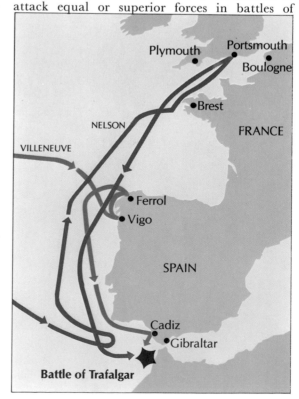

extermination. He counts for nothing the loss of his ships, if they are lost with glory.'

With that fatally furious command, on 19 October, the fleets began to straggle out of harbour. Before they were out, the frigates' signals had been relayed to Nelson, and the *Victory* hoisted the flags: 'General chase south-east'.

There followed a night and a day and another night of shadowing, suspense and manoeuvre. At 6 am on the 21st, in the British ships, thirty-three sail of the enemy were sighted against the dawn. Nelson, seeing them at last where he had always longed to see them, said, 'I shall not be contented with capturing less than twenty.' He signalled: 'Prepare for battle. Bear up in succession on the course set by the Admiral.'

The approach to battle was a prolonged ordeal. With all sail set in a feeble breeze and a heavy swell astern, the ships bore down on the enemy at less than a walking pace. The scene became almost festive. Ships that had bands put them up on their poops, where they could plainly be heard by the ships that had none. They all played different tunes, not very well. Boats rowed from ship to ship, and captains hailed each other and wished each other an enemy prize in tow before the night.

On the deck of the *Victory*, Nelson was surrounded by friends, and all of them were worried about him. In close fighting, the *Victory* would be the most conspicuous target, and Nelson the most conspicuous figure on her decks. They suggested he should shift his flag to a frigate, or let another ship lead, or even cover the stars and decorations on his coat. But avoiding personal danger was not his idea of duty, and he would not listen. On the contrary, danger always put him in the best of spirits; and he had an air of boyish gaiety when he said to

Blackwood the frigate captain, now one of his closest friends, 'I will now amuse the fleet with a signal, do you not think there is one yet wanting?'

Blackwood said everyone seemed to know exactly what to do.

'Suppose we telegraph "Nelson confides that every man will do his duty"?'

The flag-lieutenant suggested 'England expects', because it would be quicker to signal.

Nelson agreed; and so the most famous battle signal ever made was hoisted to the yards and mastheads. England expects: it inspired generations of Englishmen. Yet it was not received with unanimous joy in the fleet. Sailors were heard to say, 'Do my duty? I've always done my duty, haven't you, Jack?' Nelson's first instinct had been right. Nelson confides: they would have cheered that all right. England was far away; 'expects' seemed mandatory; England was not the navy, and this was a naval occasion. But Nelson was there, one of them, personifying the navy: his confidence was what inspired them. When the flags were hauled down, his last signal was hoisted: 'Engage the enemy more closely.' It flew at the masthead until it was shot away.

At a thousand yards, the *Royal Sovereign* and then the *Victory* came under fire, each from the broadsides of half a dozen enemy ships. Against good gunners, Nelson's plan would have been impossible: the leading ships would have been crippled before they could reply. But the French and Spanish after those years in harbour were not good gunners, as Nelson certainly knew; and their ships that morning, with the swell abeam, were rolling heavily, which made them even worse. The *Sovereign* reached the enemy line and disappeared in a cloud of gunsmoke. The *Victory* suffered: the

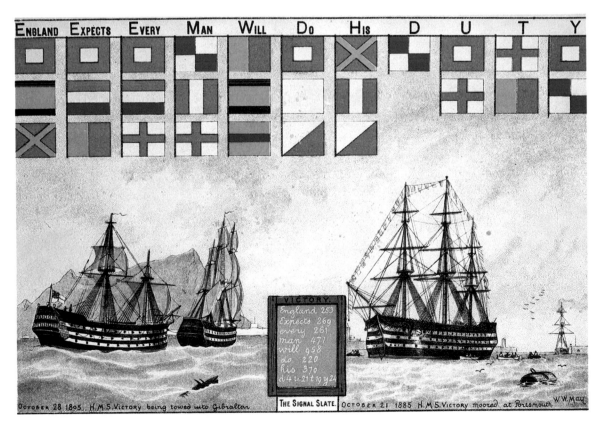

Left The flags used in Nelson's battle signal.

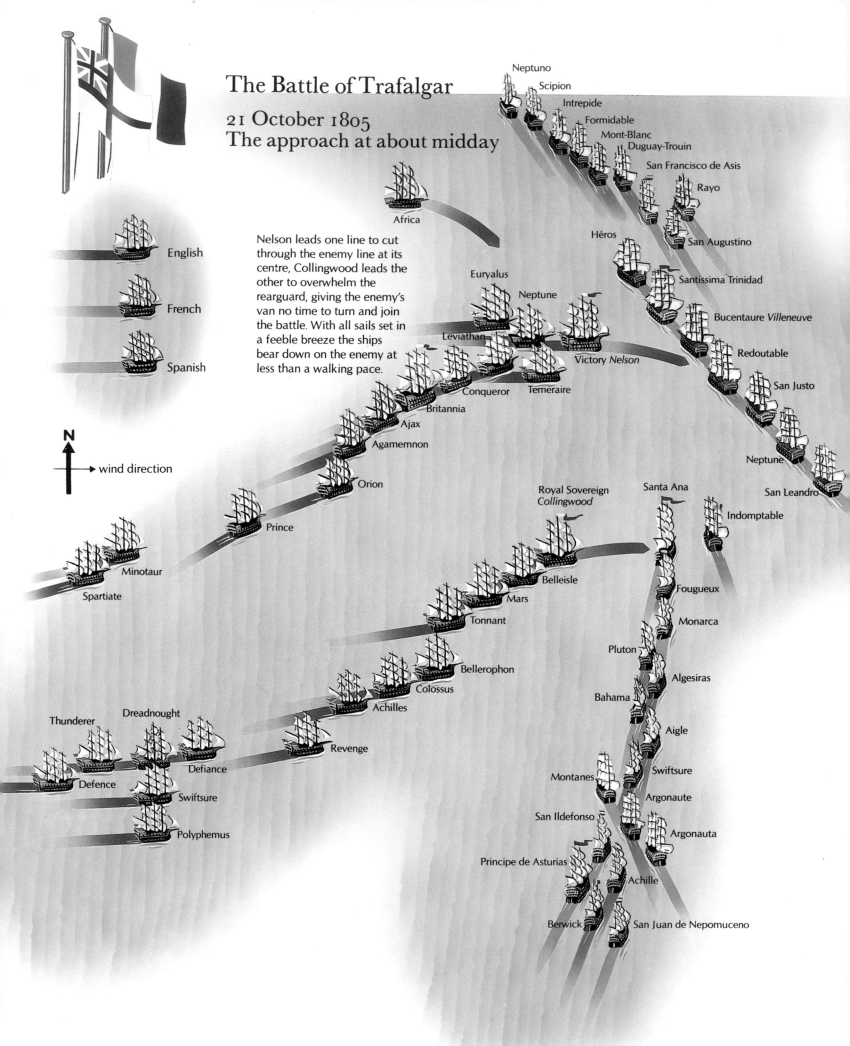

The Battle of Trafalgar
21 October 1805
The approach at about midday

Nelson leads one line to cut through the enemy line at its centre, Collingwood leads the other to overwhelm the rearguard, giving the enemy's van no time to turn and join the battle. With all sails set in a feeble breeze the ships bear down on the enemy at less than a walking pace.

English

French

Spanish

N
→ wind direction

Africa

Neptuno
Scipion
Intrepide
Formidable
Mont-Blanc
Duguay-Trouin
San Francisco de Asis
Rayo
San Augustino
Héros
Santissima Trinidad
Bucentaure *Villeneuve*
Redoutable
San Justo
Neptune
San Leandro

Euryalus
Neptune
Victory *Nelson*
Leviathan
Conqueror
Temeraire
Britannia
Ajax
Agamemnon
Orion
Prince
Minotaur
Spartiate

Royal Sovereign *Collingwood*
Santa Ana
Indomptable
Belleisle
Mars
Tonnant
Bellerophon
Colossus
Achilles
Revenge
Thunderer
Dreadnought
Defiance
Defence
Swiftsure
Polyphemus

Fougueux
Monarca
Pluton
Algesiras
Bahama
Aigle
Swiftsure
Montanes
Argonaute
San Ildefonso
Argonauta
Principe de Asturias
Achille
Berwick
San Juan de Nepomuceno

The mêlée at about 2 pm

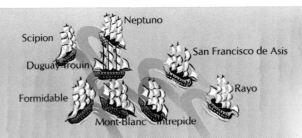

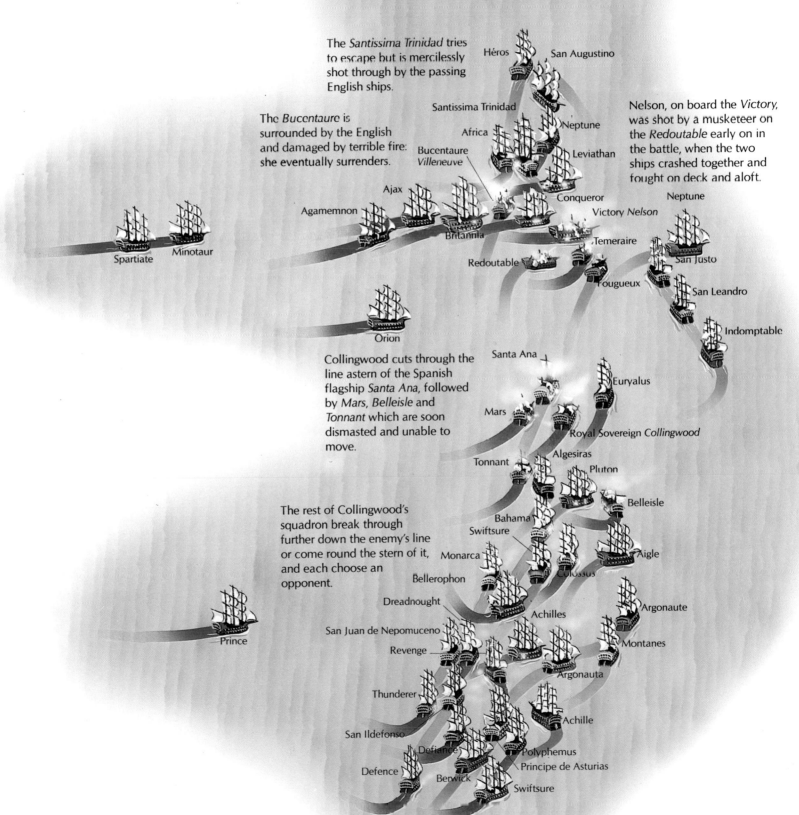

The van of the enemy, which for two hours has been sailing away from the battle, slowly turns to join the main fleet.

Neptuno

Scipion

San Francisco de Asis

Duguay-Trouin

Rayo

Formidable

Mont-Blanc Intrepide

The *Santissima Trinidad* tries to escape but is mercilessly shot through by the passing English ships.

Héros
San Augustino

The *Bucentaure* is surrounded by the English and damaged by terrible fire: she eventually surrenders.

Santissima Trinidad

Neptune

Africa

Nelson, on board the *Victory*, was shot by a musketeer on the *Redoutable* early on in the battle, when the two ships crashed together and fought on deck and aloft.

Bucentaure *Villeneuve*

Leviathan

Ajax

Conqueror

Neptune

Agamemnon

Victory *Nelson*

Britannia

Temeraire

San Justo

Spartiate

Minotaur

Redoutable

Fougueux

San Leandro

Indomptable

Orion

Collingwood cuts through the line astern of the Spanish flagship *Santa Ana*, followed by *Mars*, *Belleisle* and *Tonnant* which are soon dismasted and unable to move.

Santa Ana

Euryalus

Mars

Royal Sovereign *Collingwood*

Tonnant

Algesiras

Pluton

Belleisle

The rest of Collingwood's squadron break through further down the enemy's line or come round the stern of it, and each choose an opponent.

Bahama

Swiftsure

Monarca

Aigle

Colossus

Bellerophon

Dreadnought

Argonaute

Achilles

San Juan de Nepomuceno

Montanes

Revenge

Argonauta

Prince

Thunderer

Achille

San Ildefonso

Defiance

Polyphemus

Defence

Principe de Asturias

Berwick

Swiftsure

73

Trafalgar, 1805

mizzen topmast fell, the wheel was smashed, twenty men were killed before she could fire a shot.

Very slowly, she ploughed on to pistol-shot, and cut through the line astern of the French flagship *Bucentaure*, so close that their rigging touched. She fired her port carronade, the biggest gun in the fleet, loaded with a 68-pound (31-kg) ball and a keg of 500 musket balls, and then the awful blast of the whole of her port broadside point blank at the unprotected stern of the *Bucentaure*, and the dust of shattered woodwork drifted across her decks. Then on the starboard side she crashed aboard the French *Redoutable*, and the two ships were grappled together.

Collingwood in *Royal Sovereign* had cut through the line astern of the Spanish flagship *Santa Ana*, fired his broadside into her stern and then come up

on her lee side; those two ships were also locked together in combat. Three more ships came through the same gap, *Belleisle*, *Mars* and *Tonnant* – the latter one of the prizes from the Nile. The rest of his squadron, eight more ships in all, broke through farther down the line or came round the stern of it, and each chose an opponent. Very soon, in that part of the battle, ten ships were grappled together in pairs, each firing her guns at such a short distance that not only the shot but the red-hot blast went in through the enemy's gunports. The rest were manoeuvring, all within range of each other, trying to bring their own broadsides to bear and keep out of the way of the enemy's. In the feeble breeze, every movement in the battle was very slow. Probably, once the fighting was started, no ship made more than one mile an hour, and to turn

'Trafalgar' by J. M. W. Turner. It was commissioned by George IV for the Painted Hall at Greenwich in 1824, and shows Nelson's flagship, *Victory*.

them took many minutes. The gunsmoke grew so thick that ships hove out of it, enemies or friends, at the range of a pistol shot. Masts and spars came crashing down, covering decks and the men on them in a dreadful tangle of canvas and rigging. Here and there, furious fights flared up on the decks and then died down again. Collingwood's first four ships, *Royal Sovereign*, *Belleisle*, *Mars* and *Tonnant*, were all dismasted and unable to move.

But within an hour, two differences had shown between the fleets. The first was in gunnery. The English, through training and practice at sea, could fire their guns at least twice as quickly as the Spaniards or French, and, never without a target, they did far more damage and caused many more deaths and wounds. The second was that when things got too hot for them, the Spanish and French

ships surrendered, but the thought of surrender never crossed the minds of the English. They fought on when they were totally disabled, and they even (with their thoughts on prize money) sent boats from their own dismasted ships to accept the surrender of others. Those unable to move signalled friends to take them in tow while they laboured to get up jury masts and set some sail again.

North of Collingwood, Nelson was fighting the second of the separate battles he had planned. The *Victory* and *Redoutable* were still grappled together. The Captain of the *Redoutable* was a fiery and efficient little man called Lucas. Unable through the blockade to train his men in gunnery, he had trained them in boarding, with cutlasses, pistols, muskets and hand grenades, and had invented a tactic of his own. When the *Victory* crashed alongside, the English were astonished to see the *Redoutable* slam shut her gunports, which cut off her main armament. Lucas, knowing his gunnery was second-rate, intended to fight his battle on deck and aloft.

If Nelson's friends could have foreseen that chance would bring them alongside a man with such ideas, their anxiety for his safety would have turned into despair. When close action was joined, his work was done, and so for the moment was Captain Hardy's. And therefore they did what they always did at sea when they had no pressing business: they paced up and down the quarter-deck. Of course they could see the musketeers: some of them were only forty feet away. They could see their own people falling, hit by the unprecedented fire. But it was unthinkable that an admiral or captain should take cover, or vary his routine in deference to the enemy. The code of conduct compelled them to take no notice, and indeed they may have been so absorbed in the progress of great events that they were not thinking of the danger.

It was after twenty minutes that Nelson was shot, by a musketeer in Lucas's mizzen top, fifty feet above him. The ball, coming downwards, hit him on the shoulder and entered his chest. Hardy walked on a few paces unaware. When he turned, seamen were lifting Nelson. 'They have done for me at last,' Nelson said. 'My backbone is shot through.'

Men carried him down, deck after deck, to the

The *Redoutable* dismasted and about to surrender, by A. F. Mayer.

Trafalgar, 1805

A Spanish artist's view of Trafalgar: the approach, the battle, and the return of survivors to Cadiz.

Opposite: above Nelson on the quarter-deck of the *Victory* before Trafalgar, by W. H. Overend.

Opposite: below Nelson is carried below, by Stanley Drummond.

cockpit on the orlop deck, the lowest of all, where Dr Beatty the surgeon already had fifty wounded. There in the pool of light from a lantern, amid the roar of the guns above and the cries of the other men in pain, occurred the most famous death-bed scene in English history, the most public of private agonies.

As the *Temeraire*, second in Nelson's line, came through the gap the *Victory* had made, the smoke was so thick she could see nothing, and she ran aboard the *Redoutable* on the other side. Soon after that the French *Fougueux*, already crippled in the southern fight, drifted down on the *Temeraire*, and for a while there was a sight never seen before in battle – four ships of the line all aboard of each other, all more or less dismasted, all heading the same way, as close as if they had been moored at a pier. The main and foremasts of the *Redoutable* fell across the *Temeraire*, and the *Temeraire*'s topmast fell the other way, across the *Redoutable*, binding the ships together with hundreds of ropes and spars. The *Fougueux* had no more fight in her, and she soon surrendered. But Lucas refused, though his position was hopeless. The *Redoutable* was a two-decked ship with a three-decker on each side, and the *Victory* was shooting her to bits with her guns depressed, so that the shot would go out through her bottom. Exactly 300 of her crew were dead. 222 were in the hands of the surgeon on the orlop, and the water in the hold below them was rising fast and threatening to drown them all. The *Victory* had a prize-crew ready, but they could not cross the gap, and since the *Redoutable* had shut her gunports they could not enter her there. Neither side of her could be reached by a boat. So she remained, with her flag still flying, until at last the *Victory* broke away and sent two midshipmen in a boat to take possession.

All that time, the *Victory* had been firing her port guns at the *Bucentaure* and her next ahead, the huge Spanish ship *Santissima Trinidad*, the biggest ship in the world. Four of Nelson's squadron had followed him through the line, and each of them, as she came slowly through, had raked the *Bucentaure* with a terrible fire. The *Leviathan* brought to on her lee bow and the *Conqueror* on her quarter, and kept her under fire; and the *Britannia* and the *Ajax*, entering the fight, attacked her from the windward side. It was the fate of Admiral Villeneuve to see most of his staff and more than half of his crew fall dead or wounded, and himself to remain untouched. Towards the end, there was nothing that the few remaining men on the deck of *Bucentaure* could do, and he sent them all below to save their lives, while he remained there alone, pacing up and down like Nelson. If any man ever wanted to die in battle with a vestige of honour, he must have been one of them. In the end, all three of his masts collapsed. He could no longer even send a signal to his fleet, and after one hour of close engagement he accepted his ultimate disgrace and struck his colours.

At that the *Santissima Trinidad* made sail to try to escape, but the English ships passed on to her and mercilessly shot her full of holes. They damaged her rigging too, and the extra sail she had set put too much strain on it. Suddenly, all her masts

Death of Nelson, by A. W. Devis.

collapsed, the main and mizzen and then the foremast, and the whole majestic mass of sails, spars and rigging swayed and crumpled, plunging into the water.

By 2.15, the central part of the battle had ended. Four French and Spanish ships were lying close to the *Victory* in ruins, and the rest of Villeneuve's squadron was fleeing towards Cadiz, pursued by English ships. The smoke cleared, and Hardy was able to see that Collingwood was still in action, and that the van of the enemy, which for two hours had been sailing away from the battle, was very slowly

turning as if it meant to join. He went down to see Nelson, who had repeatedly been asking for him. Only half a dozen men were present when Nelson lay dying, although they were surrounded by other wounded and dying men. They met afterwards, and wrote down everything he had whispered, or everything they had been able to hear and remember, about Lady Hamilton and his daughter Horatia, and the pain, the battle, his duty, and Lady Hamilton again. The scene is so familiar now that it seems unreal, like a play; but for each of those men it had a poignant reality, for each of

Nelson's funeral procession passes London Bridge and St Paul's on its way from Greenwich to Whitehall.

them felt their best friend was dying there. The last thing they heard him say was, 'Thank God I have done my duty.' At 4.30 an unknown hand wrote in the *Victory*'s log, 'A victory having been reported to the Right Hon. Lord Viscount Nelson, K.B., and Commander-in-Chief, he died of his wound.'

Eighteen enemy ships had surrendered, and one was uncontrollably on fire. It was a victory so devastating, so complete, that sea warfare practically ceased for a century. Yet Captain Blackwood wrote to his wife that night, 'On such terms, it was a victory I never wish to have witnessed.' As night fell, and the news of Nelson's death spread through the fleet, men of all ranks expressed the same emotion: the elation of victory vanished in an astonishing outburst of grief; the commander they had lost seemed more important than the battle they had won. And the next day, oppressed by this news and exhausted by the fight, they were faced by a worse ordeal, a storm which blew straight towards the enemy coast.

Many veterans said they had never seen such a wind and sea as they saw in the week after Trafalgar. And no sailing fleet was ever in such a perilous position: nearly fifty ships on a lee shore, including the prizes, about half of them dismasted, and each with scores and some with hundreds of wounded and dying men down on their orlop decks. At first the English tried to tow their prizes away from the coast. Waves swept the decks, guns broke adrift, men worked aloft day and night on swaying masts and yards, supported by rigging already weakened and hastily knotted or spliced. Seamanship was stretched to its limit. Both fleets were united against this common danger, and men who had fought each other struggled now to save each other's lives. But after three days it became impossible. Collingwood, now in command again, signalled the fleet to abandon the prizes, take the men out of them and sink them or let them drive ashore. So a new struggle began: to drag the wounded up from the orlop decks of the French and Spanish ships, lower them into heaving boats, and row them to English ships that were under control. Hundreds were saved, and many men were drowned in trying to save them; but many hundreds still lay helpless down below and died when their ships went down or were pounded to wreckage on the rocks and shoals.

Not one of the British ships was lost, and that was an astonishing achievement. But only four of the prizes could be saved, one French and three Spanish and that, to the fleet, was a bitter disappointment which took away what glory remained in the victory. Since the prize money they had fairly won was gone, they felt they had nothing to show for their success. One by one, in the following fortnight, the ships limped into Gibraltar to look for repairs for the voyage home. Their crews were dead weary, and already the battle seemed long ago.

The *Victory*, dismasted, is towed into Gibraltar.

Navarino

1827

THE BATTLE OF NAVARINO was the last great battle entirely under sail. It was fought in 1827 in the Bay of Navarino at the south-west corner of Greece, with British, French and Russian fleets on one side and Turkish and Egyptian fleets on the other. The immediate cause of it was a small battle fought by a steamer.

Plenty of paddle-steamers existed by then, but navies, especially the British navy, disliked them and refused to use them except as tugs for taking their ships out of harbour: officers complained that engines covered their immaculate sails with smuts, and their holystoned decks with coal dust. There was, however, one steamer close by in Greece: a four-masted gunboat called *Karteria* with paddle-wheels and a funnel of enormous height, commanded by a young Englishman named Frank Hastings who had been cashiered from the navy for challenging a senior officer to a duel. For several years, he had been fighting with great spirit for the Greeks, and it was he who unwittingly struck the spark that started Navarino.

The political background of the battle was long and complicated. For six years past, the Greeks had been fighting to free themselves from the rule of Turkey. European sentiment was on the side of the Greeks, and a great many eccentric volunteers had gone to Greece to help them, including Lord Byron. But by 1827 they were on the verge of final defeat. Only a tiny strip of land was still in their hands, and the seas around were controlled by the Turkish fleet

Previous pages The Battle of Navarino, by L. Garneray.

Right Admiral Lord Cochrane had been dismissed from the Royal Navy and at the time of Navarino was fighting independently for the Greeks.

Below 'Serving the Guns': a scene on the gundeck of a British warship in the early nineteenth century.

and the fleet of Egypt, which was Turkey's vassal. The only challenge at sea came from Hastings' gunboat and a few ships led by the British admiral Lord Cochrane, who was as eccentric as any and had been dismissed from the navy in 1814 for many offences including frauds on the Stock Exchange.

Two things finally decided the European powers to put an end to this cruel war. One was that the Egyptian naval commander Ibrahim Pasha, the son of the ruler of Egypt Mehemet Ali, announced that he meant to annihilate the Greeks in the Peloponnese and turn it into an Arab state. The other was that many Greek ships had turned from war to piracy and were molesting peaceful shipping. Accordingly, the British and the French despatched their Mediterranean fleets to demand an armistice, announcing that a Russian fleet was also on its way from the Baltic. The Greeks agreed to the armistice, but the Sultan of Turkey refused it. He needed only one more blow to finish the Greeks – to capture the island of Hydra – and he had assembled his own fleet and the Egyptians at Navarino to do it: eighty-nine warships in all, with fire-ships.

The British commander-in-chief was Admiral Sir Edward Codrington, the French commander-in-chief was Compte Henri de Rigny. Codrington, the senior of the two, was a man of long experience – he had been the youngest of Nelson's captains at Trafalgar. But the orders he now received were very difficult to understand or interpret. Since one belligerent had accepted the armistice and the other had not, it became his duty to stop the Turks and Egyptians sending men and supplies to Greece;

but he was told to do it by persuasion, and not to fight except as a last resort. Everything was left to his judgement and de Rigny's, or in their absence to the judgement of their captains.

The two admirals therefore sailed straight to Navarino in their flagships, the *Asia*, eighty-four guns, and the *Sirène*, sixty, to explain to Ibrahim Pasha that they were obliged to enforce the armistice the Sultan had refused. They stood into the bay, through the enormous fleet assembled there. The band of the *Asia* played on deck, and her crew gave a confident display of naval seamanship by coming precisely to anchor in front of Ibrahim's tents, which were pitched on shore.

The meeting was surprisingly friendly. Codrington explained his orders. Ibrahim said his duty was to obey the Sultan's orders, not to negotiate. Those orders were to capture Hydra and bring the war to an end. His troops were embarked, he was ready to sail, and sail he must. Codrington replied that if Ibrahim left the bay, he would be obliged to destroy his fleet, much though he regretted it. The Sultan, he pointed out, had not known of this when he issued his orders, and he surely could not wish it to happen. After a long and reasonable discussion, Ibrahim agreed to report to the Sultan and to do nothing until he had an answer, which would take three weeks. After that, the three men sat chatting and pulling on ten-foot-long jewelled hookahs which Ibrahim had provided. Then the two admirals left the bay. Relying

Left Admiral Sir Edward Codrington, the youngest of Nelson's captains at Trafalgar, commanded the allied fleets at Navarino. Portrait by H. P. Briggs.

Below Ibrahim Pasha, the Viceroy in Greece of the Sultan of Turkey, who commanded the Turkish and Egyptian fleet.

on Ibrahim's promise, the French retired to the Aegean Sea, and Codrington dispersed his fleet, taking station himself at the nearby island of Zante with a frigate posted to watch Navarino.

Ibrahim had said it was unjust to restrict his fleet and let the Greek ships fight on, especially Lord Cochrane, who was in the only real warship the Greeks possessed. Codrington said the Greeks were justified in fighting until the Sultan accepted the armistice, and pointed out that Cochrane was not under his orders. However, he promised to restrain him. But nobody thought of telling Frank Hastings. Probably Codrington thought the steamship was part of Cochrane's fleet, but it was not. Hastings had always fought independently of anyone, and at that moment he was 150 miles (240 km) away,

steaming up the Gulf of Corinth towards an anchorage just below the ruins of Delphi, where he had heard some Turkish ships were lurking. And so they were: a schooner mounting twenty guns, six brigs of war, and two Austrian merchant ships which were loading a cargo of currants.

Hastings was a great innovator: in many ways his ideas were twenty-five years ahead of the navy's. He still used smooth-bore cannon, but he had somehow obtained 68-pound (31-kg) explosive shells; sometimes he used them with the charges in them, and sometimes he heated them red hot in the *Karteria*'s furnace. Moreover, he was probably the best shot in history with the old-fashioned cannon, which he aimed himself. On this occasion, at 500 yards, he fired one salvo each at the four largest

The Battle of Navarino Bay by L. Garneray: the fleet under fire from a battery on the Island of Sphacteria.

ships, and all four of them burst into flames. The schooner's crew abandoned her and fled. But she was hard aground within musket shot of a hundred troops ashore. Hastings steamed right in, got hawsers aboard her and tried to tow her off. But with his paddles thrashing the water the hawsers broke, so he boarded her, took her brass guns, and set her on fire. That left two brigs which had also run immoveably aground, and Hastings destroyed them with shells.

This completely successful battle, which lasted only half an hour, was the second battle in history fought by a steamship. (The first had been fought, also by Hastings, with equal success six months before.) Its importance was that it precipitated the final battle under sail.

The height of the battle, by Thomas Lang.

When Ibrahim heard of it, which was soon, he assumed that Codrington had broken his promise; so he felt absolved from his own promise to wait three weeks before he did anything. He made two sorties from Navarino. Both times he met Codrington outside. Codrington had not yet heard of the fight, and on both occasions, with one ship and two brigs against a fleet of fifty, he ordered Ibrahim back into port. The confidence of the British navy in those days was supreme, though afterwards Codrington confessed he was surprised and flattered when Ibrahim did as he was told.

What was worse than the sorties was that Ibrahim landed his troops, and began a devastation of the Greeks of the Peloponnese which was obviously meant to be final. He burnt their villages, killing many of the inhabitants, uprooted their vineyards and orange and lemon groves, and set their olive and fig trees on fire. The survivors were driven to hide in caves, where they tried to keep themselves and their children alive on boiled leaves and grass. Codrington wrote to Ibrahim requesting him to stop this outrage, and he sent a frigate into Navarino with the letter; but Ibrahim's staff said he had gone inland and they did not know where he was.

Codrington hastily reassembled his fleet. By luck the French came back, and at the crucial moment the Russian fleet arrived from the Baltic. The three admirals, Codrington, de Rigny and the Russian Count Heyden, met outside Navarino Bay and all signed a protocol recording their agreement: to stop the slaughter they would have to enter the bay. None of the countries were officially at war with each other, and the bay was spacious, with plenty of room for all the fleets. They hoped their mere presence there would make Ibrahim call a halt. But of course they knew they were risking a fight. In case a battle began, Codrington wrote in the orders to the fleet, 'It is to be observed that, in the words of Lord Nelson, "No captain can do very wrong who places his ship alongside that of an enemy."'

The frigate that took the letter had told him the fleets inside were anchored in a defensive three-quarter circle facing the entrance, the largest ships in front and the smallest behind, with fire-ships ready on each flank and batteries on each shore. The army transports were in the farthest part of the bay, and there were something like 140 ships all told. It was a trap arranged by some renegade Frenchmen who were Ibrahim's advisers. In theory, ships that came in with a following wind would be caught by fire all round before they could beat out again. Codrington could have sailed through the ring and anchored behind it, but he thought that would look like a hostile act. He chose to anchor inside the trap they had set.

On 19 October 1827 it was calm: there was not enough wind to go in. But early the next afternoon, a gentle westerly breeze came up, and he led the combined fleets into the bay, not in the single line of battle but in the peaceful double line that was the usual sailing formation: ten ships of the line, ten frigates, four brigs and three small cutters – twenty-seven in all against eighty-nine. The ships were cleared for action but the lower gunports were only half open, the normal position for sailing in fine weather. Again, the *Asia*'s band played cheerful music on the poop. All this, in naval eyes, was a clear indication of what he intended: he was willing to share the harbour in peace, but ready to fight if he had to. All three admirals had ordered their ships not to fire unless they were fired on.

They entered very slowly, past the shore batteries, into the waiting circle. There was a tense silence, broken only by the *Asia*'s incongruous music. The *Asia* anchored within a ship's length of the Turkish and Egyptian admirals, whose gun crews stood ready with the guns run out and loaded almost to the muzzles with shot and scrap iron. Two by two the ships astern took station, each within pistol shot of a chosen opponent.

It was a scene so charged with suspense that what happened was probably inevitable. It began with a

A contemporary plan of the Battle and Bay of Navarino.

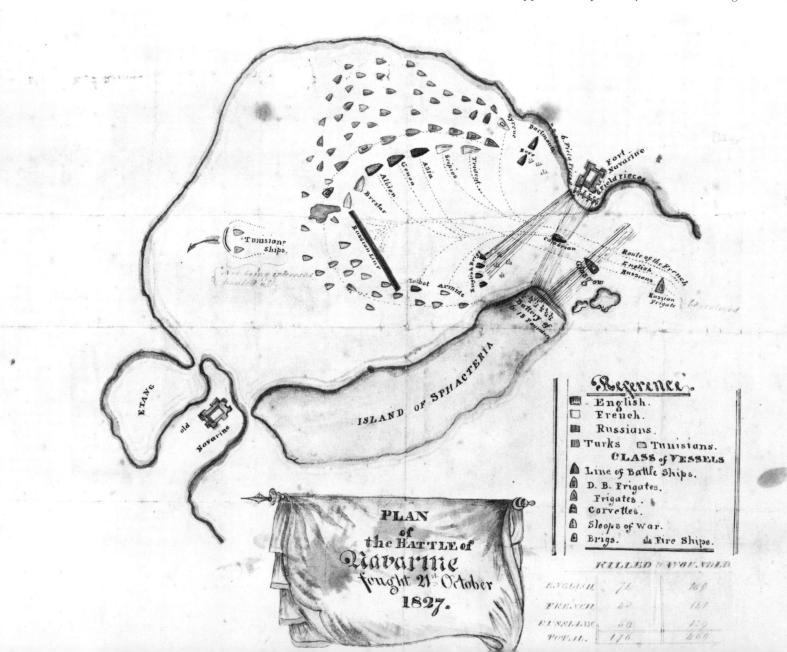

PLAN
of
the BATTLE of
Navarino
fought 21ˢᵗ October
1827.

Reference.

	English.
	French.
	Russians.
	Turks Tunisians.

CLASS of VESSELS

Line of Battle Ships.
D. B. Frigates.
Frigates.
Corvettes.
Sloops of War.
Brigs.   Fire Ships.

KILLED	WOUNDED	
ENGLISH	74	169
FRENCH	42	141
RUSSIANS	60	150
TOTAL	176	460

The French frigate *La Provence,* under repair in Navarino Bay after the battle.

single Turkish musket shot, and grew into the most destructive gunnery battle ever fought under sail. A British frigate sent a boat to request a fire-ship to move. Someone fired a musket at the boat and an officer was hit; the frigate fired muskets in retaliation; an Egyptian ship fired one cannon-shot at the French flagship, and the flagship fired back. Within minutes, the roar of gunfire filled the bay and echoed from the mountains round it. By the time the sternmost ships were in the bay the gunsmoke was so thick they could not find their stations. The battle, like so many others, was short. It lasted only four hours till darkness fell; but 'the scene of wreck and devastation', Codrington wrote, 'was such as has been seldom before witnessed.'

It was true: never since the Middle Ages had there been such slaughter at sea. To the survivors in the allied fleet it seemed a glorious victory: the concept of glory was always the comfort of men in war, and they needed comfort. They had 450 killed or wounded. They lost no ships, but nearly all were damaged, the *Asia* worst of all. She was dismasted, and at one moment Codrington himself, with two bullet holes in his coat and one in his hat, was the only man on his feet on the upper deck. The Turkish and Egyptian fleets were destroyed, partly at their own hands, and an untold number of their crews met sudden or lingering deaths. Codrington reported: 'As each ship of our opponents became effectually disabled, such of her crew as could escape from her endeavoured to set her on fire.' An uncontrolled fire in a wooden warship was certain to blow her up. 'During the whole night', Codrington wrote more flippantly to a friend, 'we were entertained with most beautiful though awful explosions.' In one British wardroom, the officers

cheered at each shattering bang and opened another bottle. At dawn, the bay was seen to be full of corpses and floating planks and spars with thousands of men clinging onto them and calling for help. At least sixty of the Sultan's warships were wrecked beyond repair.

Even at the time it did not seem glorious to everyone. The British government, which had really caused the battle by the muddled orders it had given to Codrington, affected afterwards, with more than a hint of hypocrisy, to be embarrassed at having demolished the fleets of two nominally friendly powers; and in the Speech from the Throne at the subsequent Opening of Parliament the battle was described as an untoward event. It seems sad in retrospect that the centuries of navies under sail, which on the whole had not been inglorious, ended with what can only be called a sordid slaughter. Navarino was fought at anchor, without the redeeming skill of handling ships and canvas in the open ocean. It was fought at a range that needed no skill in gunnery. It only proved that the efficient drill of a western fleet, even a mixed one, could devastate an eastern fleet at any odds.

However, it had one merit: it was fought to end a war, and it succeeded. Not that the fighting in Greece stopped at once: it went on in a desultory way for five more years. But deprived of his fleet, the Sultan could not maintain his grip on Greece. His armies slowly faded away. Four hours at Navarino ended four hundred years of Turkish rule in Greece, and gave the Greeks the freedom they had fought for.

海軍大将東郷平八郎

BETWEEN THE LAST great battle under sail and the first under steam were seventy-eight years of peace at sea, interrupted only by the offshore fights of the American Civil War and the support that navies gave to armies in the Crimea; and even those who disapprove of imperial power must admit that this unprecedented peace was due to the policing of the seas by the British navy. What brought it to an end was a devastating battle fought in the China Seas by two newcomers to naval power, Japan and Russia.

The cause of this battle was a long-standing territorial quarrel, especially over the harbour the British called Port Arthur, an important place because it was the only base for big ships on the mainland of that part of the world that was free of ice all winter. Originally, Port Arthur had been Chinese, but it was captured by Japan in 1895. Russia protested, and was backed by the governments of Germany and France, and under their diplomatic pressure and threats of naval action, Japan agreed to return it to its owners. As soon as they had done so, the Russians took it themselves.

The Japanese had never had a navy of any strength, but they patiently and secretly set to work to create one. They sent their most promising recruit to England for training, a man named Togo. He served two years in a British ship, and completed a mathematics course at Cambridge, an engineering course at Greenwich, and a gunnery course in HMS *Victory*. He was an impassive man, as the English expected all Japanese to be. It was said the only time he showed emotion during his years in England was at the commemoration on Trafalgar Day of Nelson's death in the *Victory*.

They also ordered the best and newest of ships, mostly built in England. In eight years they had a navy, including six first-class modern battleships,

帝國艦隊旅順攻擊手

Previous pages The Russo-Japanese war by the Japanese artist Toshikide.

浦潮港海軍之攻撃
八雲艦の砲撃八敵に多大
の損害を加え大勝利にて引揚
水哥勾の圖

twenty cruisers, nineteen destroyers and eighty-five torpedo boats; and Togo was its admiral. In 1904 they attacked Port Arthur, destroyed the Russian warships that were there, and started a war on land to recapture the place. Thereupon, the Tsar of Russia decided to mobilize his Baltic fleet and send it half way round the world to defend the port.

Even by the accounts of its own officers, it was a pathetically inefficient fleet, and its voyage was first comic but later tragic. It had four new battleships – one so new that she had not run her trials. Each had four up-to-date 12-inch (305-mm) guns and twelve 6-inch (152-mm) quick-firers; but the ships had had so much extra equipment added since they were designed that they were all top-heavy, unstable and two knots slower than they should have been, even when their engines were working well, which they seldom did. There were also three much older ironclads, five cruisers (one thirty-five years out of date), nine very small destroyers and a tail of colliers, repair ships and hospital ships – some forty ships in all. Their crews were reservists and merchant seamen, with a large proportion of ignorant peasants who had never been to sea. Among them were revolutionaries who saw a victory over Japan as a hindrance to their hopes and plans. All were commanded by Admiral Zinovy Rozhastvensky, who at least was a professional naval man.

Their voyage began in October 1904. The flagship *Suvarof* ran aground before she was out of harbour, and a destroyer rammed a cruiser and holed her, but no serious damage was done. Everyone, even the Admiral, was nervous. A rumour had spread that Japanese torpedo-boats were lying in wait for them in the North Sea – a most unlikely story, because the nearest Japanese were at least 10,000 miles (16,000 km) away – but the Russians were in a mood to believe anything. Sure enough, at night in the North Sea, action stations were sounded. One officer in the flagship remembered rushing up to the bridge among blazing guns and shouts of 'torpedo attack'. Between the lights of the two divisions of the fleet, he saw 'a small steamer with one mast and one funnel slowly moving away to starboard. A second vessel was heading straight for the battleship *Alexander* as if she intended to ram her; and the *Alexander* was pouring a hail of shot at her. The steamer sank before my eyes.' But in the glare of searchlights men in the strange ships were seen to be waving fish above their heads. They were not

Opposite: above Admiral Heihachiro Togo, the victor of Tsushima.

Opposite: below The Japanese navy bombards Port Arthur.

Above Action off Vladivostock in the Russo-Japanese war.

Below Caricature by Toshikide of the Tsar Nicholas II.

Japanese torpedo-boats, but the English fishing fleet on the Dogger Bank. Only an abject apology from Russia averted another war.

After that, a British fleet escorted the Russians down the Channel and safely out of the way, as far south as Tangier, where Rozhastvensky divided his forces, part to go round the Cape of Good Hope and part through the Suez Canal. They met again in Madagascar, and there also met the news that Port Arthur had fallen to the Japanese. They would have to go farther, to Vladivostok.

Any large naval fleet at that time would have found such a voyage difficult. Design was evolving so quickly that a ship could be obsolete before it was launched; reciprocating steam engines were still somewhat primitive, and the training of engineers in all navies was far from thorough. Deck officers still affected to despise steam and looked down on engineer officers whom they called greasers. But the Russian ships broke down much more often than most, and the fleet was always having to stop, or reduce its speed to 3 knots, while one ship or another was being mended. Coaling was a constant nightmare, especially in the tropics, where the bunkers became so hot that even the strongest men could only work in them for twenty minutes. No nation except the French would let the fleet enter its colonial harbours, so all the coaling had to be done at sea. The battleships normally carried 1,100

tons, but they had to take on twice that amount: coal was stowed in cabins, bathrooms, boats and lockers, and heaped in bags on the open decks. It was soft coal, and the fleet could be seen miles beyond the horizon by its clouds of smoke. A voyage to the Far East was a bigger undertaking than it had been at the height of the age of sail, because it depended on unpredictable machinery and the supply of fuel.

One minor incident was typical of both the comedy and the tragedy. The fleet tried to practise a few elementary manoeuvres, and in one of them the commander of the destroyers hoisted the signal for line ahead. 'Great was my astonishment,' he wrote afterwards, 'when all my boats, instead of taking up their stations in line, steamed off in every direction at full speed. I had some trouble collecting them again.' He found he had an old signal book and they had a new one, in which the signal he had hoisted meant 'Search the Coast'. He saw the funny side of it, but dreaded that something like that might happen in battle.

In Madagascar there were orders to wait for reinforcements. Rozhastvensky did not want the reinforcements, which he knew were ships too old and derelict to have sailed with him; but he waited two months. To the peasants who had never dreamed of anything beyond the cold plains of Russia, the island gave a glimpse of an earthly paradise, and discipline broke down. There was a mutiny, led by the revolutionaries, which the Admiral had to put down by force. After that, in the enervating heat, the fleet fell into a mood of apathy. None of the ten thousand men expected to live much longer.

Left The destruction of the Russian flagship *Suvarof*.

Opposite: below The defeated Russian Admiral Zinovy Rozhastvensky.

Below The Russian fleet at Tsushima.

In March, the reinforcements had not come, but the fleet set sail again and crossed the Indian Ocean. Everyone, including Japanese, saw it pass through the Straits of Singapore, where the Russian consul came off in a boat to deliver more bad news from Port Arthur – 20,000 Russian dead and 40,000 prisoners. He also repeated the order to wait for the reinforcements; so the fleet hovered around the South China Sea until the useless ships caught up with it. Even Admiral Rozhastvensky, after six months at sea, was suffering a deep fit of depression.

To reach Vladivostok there were several ways they could go, but they chose the shortest, the strait between Korea and Japan. In the middle of that strait is the island of Tsushima.

They almost made it. After coming 18,000 miles (30,000 km), they were only 600 (1,000 km) from their journey's end. So far as they knew, they had not been seen since Singapore, and as they approached the strait the weather was so misty they could not see the whole of their own fleet.

But the Japanese Admiral Togo had guessed the choice they would make. He had stationed his fleet at the tip of South Korea, and his cruisers were on patrol in the strait. At dawn on 27 May, one of them almost ran down a Russian hospital ship. The fleet was discovered.

Among the modern inventions which Togo possessed and the Russians did not was wireless telegraphy. His cruiser used it. Even he seemed impressed by its miracle. 'Though a heavy mist covered the sea,' he wrote, 'and visibility was only five miles, the enemy's disposition was as clear to us, forty or fifty miles away, as if we had seen it with our own eyes.' His fleet got up steam, weighed and took formation with the clockwork efficiency the Russians lacked, the efficiency he had learned to admire in England. At 1.45 pm the fleets were in sight of each other, and ten minutes later Togo hoisted a signal he must have half-remembered from the *Victory*: 'The fate of the Empire hangs on this event. Let every man do his utmost.'

Only one European, so far as we know, was a witness of what happened that day. He was a colonel of Royal Marines named Pakenham, who was aboard a Japanese battleship as an observer from the Royal Navy. Of sighting the Russian fleet he wrote, 'In the right column the four biggest battleships loomed enormous, dwarfing all others into insignificance. It was not easy to realise that the battleships of Japan were probably producing at least equal effect on the minds of the Russians.' But they were.

Since Togo had known the Russians' position and course and they had not known his, he started with an advantage. His fleet was in the conventional line of battle, the Russians still in a double line. Togo was able to 'cross the T' of the Russians, a manoeuvre that was the hope of most naval tacticians because it exposed the leaders of the enemy line to simultaneous broadsides. But Togo seems to have scorned that opportunity: he did it out of range. Then he turned at right-angles, on the opposite course to the Russians, turned again towards them, and then a third time, within

range, on to a parallel course. No sailing fleet could have done that, and nobody in battle had ever tried. It was very rash. On the final turn, the Russians had only to find the range of his leading ship, and then use the same range for all the following ships as they crossed the same spot in the ocean.

The Russians saw the chance, and for a moment they had a wild hope of success. Indeed, they did better than they or anyone else expected. Their first salvo fell only 20 yards astern of Togo's flagship *Mikasa*, and their 6-inch guns began to score hits on him and the following ships.

Their hope soon died. As the Japanese came on to the parallel course, they opened fire with their 12-inch guns. This was not only the first great battle under steam, it was also the first with 12-inch explosive shells. Nobody before had ever had the awful experience of being under fire from such monstrous weapons. Consequently, the Russians had not been prepared for it by reading or hearing what it was like from people who had been through it and survived.

For the most part, they stood paralysed by terror. After their first successful salvoes their gunnery went to pieces. Even a veteran of the fighting at Port Arthur, who was in the flagship *Suvarof*, was amazed: 'The missiles hitting our sides and falling on deck seemed more like mines than shells. They burst as soon as they touched anything. Even handrails were enough to cause a thoroughly efficient burst. Iron ladders were crumpled into rings, and guns were hurled from their mountings. The air was filled with flames and blood and flying metal.' One shell fell in the temporary first-aid post of the flagship, next to the ship's image of Christ and His Mother. The Chaplain was terribly wounded, and many already wounded were killed, but the same observer said that 'the ship's image

Opposite Togo's flagship *Mikasa* in action.

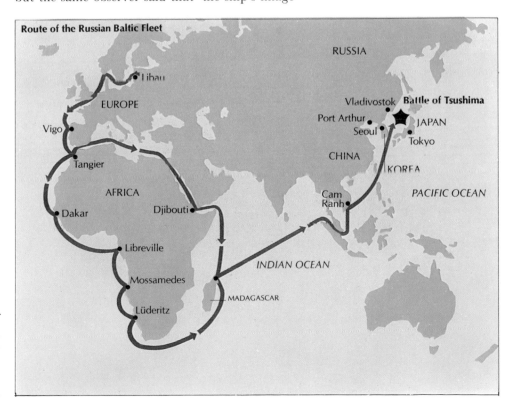

Route of the Russian Baltic Fleet

RUSSIA

Libau

EUROPE

Vladivostok · Battle of Tsushima

Port Arthur

Vigo

Seoul · JAPAN

Tokyo

Tangier

CHINA

AFRICA

KOREA

Cam Ranh

PACIFIC OCEAN

Dakar

Djibouti

Libreville

INDIAN OCEAN

Mossamedes

MADAGASCAR

Lüderitz

The Battle of Tsushima

Above After the battle very few of the remaining Russian ships survived; scattered far and wide and hopelessly demoralized, the Japanese could pick them off at their leisure.

Japanese fleet *Togo*
6 battleships
19 destroyers
cruisers

An armoured cruiser is hit and leaves the line damaged.

The battleship *Suvarof* is badly damaged and leaves line.

The battleship *Osliabia* explodes and drifts out of line.

Osliabia sinks.

Togo makes the dangerous manoeuvre of turning at right angles, on the opposite course to the Russians, turning again and then a third time, within range, onto a parallel course.

Russian fleet *Rozhastvensky*
7 battleships
9 destroyers
cruisers

96

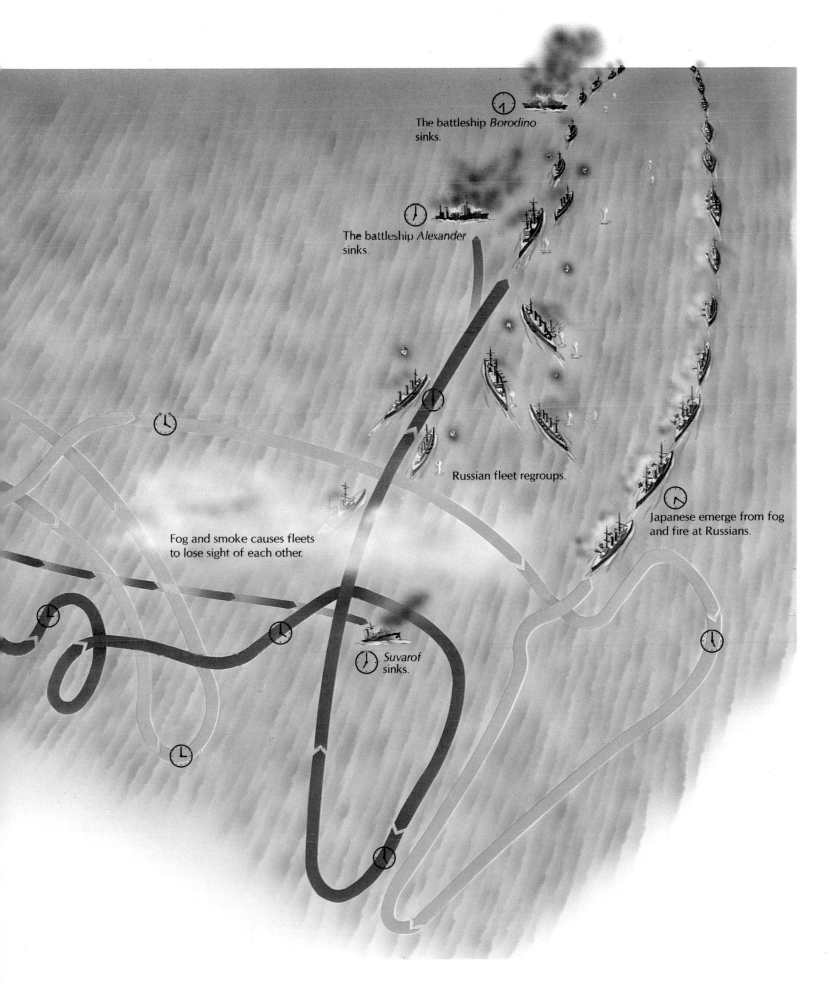

The battleship *Borodino* sinks.

The battleship *Alexander* sinks.

Russian fleet regroups.

Japanese emerge from fog and fire at Russians.

Fog and smoke causes fleets to lose sight of each other.

Suvarof sinks.

was untouched. Even the glass of the big image case was not broken, and in front of it, on hanging candlesticks, candles were peacefully burning.'

The most destructive result was fire. The heat of the explosions made everything combustible burst instantly into flames, and even the new Russian battleships had been built with far too much material that would burn – wooden decks and doors and furniture – and most were still carrying coal in unprotected spaces. Fires broke out all over the flagship, and the fire hoses were cut to bits by splinters. Togo noted with evident satisfaction: 'The flagship *Suvarof* burst heavily into flames and left the fighting line, so that the enemy's order was deranged.' At 2.45 pm, less than an hour from the opening shot, he added: 'The result of the battle had already been decided.' Nevertheless, he continued to pound the Russians all the afternoon. When he called off his main fleet in the dusk, three of the four new battleships had sunk, and so had an older battleship and an auxiliary cruiser. All the rest were damaged, disorganized and helpless. It had proved far easier to sink a steel ship with explosive shells than it had ever been to sink a wooden ship with cannon balls.

During the night he ordered his torpedo boats in to complete the rout. By dawn the Russian fleet was scattered far and wide and hopelessly demoralized, so that the Japanese could pick off single ships at their leisure. Admiral Rozhastvensky, severely wounded and barely conscious, had been taken off the burning flagship and transferred to one of the small destroyers. Although he was still alive and nominally in command, his vice-admiral offered surrender. 'I accepted it', Togo wrote, 'and as a special measure allowed the officers to retain their swords.' Soon after, the destroyer with Rozhastvensky on board was captured.

There was very little left to surrender. Twenty Russian ships, just about half the fleet, had been sunk. Of the rest, seven had been captured; two were foundering and sank after the battle ceased; one disappeared and was never seen again; six sought refuge and were interned in Shanghai or Manila; and two, only two, reached their destination at Vladivostok. 6,000 Russians were taken prisoner, and 3,000 lost their lives. The Japanese fleet lost 116 men and three torpedo-boats. It was a shattering victory.

In his report, Togo said there was not much

Below The brand-new Russian battleship *Orel* after the battle.

Opposite: above Another Russian battleship, the *Tzarevitch*, which survived the battle but only just.

Below right Russian sailors at Tsushima take to their boats to leave two sinking ships.

difference in the strengths of the fleets, and the Russians fought with energy and courage. Victory had been won through the virtues of His Majesty the Emperor, not through any human prowess. 'One has to believe', he added, 'that the small number of our casualties was due to the protection of the Spirit of the Imperial Ancestors.'

All nations use some such form of words, but the leaders of all other navies studied Tsushima with a purely technical interest. As the first test in action of steel-built steamers and high-explosive shells, it had a profound effect on naval development in the next ten years, and thus on the fleets of the First World War. It proved two things. The first was that training and discipline were just as important with steam as they had been with sail. The second was that a fleet that was planned as a homogeneous unit was far more powerful than a larger fleet that was only a chance collection of miscellaneous ships. The British in particular had always known the first of these lessons, indeed they had taught it to Togo. But they badly needed to be reminded of the second.

Coronel and
the Falkland Islands
1914

BRITISH POLICY AT that time was to have a navy that was bigger than any other two navies put together, and she succeeded. But the policy put too much emphasis on size, on mere numbers of ships, and not enough on quality. The British navy suffered from one of the faults of the Russian fleet: its ships were a mixed collection, and many were old-fashioned and slow. It policed all the seas in the world and did it very well, but it was not equipped to fight a great sea battle.

Luckily for Britain, there was one man in the navy who saw this weakness and was determined to put it right, and in the same month that the Russians left the Baltic, October 1904, he was appointed First Sea Lord. This was Admiral Sir John Fisher (Jackie Fisher, to the fleet), an abrasive, rude and ruthless little man of enormous energy. Almost his first act as First Sea Lord was to take a list of 154 ships, including seventeen battleships, and scrawl across it three words: 'Scrap the lot!' He had conceived the idea of a new kind of warship: a battleship faster than any before, with turbine engines and a main armament entirely of 12-inch (305-mm) guns. The first of these was laid down at Portsmouth in October 1905, four months after Tsushima, and she put to sea for her trials a year and a day later – a record in ship building that has probably never been equalled. She was given the old naval name of *Dreadnought*, and at once every other battleship in the world was obsolete.

Under Fisher's sense of urgency, the British set to work to build a whole fleet of dreadnoughts, and of another of Fisher's concepts, dreadnought cruisers, later called battlecruisers. These were faster than any battleship that could possibly be built, but were amoured and carried a formidable punch of eight 12-inch guns. Other nations began to follow suit, especially the Germans. In the summer of 1914, when war was plainly imminent, Britain had twenty dreadnoughts and four battlecruisers; Germany had thirteen dreadnoughts and three battlecruisers. Each of these ships could fire broadsides of over two tons of shells to a distance of ten miles. It was the greatest revolution in sea power since the British put their faith in gunnery at the time of the Spanish Armada, and it had all come about within less than ten years.

But when the First World War began, Fisher was out of office – his bad manners had gone too far and offended too many people – and his plan was not complete. The British still had many old ships, some already patrolling in distant seas, and some which had been laid up and were quickly re-manned with reservists. So it happened that the first major naval battle of that war reinforced the lesson of Tsushima.

A squadron of the elderly ships was based in the Falkland Islands, to the east of Cape Horn, which was one of the coaling stations the British maintained at strategic points all over the world. It was commanded by Rear-Admiral Sir Christopher Cradock. At the end of October 1914 his flag was in the armoured cruiser *Good Hope*, which had been completed in 1902, and had two 9·2-inch (234-mm) guns and ten 6-inch (152-mm) guns, though half of these, in the old-fashioned manner, were mounted so low in the ship that they could not be used in a high sea. Under his command were the cruiser *Monmouth*, completed in 1903, a converted liner called the *Otranto*, and one new ship, the *Glasgow*, which however was only a light – that is an unarmoured – cruiser with two 6-inch and ten 4-inch (102-mm) guns. And coming very slowly down the coast of South America to join him was one battleship, the *Canopus*. She had four 12-inch guns, but she had been designed nearly twenty years before to do seventeen knots; now, with her aged engines she could do only twelve. All these ships except the *Glasgow* had been manned by reservists within the past few weeks. It was just the sort of police force the British had kept around Cape Horn for generations past, good enough in peacetime but too old for war.

At the same time, the Germans had a much more modern squadron in the Pacific Ocean under Admiral Graf von Spee: the armoured cruisers

Previous pages The review at Spithead for the coronation of King George V in 1911.

Below Admiral Sir John Fisher by H. von Herkomer, 1911.

Scharnhorst and *Gneisenau* and three light cruisers. They had been posted there to destroy British merchant shipping and coaling stations. They were almost hopelessly isolated, with scarcely a single friendly port in the world, depending on coal from the merchant ships they captured. 'I am quite homeless,' von Spee had written. 'I cannot reach Germany. We possess no other secure harbour. I must plough the seas of the world doing as much mischief as I can, until my ammunition is exhausted, or a foe far superior in power succeeds in catching me.' But, though he knew he was doomed, von Spee was an inspiring commander and his small squadron was impeccably trained.

This was the beginning of the first war in which admiralties at home could give orders to commanders at sea by radio. It was a mixed blessing, to say the least. In the old days, if an admiral on a distant station waited for orders, he would have to wait for months, or perhaps even a year. So he used his own judgement. But now, orders could reach him at any moment. They were not always up to date, because the range of shore-to-ship signals, or ship-to-shore, was only a few hundred miles: so signals had to be sent by cable to the nearest colony, or an obliging neutral country, and transmitted from there – a process that sometimes took a week. The German Admiralty used radio wisely. It sent the latest intelligence to its isolated commanders like von Spee, but it did not send him orders. The British, on the other hand, could not resist the power to order the movements of ships all over the world – perhaps because the First Lord of the Admiralty was Winston Churchill, a man who liked to order everything. Often their orders were ill-considered and badly worded, because they did not yet possess a naval staff that was trained for the job. Admiral Cradock, thousands of miles from home, was plagued by contradictory orders. When he puzzled them out, the only possible conclusion was that the Admiralty wished him to sail round Cape Horn and intercept von Spee in the Pacific. It was plainly useless to hunt those thousands of miles of sea if he was hindered by the twelve knots of the *Canopus*, so he left her to follow behind. With his remaining four ships he believed his mission was suicidal, but tradition compelled him to try it.

On the way up the west coast after rounding the Horn, the captain of the *Canopus* made a strange discovery. His engineer commander, he found, was a sick man, apparently suffering from an acute depression which he had managed to conceal. He had greatly exaggerated the trouble with her engines. She could, after all, do sixteen knots. The captain, however, did not tell Cradock, who was twenty-four hours ahead, because he did not want to break radio silence and did not believe, in any case, that Cradock would wait for him.

On the afternoon of 1 November, Cradock was steaming at fifteen knots up the coast, with his four ships *Good Hope*, *Monmouth*, *Otranto* and *Glasgow* fifteen miles apart on a line of search – that is, a line abreast. At four o'clock the *Glasgow* sighted smoke and altered course towards it. Twenty minutes later she signalled that she had sighted the *Scharnhorst* and *Gneisenau* and the light cruiser *Leipzig*.

Cradock could have escaped to the south. He was almost hopelessly outgunned, but faster than the Germans; and it would not have been contrary to Admiralty orders to have fallen back on the *Canopus*. But he was not that sort of man, and was not in that sort of navy: another admiral at that moment was awaiting court martial for failing to engage the enemy in the Mediterranean under very similar circumstances. So he formed line of battle on a course to intercept. Von Spee did the same. The wind at that time was force six, and the fleets were on a collision course, both plunging into high head-seas. Just after six o'clock, Cradock turned four points towards the enemy, trying to bring him to action before it was dark. But von Spee turned away. With the British to the west of him, the setting sun was in his gunners' eyes. He deliberately waited until the sun was down, when the British were silhouetted against the afterglow, while his own ships were scarcely visible. He then closed the range, and at seven o'clock he opened fire at over 12,000 yards (11,000 m).

Admiral Sir Christopher Cradock, defeated and killed at Coronel.

Cradock's flagship the *Good Hope* blazes at Coronel and sinks with all hands.

Most sea battles were short, but the battle of Coronel was one of the shortest of all. Its outcome was certain within ten minutes: in forty-five minutes it was all over, except for a macabre encounter in the night. At the beginning, the British were in range of twelve of the Germans' 8·2-inch (208 mm) guns, while only the *Good Hope*'s two 9·2-inch (234 mm) could reply. Moreover, von Spee had cleverly manoeuvred in the evening light so that he could see what he was doing and the British could not. Cradock continued to close the range until it was down to 5,500 yards (5,000 m), but before then his own ship the *Good Hope* had been hit time and again and she was blazing: her burning interior, the Germans said, could be seen through the portholes, and at times the flames burst out and rose over 200 feet above her. The *Monmouth* too was hit, between thirty and forty times. A shell blew off the roof of her forward turret, and very soon after a huge internal explosion blew the whole turret off the foredeck. By 7.45 pm, an officer in the *Glasgow* wrote, she had 'Yawed off to starboard

burning furiously and heeling slightly. *Good Hope* was firing only a few of her guns, with the fires on board increasing their brilliance. At 7.50 pm there was a terrible explosion between her mainmast and her after funnel, after which she lay between the lines, a black hull lighted only by a dull glow.'

The merchant cruiser *Otranto* had never a chance to use her 4·7-inch (119-mm) guns, and she stayed out of range and escaped in the darkness. The *Glasgow*, unarmoured, was surprisingly lucky. She was in action and had a few hits but no serious damage. Neither she nor the German light cruisers could shoot effectively in the heavy sea. Seeing both the bigger ships out of action, her captain turned back in the dark to try to help the *Monmouth*. 'Are you all right?' he signalled at 8.15 pm. The *Monmouth*'s captain replied, 'I want to get stern to sea. I am making water badly foreward.' 'Can you steer NW?' the *Glasgow* asked; but no answer came, and the *Glasgow* turned south at full speed to warn the *Canopus*, which would certainly be sunk if the five Germans found her alone. 'It was awful having

to leave the *Monmouth*,' an officer wrote, 'but I don't see what else the skipper could have done.'

Nobody saw the *Good Hope* go down. She vanished in the stormy night, with Cradock and her entire complement of 900 men. But by chance, the last moments of the *Monmouth* had a witness. The German cruiser *Nürnberg*, which had been far astern in the battle, came upon the *Monmouth* in the dark. 'Her forward turret was missing,' the Germans reported, 'but her engines were still running and her steering gear was undamaged. As she did not haul down her flag, the *Nürnberg* opened fire at between 1,000 and 600 yards.' No answering fire came, so the *Nürnberg* ceased. But the *Monmouth* turned towards her. The Germans thought she meant either to ram or to bring her starboard guns to bear, so they opened point-blank fire again, 'tearing open the unprotected parts of the *Monmouth*'s hull with their shells. She heeled further and further, and at 9.28 capsized and went down with her flag still flying. There was no chance of rescue work because columns of smoke were reported from two directions. Moreover, the *Nürnberg*'s boats could not be launched in the heavy sea.' The British would not have thought the columns of smoke were a reason for not attempting rescue, but the second reason may have been adequate. A further 675 men were lost, many hundreds clinging to wreckage until they drowned.

At the very beginning of the war, von Spee's victory was ammunition for German propagandists: one called it 'the most severe blow that British prestige had suffered for over a century'. So it was, and the British felt it too. 'Individually and collectively,' an officer in the *Glasgow* wrote, 'we were humiliated to the very depths of our beings. We hardly spoke to one another for the first twenty-four hours. We felt so bitterly ashamed of ourselves.' Yet, ghastly though it was, the loss of two second-rate cruisers was of little consequence to British strength. Furthermore, the German Admiralty knew the victory made von Spee's position doubly hopeless – and von Spee knew it too. He had used more than

Admiral Sir Doveton Sturdee, Commander-in-Chief at the Falkland Islands.

half his ammunition, and the British now knew where he was. He could not doubt they would deploy the whole of their enormous power, if necessary, in revenge. His Admiralty, as usual, did not send him orders. They 'left it to his discretion' whether to try to reach Germany, which was his only slender chance.

Revenge was made even more certain by a coincidence in London. In November the First Sea Lord resigned, and two days before the battle Churchill as First Lord recalled Admiral Fisher to his old post. Fisher was then seventy-four, but still had plenty of his fire and determination. Both he and Churchill knew that many senior officers were putting the blame for the disaster on the Admiralty's muddled orders, and though Churchill later rejected any blame, his conscience at the time could not have been perfectly clear. That may have made him all the more determined to get von Spee. He and Fisher agreed on drastic action. The only ship that certainly had the speed and strength to catch and defeat von Spee was a battlecruiser. Churchill proposed sending one from the Home Fleet at Invergordon in Scotland. 'But I found Lord Fisher in bolder mood,' he wrote. 'He would take two of these powerful ships.' Accordingly, they ordered two battlecruisers, the *Invincible* and *Inflexible*, to 'proceed with all dispatch' to Plymouth. At

Plymouth, they were put under the command of Vice-Admiral Sir Doveton Sturdee.

The reason for Sturdee's appointment was very odd. He was a popular and respected officer, and he was Chief of the War Staff. But he was one of the many men that Fisher detested, and so fierce was the old man's hatred that he absolutely refused to keep him on the Admiralty staff. If Churchill had let him be sacked and given a lesser appointment, it might have seemed an admission that the Admiralty was at fault over the battle at Coronel. So he hit on the idea of sending him to command the expedition of revenge.

Then began a comedy of errors – a comedy which, without a stroke of luck, might have led to another British disaster. When the battlecruisers reached Plymouth, the admiral commanding the dockyard reported they could not be ready for five days. Churchill replied with a signal that they must be ready in two and 'Dockyard arrangements must be made to conform.' The admiral took a train to London to protest in person: both ships, he said, needed new brickwork in their furnaces. Churchill told him the ships would be gone before he was back at his post; and so they were, taking with them civilian bricklayers to finish the job on the way.

In later years, that voyage from Plymouth to the Falkland Islands was made to seem a heroic dash throughout the length of the Atlantic. But in fact, nobody had impressed on Sturdee the need for haste or secrecy. He steamed well below top speed, spent time in searching for enemy merchant ships, called at the Portuguese Cape Verde islands for coal and at a rendezvous off Pernambuco to pick up other ships, and he ordered gunnery practice; and when the wire towing the target fouled one of the *Invincible*'s propellers, he stopped the whole fleet for twelve hours while divers unwound it. Consequently, he was five days later in reaching the Falkland Islands than the Admiralty expected. There, he took the entire fleet – two battlecruisers, three armoured cruisers and two light cruisers – into the harbour of Port Stanley to coal again, leaving only an armed merchantman outside on watch. The old *Canopus* was already in harbour: she had been grounded there to act as a fort.

The British stroke of luck was that von Spee was also hesitating to round Cape Horn and begin the well-nigh impossible voyage back towards Germany. A vague message reached him by a roundabout route from the Cape Verde islands that the big ships were coming south, but he believed they were bound for South Africa. Other reports told him there were no ships in the Falkland Islands. So when he made up his mind to go, the first orders he gave his fleet were to attack the harbour of Port Stanley and burn the English stocks of coal. Sturdee arrived there at 10.30 am, 7 December. At dawn next morning, lookouts on the neighbouring hilltops sighted the German fleet. Both the battlecruisers had colliers alongside them. Two cruisers were repairing their engines, and only one had steam up. Sturdee had a reputation for imperturbability: he confirmed it by ordering all ships to get up steam, and then going below to shave and have breakfast.

At first, von Spee's leading ships saw only a cloud of smoke over the harbour, and concluded that the British had sighted him and were burning their stock of coal so that he should not get it. It was not until nine o'clock that they saw the funnels and masts of warships in the harbour. They held on, refusing to believe there were any ships there that they could not deal with. Next, observers in their fighting-tops reported four tripod masts. The only British ships that had tripod masts were dreadnoughts and battlecruisers, and von Spee disbelieved this report. Then the *Canopus*, aground on her sandbank, fired two salvoes, and another extraordinary chance occurred in this tale of chances. The day before, a practice shoot had been ordered for that morning, and the crew of one turret had loaded their 12-inch (305 mm) guns with dummy shells. The salvoes fell short – the Germans were still out of range – and the live shells exploded when they hit the water. But the dummies ricocheted, and one of them struck the funnel of the *Gneisenau* and made a hole in it. At this evidence of heavier guns than his own, von Spee broke off his intended attack and turned away to the east. Had he carried on, he would have caught the British in harbour before they were ready. But he could not know, and he still believed his ships were faster than anything else in the South Atlantic. It was past ten o'clock before the battlecruisers had steam to leave Port Stanley, when Sturdee hoisted the time-honoured signal 'General chase'. And it was eleven o'clock before von Spee recognized them and knew the doom he had been expecting had come.

Sturdee still took his time. The battlecruisers

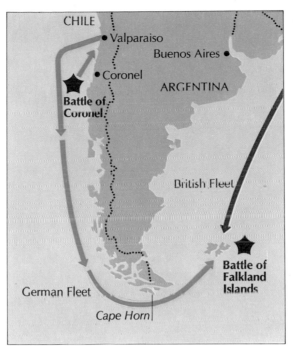

could do twenty-five and a half knots, three knots more than von Spee's fastest ships at their best – and they were not at their best after many months at sea. Sturdee reduced speed to nineteen knots to let his cruisers catch up, and signalled the fleet that they should have dinner before the action began. At about 12.20 am, an officer remembered in the flagship, 'the Skipper came aft and said that the Admiral had decided to get on with the work. The men on deck cheered.'

After the crushing British defeat at the Battle of Coronel the Admiralty sent two battle-cruisers, which joined five smaller cruisers, to intercept von Spee's ships on their way home to Germany.

Sinking of the *Scharnhorst* at the Falkland Islands, by C. E. Turner.

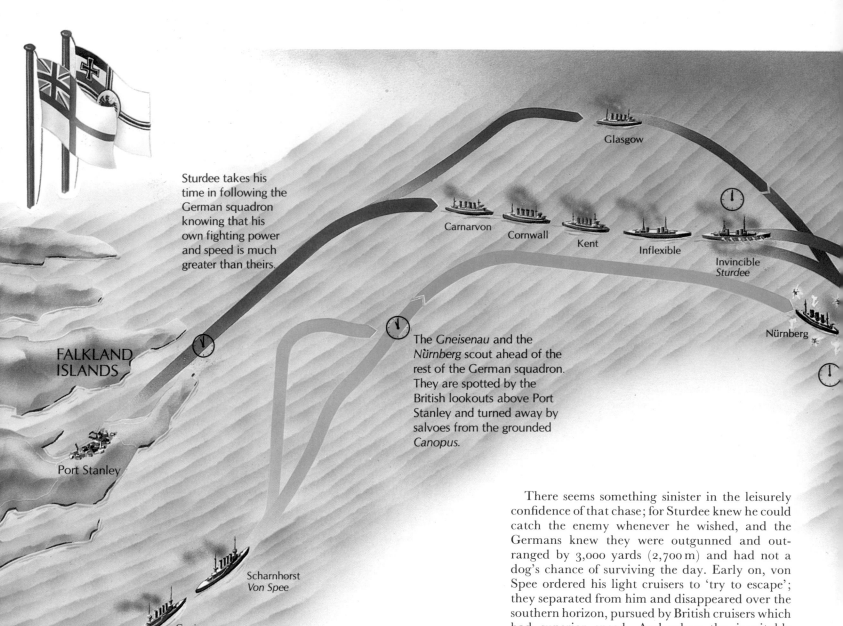

Sturdee takes his time in following the German squadron knowing that his own fighting power and speed is much greater than theirs.

The *Gneisenau* and the *Nürnberg* scout ahead of the rest of the German squadron. They are spotted by the British lookouts above Port Stanley and turned away by salvoes from the grounded *Canopus*.

Glasgow

Carnarvon Cornwall Kent Inflexible Invincible *Sturdee*

Nürnberg

FALKLAND ISLANDS

Port Stanley

Scharnhorst *Von Spee*

Gneisenau

Dresden

Leipzig

Nürnberg

The Battle of the Falkland Islands

8 December 1914
From about 11 am to 9 pm

There seems something sinister in the leisurely confidence of that chase; for Sturdee knew he could catch the enemy whenever he wished, and the Germans knew they were outgunned and out-ranged by 3,000 yards (2,700 m) and had not a dog's chance of surviving the day. Early on, von Spee ordered his light cruisers to 'try to escape'; they separated from him and disappeared over the southern horizon, pursued by British cruisers which had superior speed. And when the inevitable slaughter of the big ships started, it was very terrible. The two battlecruisers, with sixteen 12-inch guns between them, began methodically to smash the *Scharnhorst* and *Gneisenau* to pieces. It took a long time, the whole of that summer afternoon, because Sturdee had determined to do it at extreme range, beyond the range of the Germans. One by one, the Germans' guns went out of action. Both ships were on fire, both were holed below the waterline and floating lower and lower. But they continued to fire with diminishing strength and effect.

The scene on board the flagship must have been appalling, with men dying by the hundreds and the medical teams entirely overwhelmed. But von Spee would not give up. Perhaps, with no hope left for his own life or his ship, he believed that if he fought to the end the light cruisers might have a chance to get away.

At four o'clock the *Scharnhorst* abruptly ceased fire, 'as when a light is blown out', the *Inflexible*'s gunnery officer wrote. Sturdee's report, in the dispassionate language of such documents, said 'At 16.04 the *Scharnhorst*, whose flag remained flying to the last, suddenly listed heavily to port, and it became clear that she was doomed. The list

The armoured cruiser *Carnarvon* joins the two battlecruisers *Invincible* and *Inflexible*.

Invincible

Inflexible

Fire opens.

Scharnhorst

Gneisenau

Leipzig

Dresden

Von Spee orders his light cruisers to try to escape. They separate from the *Scharnhorst* and *Gneisenau*.

Scharnhorst sinks.

Carnarvon

Inflexible

Gneisenau sinks.

Invincible

The *Glasgow* leads the two armoured cruisers in their pursuit of the German light cruisers.

Cornwall

Kent

Glasgow

Kent

Nürnberg sinks.

Dresden escapes.

Leipzig sinks.

Cornwall

Glasgow

N

British

German

The last of Scharnhorst and Gneisenau
W. Wyllie

Above 'The Last of the
Scharnhorst and Gneisenau',
by W. Wyllie.

Opposite: above Ships and
admirals of the Battle of the
Falkland Islands.

Opposite: below Picking up
survivors from the *Gneisenau* at
the end of the Battle of the
Falkland Islands.
Photographed from the
Invincible, with the *Inflexible*
standing by.

increased very rapidly until she lay on her beam
ends; at 16.17 she disappeared.' The British did not
stop to rescue, because they were still in action with
the *Gneisenau*, and the whole of the *Scharnhorst*'s
crew, 765 men, were lost with her; among them,
Admiral von Spee.

The *Gneisenau* lasted an hour longer. The British,
unscathed in their more powerful ships, were able
to watch her death throes with admiration and a
kind of sorrow. One wrote, 'The poor devils on
board must have known that they were doomed.'
She was under a storm of fire from ships on three
sides, for the armoured cruiser *Carnarvon* had joined
the battlecruisers; but she fought on with what
guns remained. When she was sinking and some
600 of her crew were dead or wounded, she
continued to fire a single gun, and one of her last
shots hit the *Invincible*. Finally, she ran out of
ammunition, all her boiler rooms were flooded, and
her captain gave orders to scuttle and abandon her.
At 5.40 pm the three British ships closed in. The
flag at her foretop was hauled down, but she still
flew a flag at the peak. Ten minutes later, Sturdee
ordered 'Cease fire'. She rolled over slowly and
quietly disappeared.

All three British ships stopped and lowered their
boats, and between them they picked up 190 men
from the water, which was only a few degrees above
freezing. 'We were busy getting out clothes, etc., for
them,' an officer wrote in the *Inflexible*, 'and by
dinner time we had several in the mess. Most of

them could not sleep that first night, the scenes in
their ships were so terrible. But we were all good
friends after the fight, and agreed that we did not
want to fight at all, but had to. Over 2,000 of them
must have been killed or drowned, but they fought
magnificently, and their discipline must have been
superb.'

The British were right to feel a certain remorse: it
had been too easy. Only one man had been killed in
the battlecruisers, and two slightly wounded, while
the damage was negligible. That evening, Sturdee
signalled to the senior German survivor, with
ponderous courtesy: 'The Commander-in-Chief is
very gratified that your life has been spared . . . we
sympathise with you in the loss of your Admiral and
so many officers and men. Unfortunately the two
countries are at war; the officers of both navies, who
can count friends in the other, have to carry out
their country's duties which your Admiral, captains and officers worthily maintained to the end.'
And the senior German, who was a commander,
replied: 'I thank Your Excellency very much for
your kind words. We regret, as you, the course of
the fight, as we have learnt to know during
peacetime the English navy and their officers. We
are all most thankful for our good reception.'

It was almost the same when the British cruisers
caught up with their fleeing adversaries. That same
evening, they sank the *Leipzig* and the *Nürnberg*, and
could only rescue about a score of men from the
numbing sea. The only ship that escaped was the

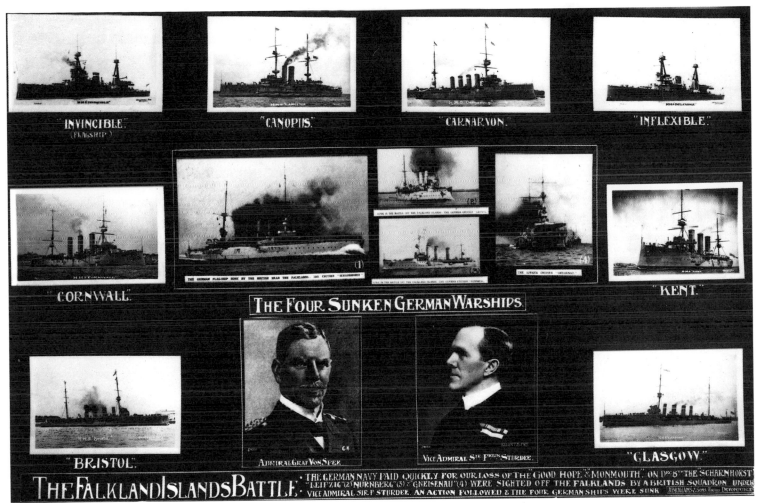

INVINCIBLE. (FLAGSHIP)   "CANOPUS."   CARNARVON.   "INFLEXIBLE."

CORNWALL.   THE FOUR SUNKEN GERMAN WARSHIPS.   KENT.

"BRISTOL."   ADMIRAL GRAF VON SPEE.   VICE ADMIRAL SIR F. DOV. STURDEE.   "GLASGOW."

THE FALKLAND ISLANDS BATTLE. • THE GERMAN NAVY PAID QUICKLY FOR OUR LOSS OF THE 'GOOD HOPE' & 'MONMOUTH'. ON DEC 8TH THE 'SCHARNHORST' "LEIPZIG" (2) 'NURNBERG' (3) & 'GNEISENAU' (4) WERE SIGHTED OFF THE FALKLANDS BY A BRITISH SQUADRON UNDER VICE ADMIRAL SIR F. STURDEE. AN ACTION FOLLOWED & THE FOUR GERMAN SHIPS WERE SUNK. ABRAHAMS & SONS Photos DEVONPORT

light cruiser *Dresden*. She rounded the Horn again and lurked in hidden bays, powerless to do anything except occupy a number of British ships in hunting for her. When at last she was found off the island of Juan Fernandez, her captain scuttled her and landed his crew to be interned in Chile. The British revenge was complete.

No sailor can look back on these two battles, Coronel and the Falklands, with satisfaction. Both were one-sided, and the result of both was cruel. Both indeed re-open the age-old question of why men will fight to the death when they know they will lose. Why did Cradock sacrifice hundreds of men by giving battle? And why did von Spee do the same, when at any moment he chose he could have scuttled his ships and surrendered his crews to live out their lives? There is no logical answer. They did it for nothing more than the ancient concept of honour, which Albemarle expressed so memorably two hundred and fifty years earlier: 'to be overcome is the fortune of war, but to fly is the fashion of cowards.'

CLAUS BERGEN

Jutland
1916

Previous pages Jutland 6.30 pm. The German destroyer attack on the British line, by the German artist Claus Bergen.

Above Admiral Alfred von Tirpitz, main architect of the Imperial German Navy before the First World War.

Right A dreadnought as a symbol of national pride.

IN HOME WATERS, in those months of 1914, a state was developing that nobody had foreseen. It was stalemate. Fisher had imagined great battles, in which the co-ordinated fleet of dreadnoughts and battlecruisers he had created would fight as one immensely powerful unit; and Admiral von Tirpitz, who had built up the German fleet, had tacitly made the same assumption. Churchill had called these fleets 'the culminating manifestation of naval force in the history of the world'. But when the time came, neither side was prepared to make the move that would start a major battle. The great fleets lurked in their anchorages, the British Grand Fleet mainly at Scapa Flow in the Orkney Islands, and the German High Seas Fleet mainly in the River Jade, guarded by an immense minefield. Between them, the North Sea was a no-man's-land, given over to lesser ships, minelayers and submarines.

The fact was that fleets of dreadnoughts were so immensely expensive and such a source of national pride that nobody who possessed them was willing to run the risk of losing them. In Germany the supreme commander of the navy was the Kaiser, and he ordered it to maintain a 'defensive attitude'. In Britain, the commander-in-chief of the Grand Fleet was Admiral Sir John Jellicoe, and he wrote to Churchill, soon after war began: 'It is suicidal to forgo our advantageous position in the big ships by risking them in waters infested with submarines.' Even Fisher concurred, when he returned to office. 'No big ships of the Fleet should go into the North Sea,' he wrote in his own peculiar style. 'WHEN the German Big Fleet comes out, THEN our Big Fleet will come out! WHEN the German battle cruisers come out, THEN our battle cruisers will also come out!' The initiative was left to the Germans and they did not take it.

As it happened, this passive strategy suited the temperaments of both the commanders-in-chief, Jellicoe in Britain and Admiral von Ingenohl in Germany: or perhaps it would be fairer to say that the command of such weapons put an intolerable strain on any man, so that they lost whatever aggressive instinct they possessed. Churchill once said that Jellicoe was the only man who could lose the war in a day. This was almost equally true of von Ingenohl. If either fleet had been destroyed, it would have been an inexorable step towards defeat: uppermost in the minds of each of these men was therefore the need to preserve his own fleet, not the need to destroy the enemy's.

But both the squadrons of battlecruisers, German and British, were commanded by men who carried marginally less responsibility, and so were able to retain a more heroic stamp. These were Franz von Hipper and Sir David Beatty. Hipper was cool, clear-headed, a master of tactics and much loved by his crews; and Beatty was the epitome, in British eyes, of the seadog of tradition – rich, handsome and slightly eccentric. Perhaps the command of battlecruisers attracted a more dashing kind of man; for the battlecruisers were faster, heavily armed but less heavily armoured than the dreadnoughts, and their primary job was to scout independently ahead of the battle fleets.

For eighteen months, the dreadnoughts lay in their harbours and made occasional indecisive sorties. It was only the battlecruisers which showed their teeth from time to time in brief encounters; but in comparison to the strength of the waiting fleets, their battles could not be reckoned more than skirmishes.

What broke the deadlock were two changes of command in Germany. The Kaiser was annoyed by Ingenohl because he lost one old battlecruiser, the *Blucher*, in a fight with Beatty. He dismissed him, and appointed an even more cautious admiral named von Pohl. Then von Pohl was found to be mortally ill, and almost by chance in January 1916 his tough and aggressive chief-of-staff was promoted to take his place. This was Admiral Reinhard Scheer. In a few weeks, Scheer persuaded the Kaiser to let him provoke an all-out battle, and three months later he had completed his plans. At one o'clock on the morning of 31 May, he left the Jade river with the whole of the High Seas Fleet. At 9.30 the previous evening, the British Grand Fleet had already left its harbours to meet him; for unknown to Scheer or anyone else in Germany, the British had decoded his signals and knew what he was doing.

This was the work of Room 40 in the old Admiralty building in Whitehall, an institution which is famous now but was then the most closely guarded secret, known only to very senior officers. At the beginning of the war, the German cruiser

Magdeburg had run aground in fog in the Baltic and was captured by the Russians, who were Britain's allies. On the body of a drowned German signalman the Russians found the Germans' naval cypher, and they sent it to England. With that as a basis the British installed a team of brilliant civilian cryptographers in Room 40. Thenceforth, these men decoded radio signals and passed them to the Operations Division. They also set up a chain of direction-finding receivers, a new invention, along the east coast of England, which supplied cross-bearings of German ships at sea whenever they used their wireless. Room 40 could predict when a German fleet would leave harbour, and say where it was when it was out.

So in the long northern dusk of that early summer evening, the most powerful fleet that had ever existed put to sea from Scottish ports, with all the elegance and majesty of this weapon of war. From Scapa Flow came Jellicoe in his flagship the *Iron Duke*, with fifteen other dreadnoughts, three battlecruisers, eight smaller armoured cruisers, eleven light cruisers, fifty-one destroyers and a minelayer. From Rosyth in the Firth of Forth, under the Forth Bridge and past the dim lights of Leith and Edinburgh, Beatty led his battlecruiser squadron: six battlecruisers, twelve light cruisers, twenty-two destroyers and a solitary seaplane carrier, together with the four most modern super-dreadnoughts with 15-inch (381-mm) guns and a speed of twenty-five knots. And thirdly, from Cromarty Firth, came the second battle squadron, of eight more dreadnoughts with their attendant cruisers and destroyers: in all, 149 warships, totalling a million and a quarter tons, and 60,000 men. The whole of this fleet was new: only the armoured cruisers were more than seven years old, and even the original *Dreadnought*, launched ten years earlier, was too old-fashioned for a place in the first-line fleet.

Scheer believed his navy was equal to Britain's.

In certain respects it was as good or better, but the fleet he led that night was far outnumbered: he had only 99 ships and 45,000 men. Moreover, only sixteen of them were dreadnoughts, and astern of the dreadnoughts in his battle line were six pre-dreadnoughts, elderly battleships which slowed the whole fleet by three knots and were known to the Germans as five-minute ships, because that was how long they expected them to last in a modern battle. Nevertheless, they steamed out with equal pride, led by Hipper with five battlecruisers 25 miles (40 km) ahead of Scheer and the battle fleet.

The two fleets very nearly missed each other, and only met by chance: despite their mechanical marvels, ships of that era had no better means of detection than Nelson's – the human eye. Officers of the watch did not merely carry telescopes, they used them; and sharp-eyed sailors were still stationed in the fighting-tops to watch the horizon, not now for sails but for smoke. On Room 40's information, Jellicoe had instructed Beatty to make for a point 100 miles (160 km) off the coast of Jutland in Denmark. If by two o'clock that afternoon he had not seen the enemy, he was to turn north to join Jellicoe, who would be 65 miles (105 km) away.

The cruiser squadron reached the spot on time and sighted nothing. At 2.30 pm Beatty signalled the turn to the north. But the cruiser *Galatea*, out on the wing of the screen of cruisers, sighted a small Danish steamer further east. It had stopped and was blowing off steam, which was unusual, so she went ahead to investigate. Behind it, she sighted two destroyers which were unmistakeably German. She sounded Action Stations (still ordered by a bugle call), signalled 'Enemy in sight' and opened fire – the first shot of the Battle of Jutland.

Jutland was a very confused and confusing battle. It had three parts. First was a running fight between the battlecruisers; next, two very short

encounters between the dreadnoughts; and last a battle in the night, when the confusion was complete. It began with a scarcely believable muddle in Room 40.

Room 40 itself was extremely efficient, but there was always a gulf of snobbery between the civilian code breakers and the naval operations staff. The naval officers seem to have thought the code breakers were very clever fellows but as civilians could not be expected to interpret signals into tactical terms. The civilians, for their part, had been snubbed so often that they had given up offering opinions and only answered literally the questions they were asked. They knew that when Scheer left harbour he transferred his call-sign, which was DK, to a shore station and used another at sea. On the morning of Jutland, Rear-Admiral Thomas Jackson, the Director of Operations, went into Room 40 and apparently asked the single question, 'Where is DK?' 'In the Jade', he was told; and he went out and signalled to Jellicoe and Beatty that the German battle fleet was still in harbour.

Beatty sighted Hipper's battlecruisers soon after 2.30 pm and believed that was all he was up against. Hipper turned to the south, and Beatty set a parallel course at his full speed, which was more than twenty-five knots. It did not occur to him that Hipper was luring him to confront the battle fleet.

A further signalling error marred that turn. The British, of course, had wireless, but they preferred not to use it unless they had to – partly because it was not entirely reliable, and partly because they knew it could be detected. Within visible range, they used flags, like Nelson, or morse with searchlights. Beatty hoisted flags to signal his change of course, but they were obscured by his own funnel smoke and the four great super-dreadnoughts did not see them but steamed on to the north. Six minutes passed before they made their turn, and by then they were 10 miles (16 km) astern of the battlecruisers.

So the great fight began beween six British battlecruisers (the *Lion*, *Princess Royal*, *Queen Mary*, *Tiger*, *New Zealand* and *Indefatigable*) and five Germans (*Lützow*, *Derfflinger*, *Seydlitz*, *Moltke* and *Von der Tann*), each in the historic formation of line ahead. At 15,000 yards (14,000 m), the Germans all opened fire simultaneously.

Many people, for the first time under fire, discovered they could see the great shells coming. One said they were like 'big bluebottles flying straight towards you, each one seeming certain to hit you in the eye. Then they would fall, and the shell would either burst or else ricochet off the water and lollop away above and beyond you, turning over and over in the air.'

The columns of water that marked the shell bursts came very quickly closer. Within four minutes the *Tiger* was hit: in ten minutes more, she was hit by eight more shells, which destroyed her forward turrets. So was the *Princess Royal*, and so was Beatty's flagship the *Lion*. One of her officers remembered a sergeant of Royal Marines staggering onto the bridge, dazed, burned and bloodstained.

I asked him what was the matter. In a tired voice he replied, 'Q turret has gone, sir. All the crew are killed and we have flooded the magazines.' I looked over the bridge amidships. The armoured roof of Q turret had been folded back like an open sardine tin, and thick yellow smoke was rolling up in clouds from the gaping hole.

Above Admiral Reinhard Scheer, German Commander-in-Chief at Jutland.

Right The battleship *Thüringen* sinks the British cruiser *Black Prince*. In reality the ships never got so close to one another.

Opposite: above The battle attracted many artists, British and German. This painting of dreadnoughts is by R. H. Smith.

Strange that all this should have happened within a few yards of where Beatty was standing, and that none of us on the bridge should have heard the detonation.

The flash of the explosion had passed down the central trunk of the turret and ignited cordite charges below. Instantly shutting the doors of the magazine and flooding it had saved the ship: the man who had ordered it was a dying major of Royal Marines, and the men who did it were found lying dead with their hands still on the door clips.

Within minutes of that near-disaster, complete disaster struck another ship. The *Indefatigable* was hit at the extreme range of 22,400 yards (20,500 m) – 12¾ miles (20·5 km) – by two salvoes from the *Von der Tann*. Like the *Lion*, she was hit on a turret, and she did not flood the magazine in time. The entire great ship disappeared in a sheet of flame and a towering column of smoke, above which, 200 feet in the air, a steamboat was seen apparently intact but upside down. The super-dreadnought *Malaya*, now coming up astern, passed over the spot where she had been. When the crew saw the debris they believed it was German, and cheered. 'We never dreamed it was one of our own battlecruisers,' one wrote. 'But it was, and over a thousand men lay in her wreck.'

The arrival of the super-dreadnoughts was turning the tables on the Germans, who had had the best of it so far. The Germans had all heard of these ships and discussed them, with their speed that was equal to a battlecruiser's and their shells which were twice as heavy. With these 15-inch shells they began to hit the *Von der Tann*, the last in Hipper's line. But twenty minutes after the *Indefatigable*, exactly the same catastrophe happened again. The *Queen Mary* was hit by five shells in quick succession. From the *Tiger*, close astern of her, an officer 'saw a dull red glow amidships, and then the ship seemed to open out like a puff ball, or one of those toadstool things when one squeezes it'. The *Tiger* and *New Zealand* abruptly had to alter course, one to port and the other to starboard, to avoid the smoke cloud and the wreckage it contained. As the *New Zealand* passed, only the stern of the *Queen Mary* was sticking out of the water, with the propellers still turning. There was no sign of life, but many people noticed clouds of white paper blowing out of her after hatch. On the bridge of the *Lion*, Beatty said to his flag captain, 'There seems to be something wrong with our bloody ships today'; and he ordered a turn of two points towards the enemy.

He also ordered a torpedo attack by destroyers; and twelve destroyers altered course for Hipper's line. Hipper saw them coming, and ordered out fifteen in counter-attack; and men on the big ships witnessed in fascination by far the fastest battle that had ever been fought at sea, the opponents closing

Admiral Sir David Beatty, commander of British battlecruisers.

at a combined speed of sixty knots – 'A wild scene, groups of long low forms vomiting heavy trails of smoke and dashing hither and thither at thirty knots or more through the smother and splashes, and all in a rain of shell from the secondary armament of the German battlecruisers, with the heavy shell of the contending squadrons screaming overhead.' Two German destroyers sank; two British, hit in their engine rooms, lay helpless between the lines. Both sides had fired about twenty torpedoes, but only one succeeded. That hit the *Seydlitz*, and she went through the rest of the battle with a hole in her bow that the Germans said was the size of a barn door, and sinking slowly by the head. Before the mêlée died away, a wireless signal came from the cruiser *Southampton*, scouting ahead of the fleet, which transformed the scene and the problems: 'Urgent. Priority. Have sighted enemy battle fleet bearing approximately S.E., course of enemy N.'

Beatty, of course, was right when he said there was something wrong with his ships. It was a fault of design in all the battlecruisers that nobody had suspected. If the turret was penetrated by a shell

The battlecruiser *Seydlitz*.

which exploded inside it, there was nothing to stop the flash spreading down the central trunk and igniting cordite charges on the hoists that took them from the magazines to the guns. Only shutting the magazine door and flooding it could then prevent disaster, and it was chance if anyone was left alive to do it. The German battlecruisers had had exactly the same defect. But in a previous encounter with Beatty, the *Seydlitz* had experienced a narrow escape exactly like the *Lion*'s, and the Germans had seen what was wrong and corrected it. The British had not had the same experience, and had not known until now that the battlecruisers had this lethal defect.

On the *Southampton*'s report, Beatty instantly understood what Hipper had been doing: luring him south towards the guns of the High Seas Fleet. Now it was his job to do the same to Hipper and to Scheer: lure them north to encounter Jellicoe, whose presence, he correctly believed, they did not suspect. His own wireless had been hit, so he signalled by morse lamp to the *Princess Royal*, next astern, to transmit the electrifying news to Jellicoe, and he hoisted flags to reverse the course of his squadron. Hipper did the same, but the four super-dreadnoughts did not. It seems incredible they had again missed the signal – especially when Beatty passed them going flat out in the opposite direction. Perhaps their admiral, bringing up the rear, meant to delay his turn and bring up the rear again. At all events, he stood on until he was in range of the High Seas Fleet, and the world's first encounter between dreadnoughts began: four British against twelve Germans.

That private battle proved one thing: that in dreadnoughts, unlike any other warship, defence was more powerful than attack. All four British ships, and all the leading Germans, took a tremendous pounding but none of them was mortally damaged. They were so solid and so well armoured that when they were hit by 12-inch (305 mm) shells many men on board were unaware of it. 'Felt one or two very heavy shakes,' the executive officer of the super-dreadnought *Warspite* wrote, 'but didn't think very much of it at the time, and it never occurred to me that we were being hit. Told everybody in the turret that we were doing all right and to keep her going; machinery working like a clockwork mouse.' Only later, when he was doing his rounds, did he discover at least a dozen hits which had started leaks and fires and killed and wounded a number of men.

On the run to the north, Beatty brought off a very successful manoeuvre. What he had to do was get Hipper out of the way, so that he would not sight the Grand Fleet and warn Scheer what lay ahead. Though Beatty's surviving ships were badly battered, they could still work up to twenty-eight knots, and at that speed he drew ahead of Hipper and engaged him at the extreme range of his 12-inch (305 mm) guns, out of range of the Germans' 11-inch (279-mm). Between five and six o'clock, Hipper was struggling to survive: the *Lützow* and *Seydlitz* suffered several hits, the *Derfflinger* was hit in the bow and began to sink by the head, and the *Von der Tann* had all her guns out of action. Beatty began a slow turn to starboard, and so forced Hipper also to alter course to the east. Scheer, following at the best speed of his oldest battleships, saw the fighting vanish out of sight ahead, leaving the northern horizon empty and obscured by gun and funnel smoke and a rising mist. Preoccupied with battle, Beatty omitted to tell Jellicoe what was happening. The signal he had sent reporting the battle fleet had read, 'Have sighted enemy's battle fleet bearing S.E.' It did not give the enemy's course or speed or distance, and by the time it had been flashed to the *Princess Royal*, encoded, transmitted by wireless and decoded, it was garbled to the point of absurdity. What Jellicoe received was, '26–30 battleships, probably hostile, bearing S.S.E. steering S.E.' Nobody ever explained how '26–30' crept into it, or the word 'probably' or the course that was the opposite of the truth. After that misinformation, Jellicoe received no news whatever for an hour.

He was steaming south-east at twenty knots with twenty-four dreadnoughts, for he had been joined by the eight from Cromarty. They were in the defensive sailing order, six parallel columns of four ships each. Somewhere ahead of him, he did not know where, was the High Seas Fleet, and before he met it he had to deploy into a single line of battle – a prolonged manoeuvre. There were three ways it could be done, with the port column leading, or the starboard column, or one of the centre columns. The right choice might well make all the difference between the advantageous position of crossing the enemy's T, or of finding himself, with his own T crossed, approaching the centre of the enemy's line. To make the choice, he had to know where the enemy was, and nobody told him. Mist was forming, and visibility was already less than gun-range: at any moment, an enemy ship, or a whole fleet, might loom up already in range.

Towards six o'clock, news came not from Beatty but from the leading dreadnought in his own starboard column, which reported gun-flashes and heavy firing on the starboard bow. In his only hint of tension, Jellicoe said, 'I wish someone would tell me who is firing and what they're firing at.'

Moments later, Beatty's ships came suddenly charging out of the mist on Jellicoe's starboard bow. The *Lion's* guns were blazing and she was surrounded by the splashes of shells from an enemy still out of sight. 'Where is the enemy's battle fleet?' Jellicoe signalled. Beatty replied, 'German battle-cruisers bearing S.E.' That was not what Jellicoe needed to know. But, in fact, it was a long time since Beatty had seen Scheer's battle fleet, which had fallen astern of the fight. Soon after, he glimpsed it through a break in the mist and signalled that it was bearing south-south-west. Still no distance, course or speed. But Jellicoe had to act, and quickly. He ordered deployment on the port column. Each of the other columns turned ninety degrees to port, and then ninety degrees to starboard in the wake of the leaders. Soon after six o'clock the whole fleet was in a single curved line, immensely long.

Around six, a great deal happened. The dreadnought fleets were still out of sight of each other, and Scheer still did not know that Jellicoe was

HMS Warspite.

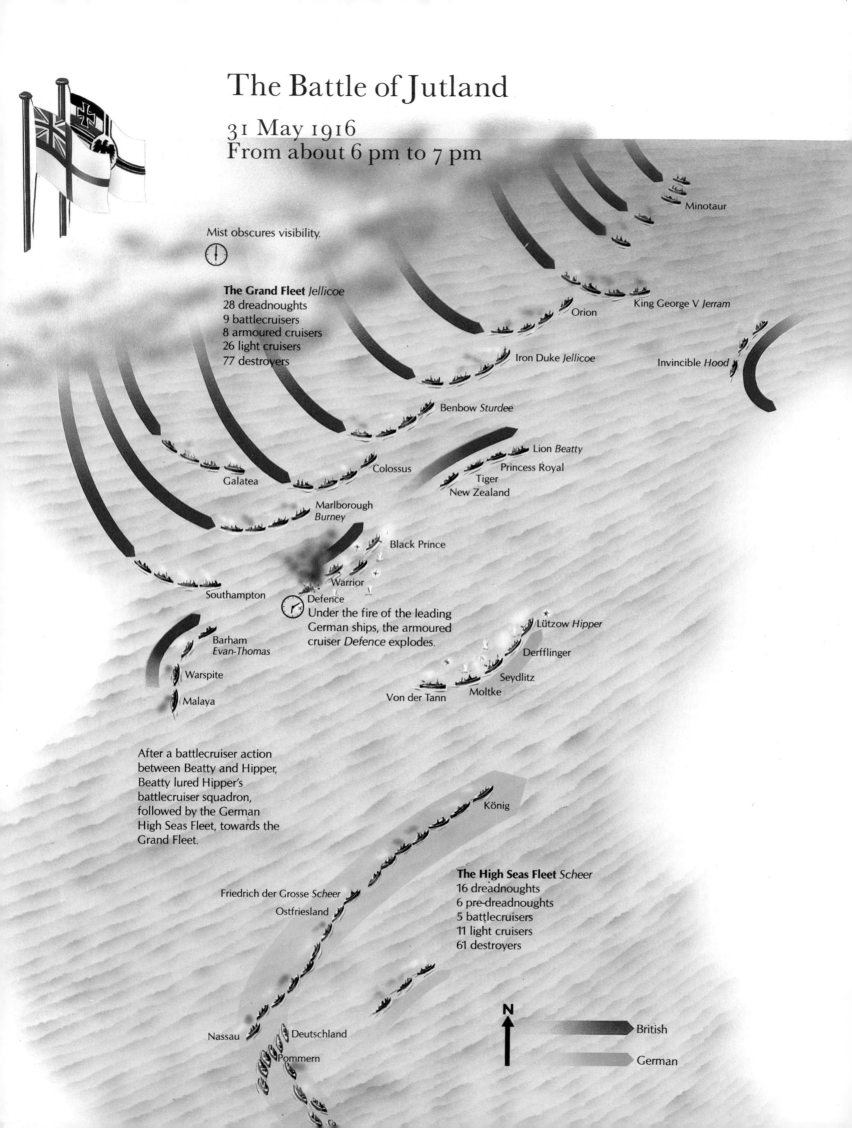

The Battle of Jutland

31 May 1916
From about 6 pm to 7 pm

Mist obscures visibility.

The Grand Fleet *Jellicoe*
28 dreadnoughts
9 battlecruisers
8 armoured cruisers
26 light cruisers
77 destroyers

Minotaur

King George V *Jerram*

Orion

Iron Duke *Jellicoe*

Invincible *Hood*

Benbow *Sturdee*

Lion *Beatty*

Princess Royal

Colossus

Tiger

New Zealand

Galatea

Marlborough
Burney

Black Prince

Warrior

Southampton

Defence
Under the fire of the leading
German ships, the armoured
cruiser *Defence* explodes.

Lützow *Hipper*

Derfflinger

Seydlitz

Barham
Evan-Thomas

Warspite

Moltke

Von der Tann

Malaya

After a battlecruiser action
between Beatty and Hipper,
Beatty lured Hipper's
battlecruiser squadron,
followed by the German
High Seas Fleet, towards the
Grand Fleet.

König

Friedrich der Grosse *Scheer*

Ostfriesland

The High Seas Fleet *Scheer*
16 dreadnoughts
6 pre-dreadnoughts
5 battlecruisers
11 light cruisers
61 destroyers

N

Nassau

Deutschland

Pommern

British

German

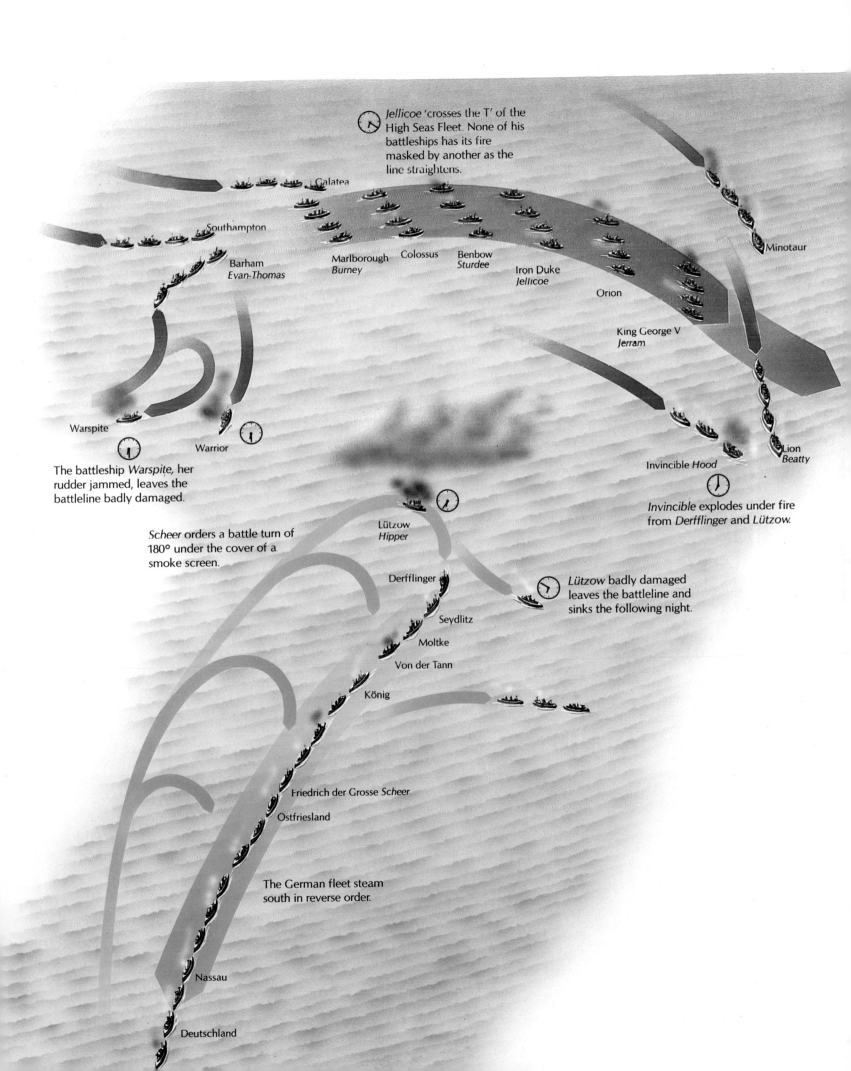

Jellicoe 'crosses the T' of the High Seas Fleet. None of his battleships has its fire masked by another as the line straightens.

Galatea

Southampton

Barham
Evan-Thomas

Marlborough
Burney

Colossus

Benbow
Sturdee

Iron Duke
Jellicoe

Orion

King George V
Jerram

Minotaur

Warspite

Warrior

The battleship *Warspite,* her rudder jammed, leaves the battleline badly damaged.

Invincible *Hood*

Lion
Beatty

Invincible explodes under fire from *Derfflinger* and *Lützow.*

Scheer orders a battle turn of 180° under the cover of a smoke screen.

Lützow
Hipper

Derfflinger

Lützow badly damaged leaves the battleline and sinks the following night.

Seydlitz

Moltke

Von der Tann

König

Friedrich der Grosse *Scheer*

Ostfriesland

The German fleet steam south in reverse order.

Nassau

Deutschland

there. As the fleets approached, their outliers – battlecruisers, cruisers and destroyers – clashed between them at a point that the British named Windy Corner. 'The whole surface of the sea', a cruiser officer wrote, 'was heaving up and down in a confused swell caused by the wash created by the two hundred-odd ships which were moving about at high speeds.' 'The light cruisers and destroyers,' another said, 'were twisting and turning, endeavouring to avoid each other and the big ships. There was handling of ships in that ten minutes such as had never been dreamed of by seamen before.' Ships of both sides met disaster under the sudden attack of something stronger. The whole third battlecruiser squadron, which had come with Jellicoe and now was ahead, turned its guns on the German cruiser *Wiesbaden* and left her stopped and smoking. The armoured cruiser *Defence* charged across Windy Corner and suddenly came within sight and range of German battlecruisers and dreadnoughts. She was hit by two salvoes of 12-inch shells, and 'completely disappeared in a mass of spray, smoke and flame. But she came through it apparently intact, only to disappear a few seconds later in a tremendous belch of vivid flame and dense black smoke which rose to a height of some hundred feet and quickly clearing, left no sign of a ship at all.' The super-dreadnought *Warspite* was hit, and her rudder jammed. If she had stopped she would

have been a sitting duck, so she steamed at full speed in two great circles that took her in range of the head of Scheer's battle line. Six German dreadnoughts had her under fire, and she was hit thirteen times. At the end of it, she was still fit to fight, but her steering gear was still giving trouble and she was ordered back to base. The Germans, finding she had vanished, naturally claimed they had sunk her, but she reached port.

At 6.30 pm Jellicoe, in the centre of his line, sighted the head of Scheer's line approaching him abeam, exactly where he wanted it to be. At last, after nearly two years of waiting, he had caught the High Seas Fleet, and caught it in the best possible position. His deployment had been correct: he had succeeded in crossing the enemy's T. Most of his dreadnoughts opened fire at once. There was no way Scheer could reply. For him, it was a total surprise. The first thing he saw was 'rounds of firing from guns of heavy calibre on the horizon directly ahead of us. The entire arc stretching from north to east was a sea of fire. The flash from the muzzles of the guns was distinctly seen, though the ships themselves were invisible. More than 100 heavy guns joined in the fight on the enemy's side.'

Between the fighting fleets, the battlecruisers had another encounter, and a third of the British ships met a disaster exactly like the others. The *Invincible*, which had come not with Beatty but with Jellicoe,

A dramatic view of the *Seydlitz* from the stern by Claus Bergen, whose paintings were accurate to the last detail. Only one turret remains in action, firing to port at the distant gun-flashes of British ships.

was hit on a turret and after a few seconds her magazines blew up. She was blown in half, and when the smoke cleared the two ends of her were standing above the water, with the shattered middle on the shallow bottom. They stood there like immense gravestones for at least half an hour before they collapsed, and in that time most of the line of dreadnoughts went racing past them. Only six men were picked up.

Hipper's five ships were still afloat, but only just. His flagship *Lützow* had her bows awash and could only steam dead slow. He was persuaded to move to a destroyer, in order to shift his flag to another ship; but approaching each in turn he found them all except one in a desperate state, leaking, burning, with prodigious casualties and most guns out of action. The only one comparatively fit was the *Moltke*, but in the fast moving battle, the mist and smoke, he could not find her, and for three hours the suffering squadron had no commander.

Seeing that the tactical position was hopeless, Scheer ordered a 'Battle Turn'. This was a difficult and dangerous manoeuvre, in which all the ships in a line turned simultaneously back on the course they had come. The British had never contemplated any need to use it, but the Germans had practised it and in the midst of the battle they did it successfully. In twenty minutes from the first sighting, the German fleet disappeared again.

At first, Jellicoe thought it was just that the mist had thickened. Many ships at the end of his line had seen the turn, but none of them told Jellicoe, believing perhaps that he could see as well as they could. So he hesitated. Tradition demanded he should turn in pursuit, and he was strongly criticized afterwards for not doing it at once; but he was reluctant, because he believed a fleeing enemy would sow mines in his wake and lead the pursuers into a submarine ambush. In fact, the Germans carried no mines, and no submarines were anywhere near. But Jellicoe made only a tentative partial turn.

It made no difference, because twenty minutes after Scheer had made his 'Battle Turn' he made another, back to his original course, and steamed straight back into the trap he had escaped from. Neither he nor anyone else ever gave a convincing explanation for that movement. He himself said to one of his staff, 'It just happened. I wanted to help the poor *Wiesbaden*'; and to another, 'If I had done that in a peacetime exercise, I would have lost my command.' Possibly he felt he had not done enough, and might be accused of running away; or perhaps he expected to pass astern of Jellicoe's line. At all events, Jellicoe was given something rare in battle: a second chance.

Again, the brunt of the fighting fell on the battlecruisers. But the leading ships of Scheer's line also suffered. To get his fleet out of the position he had got it into, he made the drastic decision to sacrifice the battlecruisers, and he signalled them 'Close the enemy and ram'. To ram a dreadnought was certain suicide. The *Lützow* was already helpless, but the four remaining ships obeyed. As they approached, more death and destruction fell on them. Two shells penetrated two of the

Derfflinger's turrets. Thanks to the Germans' change of design they did not explode the magazines, but they instantly killed both crews, 150 men. Before they completed their ride of death, Scheer changed his signal and ordered them to 'Operate against the enemy's van'. At almost the same moment, he signalled another 'Battle Turn' and ordered destroyers to cover it with a smoke screen.

The destroyers dashing through their own smoke fired thirty-one torpedoes. Ten of them reached the British line and hit nothing, but they had a decisive effect on the battle. Obviously, a ship was less likely to be hit by a torpedo end-on, and there were two ways a line of ships could minimize the risk: by turning towards the torpedoes or turning away. Turning away was the safer of the two, because in the end the ships would outrun the torpedoes'

Admiral Sir John Jellicoe, British Commander-in-Chief.

The battle turn of Scheer's
main fleet, by Howard.

range. Jellicoe ordered a turn away. There were
some near misses, but British lookouts found to
their surprise that German torpedoes left a trail of
bubbles which could be seen two miles away: so
there was time to dodge.

When the fleet had regained its line, the
Germans had vanished again, after an even shorter
encounter than the first, barely fifteen minutes.
This time they vanished for ever in the falling dusk.

It was British policy to avoid fighting at night,
because it left so much to chance and was likely to
favour the weaker fleet. So they had not made
much preparation for it. They had no adequate

searchlights and no star-shell to light up their
targets; their destroyer captains had not been
trained for night action, and they had the most
primitive system of night recognition signals –
flashing letters by morse, which could be easily
copied by the enemy as soon as they had seen it.
The Germans were much better equipped and
trained: their recognition signals, for example,
were patterns of coloured lights in the rigging,
which could not be readily copied. The night began
with a frankly stupid action by Beatty's signal
officer, who had already made several mistakes. He
signalled by morse lamp to the *Princess Royal*,

'Please give me challenge and reply now in force as they have been lost.' As the signal came from the flagship, the *Princess Royal* did so. Unknown to them both, two squadrons of German cruisers were close by. So the Germans learned the supposedly secret recognition signals for that night. It is not known how far they managed to circulate the information through the fleet, but at least some of the German ships could reply directly to the British challenge, or – if they wished to – make the challenge themselves.

Jellicoe closed up his fleet into its night cruising order with some degree of satisfaction. So far he had

not had the success he hoped for; the battle had started so late in the day that his chance had been brief. But now, his fleet was between the German fleet and its home base, and he had every hope of catching it in the morning with a whole day's fighting ahead of him – and he was confident what the result of that would be.

There were three swept channels through the minefields by which Scheer could reach the river Jade. The main one, by which he had come out, was close to Horn Reef off the coast of Denmark. The other two were farther to the south-west. Jellicoe believed his own position effectively cut

Scheer off from Horn Reef, and he expected him therefore to make for one of the other channels. Beatty reached the same conclusion, and in the night both of them set a course of south. To extend his line, Jellicoe ordered his destroyers to follow 5 miles (8 km) astern of him; and to make sure of Horn Reef he sent the minelayer *Abdiel* to lay mines off it, which she did.

But Jellicoe and Beatty were both wrong. Scheer had determined to go by Horn Reef, and was willing to take the risk of fighting his way through the British fleet in the dark. Room 40, deciphering Scheer's wireless signals, knew of this decision as soon as Scheer's own ships, but they failed, through no fault of their own, to get the information through to Jellicoe. Late in the evening, the Admiralty sent him a signal which accurately gave Scheer's course as south-south-east 3/4 east, which was exactly the course for Horn Reef. But after the mistaken signal that morning, Jellicoe was sceptical of Admiralty intelligence, and this signal did not seem to coincide with the few sighting reports from his own ships. So he discarded it. Later, Room 40 heard six more of Scheer's signals, and two of them were conclusive: one requested a dawn reconnaissance by airships at Horn Reef, and the other ordered his destroyer flotillas to concentrate at dawn – also at Horn Reef. If Jellicoe had received those, he would certainly have altered course and fought Scheer again at dawn. But when Room 40 handed the signals to the Operations Room, the

chief-of-staff had unbelievably gone to bed and left in charge a man who had no special knowledge of operations. That man decided the signals were not important, and put them on file, where they remained as proof of the most disastrous mistake the Admiralty had made for many a long year.

So Jellicoe stood on to the south, and Scheer crossed his track only three miles astern of the rear of the main fleet. So doing, he ran headlong into the British destroyers, and scattered independent actions were fought all night, mostly lasting only a matter of minutes. 'We had absolutely no idea of where the enemy was,' a British destroyer captain wrote, 'and only a very vague idea of the position of our own ships.' Such was the confusion that nobody has ever made a complete and consecutive narrative of it, and the best one can do is pick out events that were typical of the rest: as for instance when a British flotilla saw two ships which made the British recognition signal and then switched on searchlights and opened fire. Some of the flotilla replied with guns and torpedoes, others thought they were being attacked by friendly ships – and before they could be sure the two ships had vanished again in the dark.

Another destroyer flotilla suddenly saw the German battle fleet close at hand. Two destroyers were quickly hit and sunk. One torpedoed the German cruiser *Rostock*, and in the mêlée another German cruiser was rammed by one of their own battleships. Both those cruisers sank in the night.

Jutland damage to the German battlecruiser *Seydlitz*.

The British destroyer *Spitfire* collided bow to bow with the German dreadnought *Nassau*. The *Spitfire* was left with no mast, funnel or bridge and a 60-foot hole in her side – and 20 feet of the *Nassau's* upper deck inside her messdeck. Lying helpless, the *Spitfire* saw 'what appeared to be a battle-cruiser on fire steering straight for our stern. She tore past us with a roar, and the very crackling and heat of the flames could be heard and felt. She was a mass of fire.'

The Germans also saw this macabre apparition. 'A burning ship drove past us,' one of them wrote. 'The whole ship was red hot. There could not have been a soul alive on board for some time.' Neither British nor Germans knew what ship she was, but it seemed afterwards that she must have been the cruiser *Black Prince*, which had been badly hit in the afternoon and again in the night and now steamed through the heart of the battle carrying nothing but her dead. She disappeared into the darkness and was never heard of again.

The first faint light of dawn revealed to yet another flotilla the sight of the German battle fleet steaming past at close range. The destroyers fired torpedoes, and one hit the old battleship *Pommern*. She blew up like the British battlecruisers, and when the *Derfflinger* passed the spot a few minutes later, not the slightest trace of her could be seen.

By then, Scheer had broken through, and nothing was left between him and Horn Reef, the safety of the minefields. All the firing had been seen and heard from Jellicoe's flagship, but he was still stubbornly steaming south, believing it was no more than a skirmish between destroyers. Only one

destroyer captain tried to report what was really happening, and that signal did not get through. Destroyer captains were not under orders to make reports. There was less excuse for the captains of the rearmost dreadnoughts of Jellicoe's line, who also sighted the enemy battlefleet but did not report it or engage it because, they explained, they did not want to give away the position of their own fleet. For this reason, which seems so inadequate, even the crippled *Seydlitz* at seven knots was able to pass right through the lines of dreadnoughts, and the *Moltke*, now with Hipper on board, after three attempts to pass through, was allowed to retreat and steam all alone round the head of the British fleet. At dawn, Jellicoe still expected to sight the Germans to the north-west of him, but the sea was empty except for the corpses and wreckage.

It was an inconclusive battle. Publicly, both sides claimed a victory, the Germans because they had sunk more ships and the British because they had forced the enemy back to port and were left in command of the battlefield. In retrospect, it can be said the Germans won a tactical victory, the British a strategic victory. Unfortunately, Scheer's claim was made before Jellicoe was back in port and was repeated in English newspapers, so that some ships returning with their battle-scars to port were greeted by boos instead of cheers. In fact, the Germans had lost one old battleship, one battle-cruiser, four light cruisers and five destroyers; the British three battlecruisers, three cruisers and seven destroyers. The loss of men was more unequal, largely because of the British battlecruiser disasters: just over 6,000 British were killed, one in ten of their total; and of Germans 2,500. Not a single dreadnought was lost on either side.

But whatever the public claimed, both navies were bitterly disappointed. The Germans felt in their hearts that their challenge had failed and could never be renewed. The British, for their part, had signally failed to win the shattering victory they had hoped for, and within the fleet a controversy began, to answer the question why, that lasted a whole generation – if indeed it has ever ended. Only one of the high commanders came through this argument without criticism, and that was Hipper.

Both battlefleets returned to the dreary business of waiting, while all the initiative of war at sea passed to humbler ships, especially submarines. Waiting was hard on the patience and morale of any fleet. The British survived it, but the Germans cracked, and naval mutiny was the first symptom of their defeat. The dreadnoughts never met again until the German fleet surrendered. In four years of war, they were engaged for forty minutes in the kind of battle they were built for.

Both sides claimed a victory. Looking back, it may be said the Germans won a tactical victory, the British a strategic victory.

The River Plate
1939

Previous pages Battle of the River Plate, by John Hamilton: *Achilles* and *Ajax* in pursuit of the *Graf Spee*.

Above Captain Hans Langsdorff (centre) of the *Graf Spee* in Montevideo with two of his officers and the German consul. Two days later he scuttled his ship and then, to the distress of his friends and his enemies, committed suicide.

BETWEEN THE TWO world wars, there was endless controversy between navies and air forces in every country that had them: were battleships so vulnerable to air attack that they were out of date? Even Jackie Fisher, the creator of dreadnoughts, had a moment of prophetic vision shortly before he died in 1920: 'Why keep any of the present lot?' he wrote. 'All you want is the present naval side of the air force – that's the future navy!' Indeed, battleships had never been much practical use except to fight other battleships. Yet all navies clung to them, partly perhaps as symbols of pride and power. When war began again, Britain, America, Italy and France all had them, and Germany and Japan were hastily building them.

By a remarkable coincidence each world war, in 1914 and 1939, began with a battle far from home, near the southern end of South America. And it was a further coincidence that the German ship in the second of these was named after the commander at Coronel and the Falklands, Admiral Graf von Spee.

The ship of that name in 1939 was what the Germans called a panzerschiff, or armoured ship, and the British called a pocket battleship. Germany had three of these ships when war began, and the British name was given to them because they had all the qualities of battleships – 11-inch (279-mm) guns, heavy armour, the most up-to-date equipment, and an air of tigerish beauty – and yet were comparatively small, only about 12,000 tons. They had been built that way to evade the treaty restrictions which limited the size of new warships between the wars. Before war was declared, the *Graf Spee* was sent to the South Atlantic, and on the day it started she was waiting secretly there, with a supply ship called the *Altmark*, ready to make attacks on British merchant shipping. Her captain's name was Hans Langsdorff.

Three weeks after the war began, in late September 1939, an old British trampship called the *Clement* was steaming sleepily down through the tropics off Pernambuco with a cargo of kerosene from New York to the South American ports. The third officer was on watch, and he saw a warship far away, but bow-on and approaching. He called the captain, but the captain was not worried: he assumed the ship was British.

Then a seaplane flew over. He still was not worried. He knew there were British cruisers off that coast, and they carried seaplanes for reconnaissance. It was flashing a morse signal, but they could not read it. And then it opened fire with a machine gun, and they saw the German cross on its fuselage.

The captain stopped his ship, swung out the boats and told the radio operator to transmit the signal for a surface raider, three Rs and their position. Close to them the warship stopped and swung broadside with its guns trained on the *Clement*, and it was only then that they saw its swastika flag.

There was nothing the *Clement* could do. The crew took to their boats, the *Graf Spee* fired a torpedo at her which unaccountably missed, and then sank her by gunfire.

Later that day, Captain Langsdorff did a most remarkable thing. He sent an uncoded signal in English to the nearest radio station in Brazil: 'Please save lifeboats of *Clement*. 0945S 3404W.' To make sure the men in the boats were rescued, he had given away his own position.

By next morning, that signal had been reported to London. The *Clement's* signal also had been heard and relayed by another ship; and two days later the crew of the *Clement* were ashore and were questioned by the British naval man in Pernambuco.

Winston Churchill was again First Lord of the Admiralty, as he had been in 1914. The news, he wrote later, 'recalled to me the anxious weeks before the action at Coronel and later at the Falkland Islands in December 1914. A quarter of a century had passed, but the problem was the same.'

One of the objects of a surface commerce raider, in German eyes, was that it occupied large numbers of enemy warships in hunting for it, and in that the *Graf Spee* succeeded right away. Churchill and the First Sea Lord, Admiral Sir Dudley Pound, brought in ships from all over the world to join the hunt – from Britain, Nova Scotia, the Mediterranean, Trinidad, South America and even China. Before long, nine battleships, five aircraft carriers, and at least fifteen cruisers were assembling round the South Atlantic, and there were many celebrated naval names among them: *Renown*, *Malaya*, *Ark Royal*, *Glorious*, and the French battleships *Strasbourg* and *Dunkirk*.

Yet for weeks the *Graf Spee* remained hidden –

hidden by nothing but the vastness of the sea. The South Atlantic is roughly 3,000 miles (4,800 km) across and 3,000 from north to south – 9 million square miles (19.6 million sq km) of ocean – and in much of it even nowadays one might wait a lifetime and never see a ship. Supposing a ship can be seen twenty miles away, at least 20,000 ships could be stationed down there so that none of them was in sight of any other.

And the hunt did depend on seeing with the human eye. These were the very earliest days of radar and of long-range aircraft. The *Graf Spee* had a radar for range-finding, but it often went out of action, and British ships had none. As for aircraft, big warships – apart from aircraft carriers – carried a seaplane which they could launch with a catapult and pick up again from the sea; but their principal use was for gunnery spotting, and their range was short.

As soon as she had sunk the *Clement*, the *Graf Spee* crossed the Atlantic and sank four more British merchant ships off the African coast. From Captain Langsdorff's point of view, the first sinking, of the *Clement*, had gone wrong. His seaplane had signalled her to stop, and not to use her radio transmitter. But she had not read the signal, and it was when she failed to stop that the seaplane opened fire.

Now Langsdorff used a new technique. He steamed straight at his victims, believing rightly that they would not recognize him head-on as a German and would probably think he was French. Sometimes he flew the French flag, and changed it at the last moment for the German swastika. When

he was close, he hoisted two flag signals in international code: 'Heave to, I am sending a boat', and 'Do not transmit or I will open fire.' His boats took off the crews and brought them on board the *Graf Spee* before he sank the ships. He could have blasted the ships to bits from a distance, almost before they saw him and certainly before they had a chance to use their radio. But he did not. He did his job the risky way, solely to save the lives of the British merchant seamen.

Of course the British were doing the same thing, when they could find a German merchant ship, which was seldom, and they were using the same care. It was naval tradition. But it was not Hitler's policy. German submarines were sinking ships without warning: the liner *Athenia* had already been sunk like that, and a hundred people drowned.

And there was this difference: there were British warships in every ocean, and it was not imperative for them to keep their position secret. But Langsdorff was alone, except for his supply ship the *Altmark*. In the long run, secrecy was his only hope of survival; and he risked it every time he gave a British ship a chance to transmit. Some of them did, in spite of his threat, and those desperate signals were the only clues the hunting forces had.

'The *Graf Spee* was daring and imaginative,' Churchill wrote in his memoirs. 'Her practice was to make a brief appearance at some point, claim a victim, and vanish again into the trackless ocean wastes. Unless she struck, she won no prizes. Until she struck, she was in no danger.'

When she vanished, she was meeting her supply

The *Graf Spee* on patrol in October 1939: painted by Captain Gerhart Ulpts, who was then one of the ship's officers.

ship the *Altmark* to refuel – and to get rid of her prisoners. The *Graf Spee* was a very crowded ship; she carried 1,120 officers and men. There simply was no room in her for a crowd of prisoners, so Langsdorff transferred most of them to the *Altmark*.

But most of the captains of the captured ships were kept in the *Graf Spee*, and all of them, when they met Langsdorff, found something which surprised them very much: in spite of what he had done, they could not help liking him. People in wartime normally fear and hate their enemies: certainly most British people at that time expected the Germans to be overbearing and cruel. But Langsdorff was sympathetic, thoughtful, kind and genuinely friendly; he always apologized for sinking unarmed ships, and pleaded it was the necessity of war. Many of the merchant service officers and men he captured spoke or wrote of him afterwards, and – a unique occurrence in war – they were unanimous in their praise. 'He impressed me as a man of great humanity,' one of them summed it up, 'with a distaste for his job of raiding unarmed vessels and a healthy respect for the British navy.'

By early December the *Graf Spee* had sunk nine British ships. Langsdorff was not proud of that: it was an ignominious job for a battleship. But he was proud, he said, to have done it without a single loss of life.

The weakest of the hunting groups was the one on the coast of South America. It was commanded by Commodore Henry Harwood in the light cruiser *Ajax*, Captain Woodhouse. Under his

command he had also the more powerful 8-inch (203-mm) cruiser *Exeter*, Captain Bell, and the New Zealand light cruiser *Achilles*, Captain Parry. He also had the cruiser *Cumberland*, but she was under repair in the Falkland Islands. With three ships, therefore, he was patrolling about 3000 miles of coast, from Pernambuco to Cape Horn.

Harwood had always known he might have to meet a pocket battleship with much more gun power than his own, and his orders in case of that event were suitably Nelsonian: 'My policy with three cruisers in company versus one pocket battleship. Attack at once by day or night.' *Exeter* was to take one side, *Ajax* and *Achilles* the other.

On 2 December, Harwood learned that a steamer called the *Doric Star* had signalled attack by a battleship off the coast of Africa. A kind of intuition told him that the raider would next come across to his side of the ocean. He calculated she might be off Rio at dawn on the 12th, off the River Plate on the 13th, or the Falkland Islands on the 14th. He had to make a guess, and he guessed the River Plate, because the most important British trade came from the cities of Buenos Aires and Montevideo in its estuary. So he ordered his three ships to concentrate at dawn on the 12th 250 miles off the river mouth.

It was a pure hunch, and nobody really believed it. But soon after dawn on the 13th, smoke was sighted. At first it was taken to be a merchant ship; but in case it was not, *Exeter* turned towards it while *Ajax* and *Achilles* steamed on to cross its bows. Then the unmistakeable upper works of a battleship

Ajax and *Achilles* in pursuit of the *Graf Spee*, by Norman Wilkinson.

came over the horizon; one witness remembered it looked like a high-rise office block. And then a cloud of cordite smoke: it was the *Graf Spee*, and she had opened fire. Two minutes later the *Exeter* replied.

The essence of a naval gunnery battle was always space. The battlefield was the open ocean, and most of the time the enemy was so far away he could hardly be seen with the naked eye.

Yet as a private experience, a battle was always claustrophobic. The majority of a crew at action stations were shut away below decks in steel compartments – cabins, engine and boiler rooms, magazines and control positions. They could not see what was happening; they could only guess from the roar of their own guns and the different menacing crash of being hit. Some were kept busy, but some like the damage-control and medical parties had nothing whatever to do unless their ship was hit. They just had to stand and wait and imagine being blown to bits or burnt to death, or imagine their escape hatch being blocked and themselves slowly suffocating or drowning down in the dark.

And that morning in the three British ships, everyone knew in the back of his mind that probably no cruiser shell could penetrate the *Graf Spee*'s armour, whereas a single lucky shot from the *Graf Spee* could sink any one of the cruisers.

But in almost any man habit and training, and the example of his friends, combine to overcome his fear. In the *Exeter* there was not long to wait. Within four minutes she was hit. An 11-inch shell destroyed B turret and most of the men in it. Steel splinters sprayed the bridge and killed everyone there except Captain Bell and two other officers. The same shell smashed the steering gear in the wheelhouse under the bridge. The Captain, with wounds in both legs and splinters in both eyes, went aft to the secondary steering position. The chief quartermaster, whose name was Jimmy Green, felt the wheel go dead in his hands and the ship go out of control. He went down to the deck below to make his way aft, and while he was there a second shell exploded in the compartment. It spun him round and knocked the breath out of him; everything was burning, and he fell in the flames and could not move, or see, hear or speak. Somebody got him up on deck, in agony with his clothes burnt on to him.

Down in the wardroom the young surgeon lieutenant had his post, and suddenly scores of terribly mutilated men were thrust in on him. In a matter of minutes, sixty-one were dead or dying. He did his best for those he could hope to save, Jimmy Green among them, who survived the battle burned, as the Captain said, like a baked potato. Someone told the surgeon the Captain was hurt, and when he could spare a minute he went up on deck to see him. He was shocked by the sight of the immaculate ship reduced to a shambles. She had taken direct hits from eight 11-inch shells. Both her forward turrets were out of action, she was burning forward and amidships, 3 feet down by the bows and listing. All her communications were gone. The gunnery officer was standing on the roof

Sailors of the *Graf Spee* watch one of her victims go down. This was the British *SS Ashlea*. Langsdorff, as usual, had taken off the crew before he sank her.

of the one remaining turret, shouting corrections of aim down through a hatch. The Captain was conning her with a boat's compass and passing his orders down to the tiller by a human chain. But she was still steaming, still hitting back. The Captain said to the surgeon, 'Our speed's down to nineteen knots, we've got a list to port and we've had to flood the forward magazines, and there's not much I can do about it. But if the *Graf Spee* comes this way and I get half a chance, I'm going to ram the b——.'

He did not get the chance. At last the final power circuit failed; the final gun fell silent. She was helpless.

But the *Ajax* and *Achilles* were helping her. To distract the *Graf Spee*'s attention they had steamed full speed towards her firing at their top rate. Thus they attracted part of the *Graf Spee*'s fire, and when *Exeter* had withdrawn from the battle the *Graf Spee* concentrated all her guns on them. They had brought the range down to 4½ miles (7 km), almost point-blank for their 6-inch (152 mm) guns and her 11-inch (179 mm). They were hitting her, but what damage they were doing they could not tell.

Achilles suffered from a near miss which sprayed the bridge and the gunnery control tower with shell splinters, wounded Captain Parry and the gunnery officer and killed some of the gunnery team. For a while, her shooting suffered. *Ajax* next had a direct hit which demolished one of her after turrets and jammed the other.

This position could not last. They were absurdly

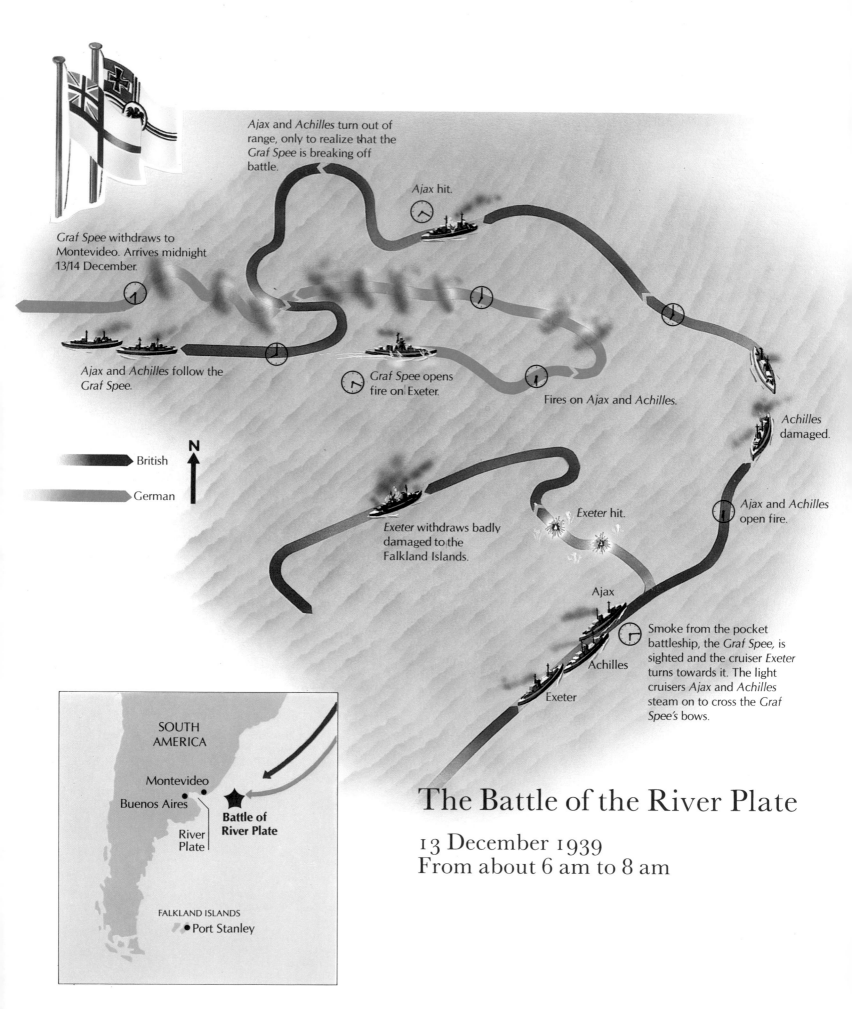

Ajax and Achilles turn out of range, only to realize that the *Graf Spee* is breaking off battle.

Ajax hit.

Graf Spee withdraws to Montevideo. Arrives midnight 13/14 December.

Ajax and *Achilles* follow the *Graf Spee*.

Graf Spee opens fire on Exeter.

Fires on *Ajax* and *Achilles*.

Achilles damaged.

Ajax and *Achilles* open fire.

British

German

N

Exeter withdraws badly damaged to the Falkland Islands.

Exeter hit.

Ajax

Achilles

Exeter

Smoke from the pocket battleship, the *Graf Spee,* is sighted and the cruiser *Exeter* turns towards it. The light cruisers *Ajax* and *Achilles* steam on to cross the *Graf Spee's* bows.

SOUTH AMERICA

Montevideo

Buenos Aires

River Plate

Battle of River Plate

FALKLAND ISLANDS

Port Stanley

The Battle of the River Plate

13 December 1939
From about 6 am to 8 am

vulnerable and were using ammunition at a prodigious rate. Harwood decided he could not win the battle that way, and he ordered both ships to withdraw under a smoke screen and then take positions for shadowing the *Graf Spee* at the limit of her range of 12 or 13 miles (about 20 km).

As they turned away, they were amazed to see the *Graf Spee* do the same, and make off at high speed to the westward, towards the distant mouth of the River Plate. She was breaking off the battle.

Not even German officers have been able to explain why Langsdorff did this. He had been controlling the ship from an upper bridge which was unprotected, and he had been slightly wounded by splinters and for a few seconds knocked unconscious by the blast. Some of them thought that affected his judgement, but if it did he very soon recovered. When the cruisers ceased fire he went round his ship to inspect the damage. She had been hit by sixteen shells. Only two had penetrated her armour. Her main armament and engines were intact, but superficial damage was widespread: she had a large hole in her port bow; her galleys and fresh-water system were destroyed; and so was the machine that cleaned her engine oil. Thirty-six of her men were dead. Langsdorff had decided she was not fit to try to reach Germany, or able to make her own repairs at sea, or to escape from the shadowing of the cruisers. He was going to the neutral port of Montevideo. Most of his officers thought he was wrong, but none of them said so.

As for the British, they could not believe it. He had put the *Exeter* out of action, and Harwood had ordered her to try to make the Falkland Islands. They all believed the *Graf Spee* had every chance of getting the light cruisers too – but that if she went into Montevideo she would never get out again.

The battle was most alarming for the merchant captains and the crew of the last ship the *Graf Spee* had sunk. They were locked below decks, and as soon as they heard her big guns firing above them they knew she was in action with British warships. All day their emotions were divided: they hoped the German ship would be sunk, but knew that if she was they would go down with her. Langsdorff was as courteous as ever. That evening, he sent them a message that he was entering Montevideo and they would be freed in the morning.

She anchored in Montevideo harbour in the middle of the night, and the moment she did so the naval occasion became a kind of international circus, the gunnery battle became a battle of diplomacy. Reporters, photographers and news-reel cameramen crowded into the city, American radio gave running commentaries and hundreds of thousands of people came down to the shores to see what was going to happen next.

Montevideo is the capital of Uruguay, which – unknown to Langsdorff – was strongly democratic then and so inclined to favour the British. The river mouth is 100 miles (160 km) across, and on the other side was Argentina, with its capital Buenos Aires, which was somewhat pro-German. Langsdorff came ashore and met the German minister, and together they asked the foreign minister of Uruguay for permission to stay fifteen

days to get the damage repaired. But the status of a warship in a neutral harbour was controlled by the Hague Convention of 1907, which only allowed a stay of forty-eight hours. The British minister, whose name was Eugene Millington Drake, therefore asked the Uruguayans to insist the *Graf Spee* should leave within that time. The Uruguayans compromised, with permission for her to stay for four days.

But then Millington Drake had a message from Commodore Harwood, patrolling off shore in *Ajax*: he did not want the *Graf Spee* to come out in a hurry, he wanted to wait until reinforcements arrived. The nearest of those, except for the cruiser *Cumberland* which came belting up from the Falkland Islands, was five days' steaming away. So Millington Drake had to change his tactics and encourage the Uruguayans to let the *Graf Spee* stay where she was. To make sure she did, he and other British diplomats began to spread rumours that strong British forces were already assembled outside the river mouth.

During those four days the Germans landed their dead for burial (the British, according to their custom, had buried theirs at sea). Some of the British merchant captains, who had so much

Exeter's fore funnel holed by splinters from the *Graf Spee's* 11-inch shells. She retired from the fight with 61 men dead and dying and all her guns out of action, but she reached home safely.

admired Langsdorff, attended the German funeral and laid a wreath inscribed 'From the British Captains to the Brave German Sailors'.

Langsdorff readily believed the British rumours – so readily that one has to conclude that he wanted to believe them. He had reported by shore radio to Admiral Raeder, Commander-in-Chief of the German Navy, and Raeder had consulted Hitler; but they sent him no positive orders, only the negative order that he was not to let his ship be interned in Uruguay. Everything was left to him. Of what went on in his mind one can only express a personal opinion. I myself believe that right from the moment when he decided to enter Montevideo, Langsdorff in his heart had never intended to go out again. He had been a naval officer all his working life; but he was essentially a man who liked his fellow men. He liked the British: his treatment of the prisoners proved it. When the test came, I believe, he could not summon up any enmity for the British sailors; he could not make the transition from the morality of peace to the different morality of war. When he saw the wreckage of battle, saw his own dead and wounded, knew what he had done to the *Exeter*, he was revolted by the stupidity of it all, and resolved that he would not do anything more to add to the suffering.

Some things he said in those few days seem to confirm this view. Of the *Exeter's* fight, he said to one of his prisoners: 'When you fight brave men like that, you can't feel any enmity, you only want to shake hands with them.' And again to a prisoner: 'I am not going out to commit suicide with all my crew.' And to one of his own crew: 'Better a thousand live young men that a thousand dead heroes.

If this is right, it was a terrible self-revelation for a captain in war; but Langsdorff had to see it through to its inevitable end, and he had to do it alone.

The climax came on the evening of Sunday 17 December, four days after the battle. Just after six o'clock, the *Graf Spee* raised her anchors and steamed out through the harbour mouth. It is said that three-quarters of a million people were crowded along the shore, expecting a grandstand view of a naval battle.

Offshore, the men in the cruisers heard the American radio commentary and braced themselves for the final battle in the dark that night. They could not really expect to survive to see another day. But four miles out of the harbour, just as the sun went down, a tremendous explosion wrecked the battleship, and she began to settle in the shallow water and the river mud.

A wave of pure horror swept through the crowds on shore, because they believed the German crew, or some of it, was still on board. But it was not. Langsdorff had summoned German-owned tugs across the river from Argentina. They had taken off all his men and landed them the next morning in the friendlier world of Buenos Aires. He went with them, saw that they were accepted for internment, spoke to them all in divisions and explained what their future would be.

He had brought with him the battle ensign of the *Graf Spee*, and alone in a room that night he wrote a letter to his wife and another to his parents; and then unfolded the flag, spread it on the floor of the room, lay down on it and shot himself dead.

That event shocked his enemies almost as much as his friends. Again, one of the merchant captains attended his funeral and laid a wreath on behalf of them all. And many British naval officers who had fought the battle expressed their admiration. 'I think there's no shadow of doubt', one said, 'that he was an extremely nice man with high humane feelings.' Another called him, 'a really tragic figure. I was profoundly sorry for the man.' And a third: 'I shall always feel myself that Langsdorff was a very fine man, and a great humanitarian.' Years afterwards, a merchant seaman who had been his prisoner said, 'I wouldn't be here today if it hadn't been Captain Langsdorff who captured us. Right through our time aboard that ship the humanitarian thread came through and through. He respected us and we respected him. He was a gentleman.'

With the end of *Graf Spee*, one problem remained for the British. Her supply ship the *Altmark* had vanished, and with her some hundreds of merchant-service prisoners. Langsdorff had told her captain to land the prisoners at a neutral port; but it is hard to see how he could have done so without getting his own ship interned, or else attacked as soon as he came out again. He decided to do what Langsdorff had thought was impossible: to run the gauntlet of the British fleet and make his way back to Germany.

He very nearly succeeded. The British did not find the *Altmark* until she was on the coast of Norway. Another problem of neutrality arose, for this was shortly before Germany invaded Norway. The Norwegians could have claimed a right to search the ship, but they did not; they accepted the captain's statement that he had no prisoners on board. The British were convinced he had. While the argument went on, the *Altmark* steamed down the Norwegian coast until she reached the southern end of it, within a day's steaming of home. Churchill decided to set the law aside. A flotilla of destroyers intercepted her, and she took refuge in a narrow inlet called Jössingfjord, which was covered with ice. In the middle of a pitch-dark night, the destroyer leader *Cossack*, Captain Philip Vian, entered the fjord and found her. The *Altmark* tried to ram the *Cossack* and there were sharp manoeuvres among the ice. The *Cossack* put herself alongside and the *Altmark* ran ashore, stern first. A boarding party jumped across, there was a short gunfight as they searched the ship and prized open the hatches. The lieutenant commanding the boarding party shouted down to the hold, 'Any British down there?' A shout came back, 'Yes, we're all British.' 'Come on up then,' he is said to have shouted. 'The navy's here.'

They brought off all the men there were, 199 of them; but in respect for the Norwegians' authority, they left the *Altmark* unharmed.

Opposite: above British merchant seamen safe in port on the deck of the destroyer *HMS Cossack*. In a Norwegian fjord, she rescued nearly 300 of them from imprisonment in the German supply ship *Altmark*.

Opposite: below The *Graf Spee*, torn by huge explosions, settled in the mud of the River Plate outside Montevideo harbour. She is lying there still, but wholly submerged

The Sinking
of the Bismarck
1941

IN MAY 1941, Britain had stood alone for a year against Germany and Italy. Her navy was hard pressed in the Mediterranean, fighting for the first time within range of aircraft, and all harbours from Norway to France were in German hands.

While Germany occupied Norway, the country was full of small groups of Norwegians who devoted themselves at great risk to overthrowing the invaders. One such group centred on a young man called Odd Starheim, who had been trained in England and had a radio transmitter hidden in a farm near the south coast. Another member of the group saw two very large warships out at sea, with a convoy of merchant ships, steering west. He knew he must tell Starheim, so that he could transmit the news to England.

But Starheim's farm was surrounded at a distance by Germans, who were homing in on it with radio direction finders. There was a detachment of them on the road to the farm, and it was a problem how to get the message to him through the German ring. A girlfriend of his volunteered to take it, because the Germans knew her by sight. She tucked the written message in the top of her stocking, and cheerfully walked through the German detachment.

Starheim had already decided he must stop transmitting, bury his apparatus and escape. But when he saw the message he knew it was so important that he must take the risk of sending one

final signal. He did, and then burying all his gear made a long and perilous but successful escape back to England. The message, received in London, was relayed to the Commander-in-Chief, Home Fleet, in Scapa Flow, though he never knew where it had come from; and all the events of this story, and all the immense forces that were deployed, were as a result of the action of that intrepid girl with the note in her stocking.

RAF reconnaissance Spitfires were sent to search the Norwegian coast, and one of them found two warships anchored in a fjord near Bergen. The photographs it took revealed that one of them was an armoured cruiser and the other was the brand new battleship *Bismarck*. That night, the weather became so thick that no other aircraft could approach the place.

Sir John Tovey, the Commander-in-Chief, had a difficult problem. The *Bismarck* was known to be bigger, more heavily armoured and probably faster than any British battleship, and the British had a great respect, dating back to Jutland, for the strength and quality the Germans put into their big ships. Tovey had a powerful fleet under his command, though nothing like so big as Jellicoe's had been: two new battleships, *King George V* and *Prince of Wales*, two old battlecruisers, *Hood* and *Repulse*, the aircraft carrier *Victorious*, ten cruisers and twelve destroyers. But the *Prince of Wales* and *Victorious* were so new that the former still had the building contractor's men at work in her turrets,

Previous pages The end of the *Bismarck*, by C.E. Turner.

Right The photograph by a reconnaissance Spitfire over the coast of Norway which first identified the *Bismarck*.

The battleship *Bismarck*.

and the latter had only flown on her aircraft for the first time the day before. The only ship that was a match for the *Bismarck* was his own flagship *King George V* – which was always known in the fleet as *KG5*.

The problem was to guess what the *Bismarck* and her escorting cruiser meant to do. With the convoy she had brought, it might have been a reinforcement of north Norway or an invasion of Iceland, or if she left the convoy she might mean to break out into the Atlantic as a commerce raider like the *Graf Spee*, but far more powerful. If so, she might come north of Iceland or south of it, or even north or south of the Shetland Islands. And Tovey could not make a move before she moved, or he would be the first to run out of fuel.

After two days of anxiety a single aircraft with a picked naval crew flew in the 200 feet (60 m) between the sea and the cloud base, found the fjord and reported that the ships had gone. The Home Fleet sailed, the *KG5* and *Victorious* to search the passage south of Iceland, the *Prince of Wales* and *Hood* for the Denmark strait between Iceland and Greenland. So began the most far-flung battle that had ever been fought, the first in which tactics were solely controlled by radio.

The 8-inch cruisers *Norfolk* and *Suffolk* were sent to patrol the strait between the north of Iceland and the Arctic pack ice. It was an eerie and forbidding place, with the edge of the ice to the north and the ice-blink always visible on the horizon, and to the south a bank of fog which seldom shifted, a minefield and the jagged rocks of Iceland. Between the ice and the fog there was a lane of clear water only about 3 miles (5 km) wide.

Both cruisers had radar, but it was still at a primitive stage of development. The *Suffolk*'s set had a rotating aerial, and so could watch all round except on a narrow arc astern; the *Norfolk*'s, with a fixed aerial, only watched a narrow arc ahead. Neither had a range of much more than 13 miles (21 km), which in clear weather was less than the range of optical telescopes, and also much less than the range of the *Bismarck*'s guns.

It was the human eye, a lookout on the *Suffolk*, that first spotted the *Bismarck* and the cruiser with her early one morning, 23 May 1941. The *Suffolk* dodged back into the fog bank, and the *Bismarck* did not seem to have seen her. It was not her job to fight the *Bismarck*, which would have been impossible, but to report and shadow her. She signalled by radio what she had seen, then watched the two dots on her radar screen. They passed her to the westward, and she came out of the fog again to follow the ships by eye at the limits of her radar range. They were travelling fast, at twenty-eight to thirty knots.

An hour after the *Suffolk*'s sighting, the *Norfolk* broke out of the fog and found the *Bismarck* only 6 miles (10 km) away. This time, the *Bismarck* opened fire. It was clear very quickly that she had radar gunnery control, which the British had not. The *Norfolk* had some minutes of near misses before she was in the fog again, and the *Bismarck*'s fire did not follow her there.

All night the four ships steamed flat out through the Arctic seas, in and out of snow and rainstorms, with the uncharted ice most uncomfortably close to

Hunting the Bismarck

From 21 May to 27 May 1941

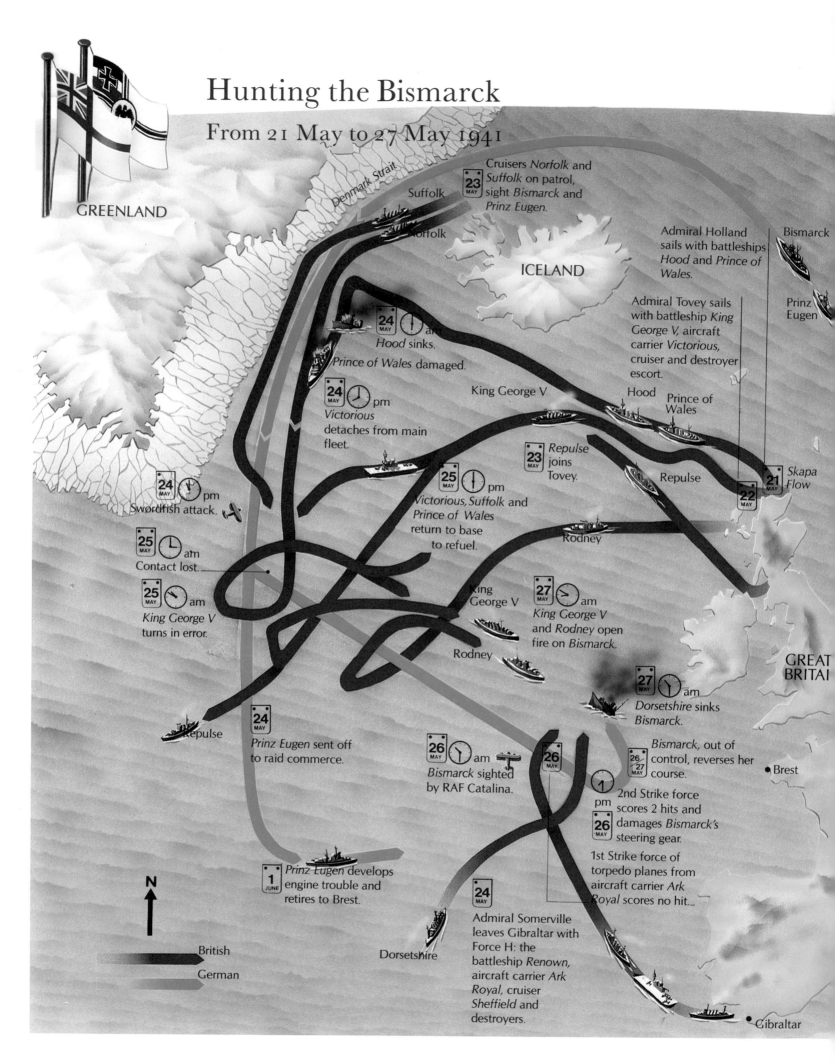

GREENLAND

Denmark Strait

Suffolk

Norfolk

23 MAY Cruisers *Norfolk* and *Suffolk* on patrol, sight *Bismarck* and *Prinz Eugen*.

ICELAND

Admiral Holland sails with battleships *Hood* and *Prince of Wales*.

Bismarck

Prinz Eugen

Admiral Tovey sails with battleship *King George V*, aircraft carrier *Victorious*, cruiser and destroyer escort.

24 MAY am *Hood* sinks. *Prince of Wales* damaged.

24 MAY pm *Victorious* detaches from main fleet.

King George V

Hood

Prince of Wales

23 MAY *Repulse* joins Tovey.

Repulse

21 MAY Skapa Flow

22 MAY

24 MAY pm Swordfish attack.

25 MAY pm *Victorious*, *Suffolk* and *Prince of Wales* return to base to refuel.

Rodney

25 MAY am Contact lost.

25 MAY am *King George V* turns in error.

King George V

27 MAY am *King George V* and *Rodney* open fire on *Bismarck*.

Rodney

GREAT BRITAIN

27 MAY am *Dorsetshire* sinks *Bismarck*.

Repulse

24 MAY *Prinz Eugen* sent off to raid commerce.

26 MAY am *Bismarck* sighted by RAF Catalina.

26 MAY

26/27 MAY *Bismarck*, out of control, reverses her course.

Brest

26 MAY pm 2nd Strike force scores 2 hits and damages *Bismarck's* steering gear.

1st Strike force of torpedo planes from aircraft carrier *Ark Royal* scores no hit.

1 JUNE *Prinz Eugen* develops engine trouble and retires to Brest.

N

British

German

24 MAY Admiral Somerville leaves Gibraltar with Force H: the battleship *Renown*, aircraft carrier *Ark Royal*, cruiser *Sheffield* and destroyers.

Dorsetshire

Gibraltar

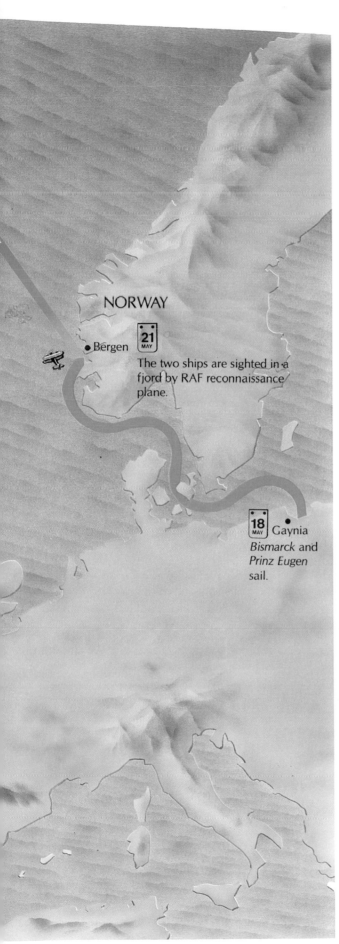

NORWAY

• Bergen

21 MAY

The two ships are sighted in a fjord by RAF reconnaissance plane.

18 MAY • Gaynia

Bismarck and *Prinz Eugen* sail.

starboard. The cruisers sent out a stream of signals of the *Bismarck*'s position, course and speed. These were received by the Admiralty, the Commander-in-Chief, and Admiral Holland commanding the *Hood* and *Prince of Wales*. He was nearest, and steamed all night to the southern end of the Denmark Strait to intercept the *Bismarck* at dawn. At 5.35 am, 24 May, he made contact, and turned towards the enemy. At 5.49 the action began.

In theory the British had an advantage in gunpower, but Admiral Holland in the *Hood* had chosen to make the attack head on, and signalled the *Prince of Wales* to do the same. This almost halved the power of the ships, because they could only use their forward guns. At 25,000 yards (23,000 m) the *Hood* opened fire, and within seconds all four ships had done the same. The shooting on both sides was accurate, though the *Hood* began by aiming not at the *Bismarck* but at the cruiser, now identified as the 8-inch *Prinz Eugen*. It was also the *Prinz Eugen* that made the first hit on the *Hood*. It started a large fire.

After six minutes Holland ordered a turn to port which would have brought all guns to bear. But before the turn was complete a vast eruption of flame was seen between the *Hood*'s masts. It blazed up hundreds of feet, some watchers said a thousand, with a great incandescent ball in the centre of it. It lasted only a second or two and left a column of smoke through which the bows and stern could be dimly seen each pointing upwards. She had broken in half, and in two minutes or so had completely disappeared.

The German ships transferred their fire to the *Prince of Wales*, which was in serious trouble with its new gun turrets. They kept breaking down with minor faults. The builders' foremen were still inside them, struggling to put things right, but in each salvo only about half the guns were fired.

A deluge of shells fell on and around her, 15-inch (381-mm), 8-inch (203-mm) and 6-inch (152-mm) – the latter from the *Bismarck*'s secondary armament. She was hit seven times. One 15-inch shell smashed through the bridge and exploded as it came out of the other side. It killed or wounded everyone there except the captain himself and the chief yeoman of signals. In the plotting room below, blood ran out of the voice pipe. There was nothing to be done but open the range and break off the action. It had lasted only about eight minutes. The *Norfolk* and *Suffolk*, still out of range, had expected to watch the battle with the satisfaction of knowing they had done their job. With the *Hood*'s disaster, the rear-admiral commanding the cruisers suddenly found himself again senior officer, with the *Prince of Wales* now under his command. It was he who sent the terse radio signal '*Hood* has blown up'.

Nobody who was at sea in the fleet that early dawn will forget the shock of that signal. *Hood* was an old ship, laid down just after Jutland. For many years, she had been the largest and most famous warship in the world, and in many people's eyes the most graceful. There were not many men in the navy who did not have friends on board her. From that

Above The destruction of *HMS Hood*: the *Prince of Wales* alters course to avoid the wreck. By John Hamilton.

Right One of the ships which took part in the hunt for the *Bismarck*: *HMS Renown* in a North Sea gale, by John Hamilton.

moment, sinking the *Bismarck* became something more than a strategic need. It became a naked revenge. Yet it illustrated well the impersonal nature of war at sea. It was revenge on the ship, not on her admiral, captain or crew, who had done their job and done it very well. The hunt grew and grew in extent, until great ships were steaming from every part of the Atlantic. And being impersonal, it became extremely exciting. For the first time, tactics were signalled from thousands of miles away. In each ship, cypher staff were kept busy night and day, navigators were plotting positions and moves on the Atlantic chart, and admirals and captains, on the information that was coming in, were planning intercepts. To take one small example, the old cruiser *Arethusa*, which happened to be in Reykjavik, was sent anti-clockwise round Iceland in case *Bismarck* went back by the way she had come. On board, it was noticeable that the regular officers were hoping she would come that way, while the few reservists, with more realism, were privately hoping she would not: for with 6-inch guns, no armour and no radar, the *Arethusa* would no doubt have been sunk before she even saw the enemy, and would have been lucky to have the satisfaction of sending a signal before she went down. But even she, alone in sight of the ice, was able to follow through radio the evolution of the drama.

The *Norfolk* and *Suffolk*, now with the *Prince of Wales*, took up the job of shadowing again. Sir John Tovey, some 300 miles (500 km) away, still had the problem of where she was bound, and now the added question of whether, or how much, she was damaged. The *Suffolk* and a flying boat sent from Iceland both reported she was leaving a track of oil behind her. So she had certainly been hit. But the damage might be nothing very serious, only a minor leak. Her firing had not been impaired, and she was steaming only a little slower. If she needed repairs, would she head back to Germany, and if so by what route; or would she make for the ports the Germans held in France, or even perhaps for a neutral port in Spain? If she did not, she might be expecting to meet an oil tanker, which might be in the Davis Strait to the west of Greenland, or somewhere down in the tropics. The possibilities were still wide open.

The hunt had spread far beyond Tovey's own command. From Gibraltar, the battlecruiser *Renown* and the aircraft carrier *Ark Royal* had put to sea, escorted by the cruiser *Sheffield* and six destroyers. Thousands of miles away, the battleship *Revenge* put out from Halifax, Nova Scotia. Out in the Atlantic, the battleship *Rodney* was on her way to Boston for a refit, the battleship *Ramillies* and the cruisers *London* and *Edinburgh* were escorting convoys. All of these left what they were doing and steamed at full speed to intercept, some on Admiralty orders and some on their own initiative.

That evening, 24 May, Tovey decided something, however desperate, had to be done to slow the *Bismarck* down, so that she could not escape the shadowers by suddenly putting on speed in the night. He asked the captain of the aircraft carrier *Victorious* what would be the range for an aircraft torpedo attack. The answer was 100 miles (160 km) – if the ship could steam towards the enemy while the aircraft were off, so that their flight would be shorter coming back. Tovey told him to make the attack when he was in that range. But it was delayed because the *Bismarck* altered course to the south-west, away from them. The aircraft flew off just before sunset, in a rising wind and heavy squalls of rain.

The only torpedo aircraft in service were Swordfish, usually known as Stringbags, single-engined biplanes with a crew of three and a top speed of about eighty knots. The *Victorious* had nine of them, and some had a new kind of radar for finding ships. They were appallingly flimsy machines to fly out in mid-Atlantic, let alone to attack a battleship, and most of their pilots had only once landed on a carrier when they joined the ship three days before. Now they would have to do it in the dark. But their leader was Lieutenant-Commander E. Esmonde, a man of great courage who later won fame and a posthumous VC in attacking the battlecruisers *Scharnhorst* and *Gneisenau* in 1943.

After an hour's flight, the planes with radar picked up a ship they thought was the *Bismarck* and dived through cloud to attack. It was not; it was an American coastguard cutter which by a billion-to-one chance was at that moment in that particular spot in mid-Atlantic. Emerging from the cloud, they also saw the *Bismarck* not far away and switched their attack to her. But the *Bismarck* had been given time to sight them too, and she put up heavy fire. All the Swordfish attacked in spite of it, and they saw one torpedo hit.

An hour after that, when it was pitch dark and

The *Bismarck* escapes her shadowers, followed by the cruiser *Prinz Eugen*. By John Hamilton.

A swordfish of the Fleet Air Arm approaching the aircraft carrier *Ark Royal*. This photograph was taken in the calmer seas of the Mediterranean.

estimate of her position. It was not to the north of where she had been lost, but well to the south-east. The officer who had made the plot in *KG5* frantically worked it out again, and found he had been wrong. For five hours the Home Fleet had been steaming in the wrong direction. The extraordinary thing, which has never been fully explained, is that the Admiralty knew what the fleet was doing but did not correct it. Not only that, but an hour after the second set of bearings, they ordered the battleship *Rodney* also to steer for the North Sea.

To Admiral Tovey, the problem had become incomprehensible. He now felt sure the *Bismarck* was heading for the west coast of France, but the Admiralty's silence made him hesitate to change his own course. He reluctantly broke radio silence to enquire, but no answer came for two hours. Meanwhile, he did change course on his own initiative. That evening, the Admiralty signalled that they also believed it was to be the coast of France.

raining, the captain of the *Victorious* was so anxious about his aircraft that he switched on all his searchlights as a beacon and flashed them round the sky. Of course that made a beacon too for any German submarines in the area, and the vice-admiral of the cruiser escort signalled him to switch them off again. He managed to disobey until he heard the welcome sound of the aircraft. Even then he expected most of them to crash; but somehow all of them found the ship and scrambled on board, haphazardly but safely.

Later that night the shadowing cruisers lost the *Bismarck* in the dark. The huge game of hide and seek began all over again. She had now been hit twice, but a hit by a single aircraft torpedo, smaller than a ship's torpedo, could not be expected to cripple her. It made it more likely she would go somewhere for repairs; but the guesses still varied from the tropics to the Arctic, and from Germany to the west of Greenland.

Later still that night, the *Bismarck* broke radio silence with a series of signals. Neither side could decipher the other's signals, but shore stations could take bearings of them, and they did. It was not much help, because all the shore stations were in Britain and the *Bismarck* was most of 1,000 miles (1,600 km) out to the west, so that the bearings intersected at a very acute angle and did not give an accurate fix. The Admiralty presumably plotted them on a chart, but for some reason never explained they did not transmit their own estimate of her position: they transmitted all the separate bearings and left each ship to plot the position as best it could. In Sir John Tovey's flagship, the plot gave a position north of where the *Bismarck* had been lost. So he concluded she was going back to Germany either north or south of Iceland, and he altered the course of the Home Fleet to north-east. The old *Arethusa*, alone by the ice, began again to expect a salvo of 15-inch shells out of nowhere.

Late next morning, 25 May, the *Bismarck* transmitted again. This time, the Admiralty broadcast not the separate bearings but their own

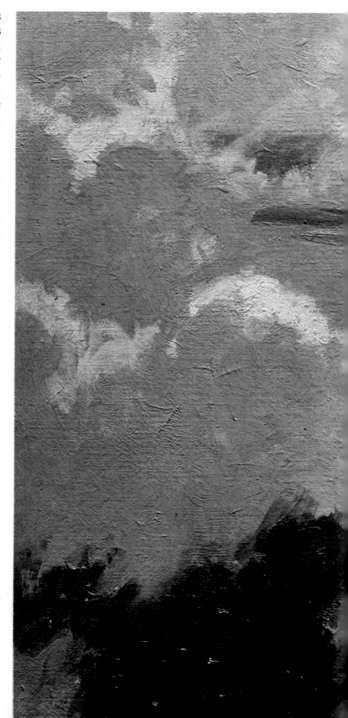

The series of mistakes had put *KG5* at least 100 miles behind in the hunt, and most of the cruisers and all the destroyers had to go back to Iceland for fuel. The *Victorious* went too, because a carrier could not be risked without an anti-submarine escort. To protect the *KG5* and the *Rodney*, which were separate but converging, five destroyers were detached from a convoy 300 miles away. They were commanded by Captain Philip Vian, who had rescued the *Graf Spee* prisoners from the *Altmark*. And Force H, including the *Ark Royal*, was still coming up from Gibraltar. But the wind was getting up from the north, and that force, plunging into very heavy seas, had had to reduce its speed to seventeen knots. Even so, the *Ark Royal* was taking green seas over her flight-deck.

At dawn on 26 May the *Ark Royal* flew off her Swordfish for reconnaissance. She was rolling so much that aircraft slid sideways on the wet flight-deck in spite of extra men to hold them down, and measurements showed that her bow and stern were rising and falling 55 feet (17 m). Her aircrews, unlike those of the *Victorious*, were well experienced, but neither they nor anyone else had flown off or on in conditions like that. On a runway like a seesaw, the takeoff was erratic, but at length they were all off for a search of three and a half hours.

At 10.30 am a battleship was sighted – not by the Swordfish but by a Catalina flying-boat from Northern Ireland. She was almost 700 miles (1,100 km) west of the English Channel. In dozens of British ships men marked her position on their charts. It was 135 miles (217 km) south from *KG5*, 125 miles (200 km) south by west of *Rodney*, 110 miles (177 km) north-north-west of *Renown* and Force H. No other British battleship was near. It had to be the *Bismarck*. If she kept going, none of them could catch her up before dark, and by dawn she could be within the range of German shore-based bombers. Somebody had to slow her down. There were only two chances, and both were very slender: the Swordfish, or Vian's five destroyers.

Commanding Force H was Admiral Sir James Somerville, flying his flag in the *Renown*. He

The *Bismarck* sighted again by a Catalina aircraft, by Norman Wilkinson.

The crew of the *Bismarck* had a long ordeal. She was ablaze from end to end before she sank.

signalled the *Ark Royal* to attack, and signalled the cruiser *Sheffield* to press on ahead, find and shadow the *Bismarck*. The latter signal was not deciphered in any hurry by the *Ark Royal* because it was not addressed to her. So the pilots flew off without knowing the *Sheffield* was ahead. They picked her up by radar and dropped through the clouds, and most of them fired torpedos before they discovered their mistake. Luckily, the torpedos had a new kind of magnetic pistol which did not function well. Five of them exploded when they hit the water. The *Sheffield* put on speed and altered course abruptly, managing to dodge the ones that were not defective. Somerville signalled to Tovey 'No hits', without explaining why, and Tovey's hopes sank almost to zero.

After seven o'clock that evening, the *Ark Royal* had fifteen Swordfish on deck for a fresh attempt, their torpedoes now fitted with the old-fashioned and reliable contact pistol that only went off when it hit something. Again the aircraft lurched unsteadily along the swaying deck and climbed into the ragged storm-swept sky. They passed the *Sheffield*, which signalled to them 'Enemy 12 miles dead ahead'. Half an hour later they came back for another bearing, having failed to find the *Bismarck*: air navigation at eighty knots in a wind of forty was not easy. They disappeared again, and this time the *Sheffield* saw anti-aircraft fire: then the flashes of big guns, and four 15-inch salvoes fell unpleasantly close to her. She turned away and made smoke, but

had a glimpse of the *Bismarck*, which seemed to have turned right round to the north-north-west. The *Sheffield* signalled this move, and at almost the same time the squadron leader of the aircraft signalled 'Estimate no hits'. Tovey could therefore not believe the *Sheffield*'s report. The *Bismarck* was in reach of safety if she steamed south-east. It seemed incredible that she was steering the opposite way.

Captain Vian with the destroyers was under orders to protect the battleships, but as soon as he heard the *Bismarck* had been sighted he altered course towards her at the highest speed the destroyers could make in the heavy sea. At 10.50 pm he made contact in the darkness. At about the same time, the Swordfish were coming in to the *Ark Royal* and their crews were being questioned. The *Ark Royal*'s captain signalled that the squadron leader had been mistaken: one torpedo had hit. Other aircraft were now reporting the *Bismarck*'s change of course. It was nearly midnight before the mystery was solved. Returning aircraft reported there had been a second hit on the *Bismarck*'s quarter, and that she had turned two complete circles after it and then stopped. The torpedo must have hit her only vulnerable part, her rudders or propellers or both.

That transformed the situation. Tovey decided to wait until dawn, leaving Vian to keep contact in the night. There was one remaining serious worry: all the big ships were in submarine waters without a destroyer screen. It seemed certain the Germans

all directions. Inside she was a blazing inferno; the flames could be seen through the shell holes in her sides. But she would not surrender and she did not sink. The *Rodney* at 10 o'clock was firing 9 gun salvoes of 16-inch shells at a range of 3,000 yards (2,750 m). She also torpedoed her, probably the only occasion in history when one battleship torpedoed another. So did the *Norfolk*. Towards the end, men could be seen running about on the *Bismarck's* upper deck, and some in despair jumping overboard. The impersonal fight against the ship became human.

At 10.15 am the *KG5* and *Rodney* had urgently to turn for home for lack of fuel. Tovey and everyone else was amazed that they had not been able to sink the *Bismarck*. But whether she sank soon or later, it was obvious she would never get back to port. He signalled that any ship that had torpedoes left should use them. The *Dorsetshire* was the only ship nearby that had any. She fired two, from very close, then deliberately steamed round to the *Bismarck's* other side and fired another. The *Bismarck*, with her flag still flying, silently heeled to port, turned bottom up and vanished.

Nothing was left but the heads of men swimming in the breaking sea. The *Dorsetshire* called a destroyer to help her to pick them up. It was too rough to launch boats, but they threw lines and let down scrambling nets. Many of the men were too wounded or exhausted to climb them, but the two ships between them rescued 110, perhaps one-tenth of her crew.

It had been a unique battle which could not have happened at any other time in the development of ships and aircraft, either before or since. From first to last, the battlefield was some 3,000 miles (4,800 km) in length. To catch one ship (for the *Prinz Eugen* was not detected) five battleships, two battlecruisers, two aircraft carriers, about ten cruisers, twenty destroyers and probably fifty aircraft had been drawn in from all over the Atlantic, and they very nearly failed. There had been serious errors: in the *Hood's* head-on attack, the gunnery breakdowns of the *Prince of Wales* (the *KG5* had them too), the flagship's wrong plotting of the radio position, the Admiralty's neglect to point it out, the *Ark Royal's* aircraft attack on the *Sheffield*. But Britannia could still claim to rule the waves – in spite of her own mistakes.

However, the British knew that times were changing. The great battleships were becoming a weapon of the past, and aircraft were the weapon of the future. Battleships might strike at twenty miles, but carriers even in the Swordfish era could strike at more than a hundred. *The Bismarck's* sister ship *Tirpitz* never reached the open sea at all, because British aircraft slowly smashed her to bits in Norway. But it was the loss of the *Prince of Wales* and *Repulse*, sunk by Japanese aircraft off Singapore within ninety minutes in 1941, that brought home to the British the chilling realization that the battleship and the naval gun, on which they had depended since the Armada, belonged to an era that was ending.

Survivors alongside the cruiser *Dorsetshire*, which had fired the final torpedoes. It was too rough to launch boats, and some were too weak to be hauled aboard, but over 100 were saved.

would send out submarines to counter-attack – and so they did, but they sent them to the wrong place. One submarine coming back from patrol in the Atlantic sighted the *Ark Royal* slowly crossing its bows, but it had already used all its torpedoes.

The destroyers that night, circling the *Bismarck* in the gale, were the first ships that had the unpleasant experience of being under radar-directed gunfire in the pitch dark. But none of them were hit and at first light, on 27 May, the *Bismarck* was still there, still steering a slow erratic course to the northward. The *KG5* and *Rodney* closed in and opened fire. So did the 8-inch cruiser *Norfolk*, which had followed the whole hunt from the Arctic ice, and *Dorsetshire* which had left a convoy on its own initiative. At 8.47 am the *Rodney* opened fire, and within two minutes the *KG5* and the *Bismarck* followed.

Ever since the torpedo had crippled her rudders, the crew of the *Bismarck* must have known they had no hope, and that death would come to most of them in the morning. But they fought back, with unsurpassed determination, until they had no guns left to fight with. The ship was so superbly built that the agony of her men was long and awful. For ten minutes short of two hours, she was pounded by 16-inch (406-mm), 15-inch (381-mm) and 8-inch (203-mm) shells. She made no hit on the British ships, and her firing grew more and more erratic. One by one her turrets went out of action. By ten o'clock she was a silent battered wreck; her mast and funnel had gone; and her guns were pointing in

Midway
1942

Norman Wilkinson

IT WAS left to the Japanese to build the ultimate battleships, the *Yamato* and *Musashi*, bigger and more powerful than any had ever been before; and it was left to the Americans to win the first sea battle fought entirely with aircraft, in which the ships never saw each other.

That battle was Midway, in June 1942, named after a minute and isolated atoll in mid-Pacific. The Japanese dispatched a huge armada to capture that hitherto innocent and insignificant pair of islands, which were only one square mile in extent: they sent in total – including a diversionary attack on the Aleutian Islands – ninety-one warships in eight separate squadrons, together with another hundred transports and auxiliaries.

This great sea operation was planned and commanded by Admiral Isoruku Yamamoto, flying his flag in the new super-battleship *Yamato*, of 65,000 tons and nine 18.1-inch (460-mm) guns. Its object was not only to capture the atoll, which was an essential link in American communications across the Pacific; it was also to lure out the American Pacific Fleet to give battle.

But the armada was led, 300 miles (480 km) ahead of Yamamoto himself, by a squadron called – after its admiral – the Nagumo Force. This force alone contained four fast heavy aircraft carriers, the *Akagi*, which was the flagship, the *Hiryu*, *Soryu* and *Kaga*, with two battleships, two cruisers and twelve destroyers. In the past six months it had taken part in battles from Pearl Harbor to Ceylon. It had steamed 50,000 miles (80,500 km), and everywhere it had gone, it had conquered: after Pearl Harbor, successful attacks against Rabaul, Java, Colombo and Trincomalee had given the force a formidable reputation and made it believe it was invincible. To take Midway and break American communications was merely the next step in an even greater plan. Its sights were set on invading Fiji, Samoa, New Caledonia and ultimately Australia and Hawaii. Its crews were supremely confident as it steamed out towards Midway, 3,000 miles (4,800 km) from home. So were the pilots of its 260 aircraft. But Vice-Admiral Nagumo was not.

Nagumo was not at all the swashbuckling warlord his Force's achievements suggest. His build was heavy, but it was said he seemed apologetic and even timid, as if he was always unsure of the right thing to do. Certainly, as this voyage progressed, he was hesitant. He was a torpedo expert, and regarded as a man of exceptional ability who in time would become a great leader; but the system of promotion had put him in command of the First Air Fleet, and he knew very little about aviation. He was in the wrong job, which is a misfortune for any man. So far, in his uncertainty, he had done the only thing he could: he had followed orders implicitly. And so far, the orders had been good. But the strike against Midway involved two orders which were contradictory; and while his men were optimistic, Nagumo was gloomy and apprehensive.

Yamamoto, who had conceived the operation, was not a ferocious war-lord either. He was old enough to have served under Togo at the Battle of Tsushima. After that, he had spent four years in America, two at Harvard and two as naval attaché in Washington. In his forties he learned to fly, and was soon well known as an advocate of naval aviation, which he saw as the weapon of the future. But when Japan slid towards war in the late 1930s, he did all he could to hold the country back: not perhaps for love of peace, but because after living in America and visiting Britain, he did not believe Japan was strong enough to beat them.

He is said to have been an expert bridge-player, and in his war plans he often took a gambler's risks and won. Pearl Harbor had been the greatest and most closely calculated risk; yet although it was a huge success for him, the complete victory he had hoped for had eluded him: no American aircraft carriers had been in the harbour, and until those carriers were sunk, he believed, Japan could not control the ocean. The Nagumo Force,

he expected, would destroy the Americans in Midway. A force of troop-carrying transports would occupy it; the American fleet would be provoked into the area; and he would come up with the *Yamato* and his battle fleet to engage them. Yet this tight sequence of events depended on risks that could not be calculated: that the weather would be perfect; that Japanese intelligence reports were correct; and above all that his intentions were a secret unknown to the Americans. Nagumo, out in front, was worried by all three of these assumptions. His orders were to attack the island and then prepare to fight the American fleet. But if weather delayed him, or intelligence was wrong, or the secret was out, the American fleet might get there first, and there was no plan for this contingency. He would have to fight first and invade afterwards; but

Previous pages 'Mitchells taking off from US Carrier *Hornet*', by Norman Wilkinson.

Right Admiral Nagumo, Japanese commander at Midway.

meanwhile, what would become of the transports and the thousands of troops which were approaching by a different route?

Nagumo had been given nine days for the outward voyage. Invasion day was set for 6 June, the night of the full moon. On 4 June, Nagumo was required to be at a point 250 miles (400 km) north-west of Midway. From there he was to launch a pre-invasion air strike to destroy the island's defences, the enemy air strength and any enemy ships that might be around. At dawn on Invasion Day, the Transport Group would land 5,000 men. Three cordons of submarines would be screening the sea towards Hawaii, ready to give warning when the American fleet came out.

By the fifth day of his voyage, Nagumo was beginning to feel more hopeful. The weather had been none too good, with a heavily overcast sky,

Admiral Chester W. Nimitz, Commander-in-Chief of the US Pacific Fleet.

rain and strong winds; but everything seemed to be going according to schedule. Yet he could not be sure, for his force was sailing deaf, dumb and blind. Ships in the Japanese navy then had no radar – though oddly enough American and British ships were using radar with a directional antenna of Japanese design. Furthermore, the radio in the Nagumo Force had very limited receiving ability, and all ships, for the sake of secrecy, had been ordered to maintain radio silence. Nagumo could only assume that Yamamoto, or naval headquarters in Japan, would send him any fresh information that was critically important, and that therefore no news was good news.

Six days out, he ran into fog, so thick that his ships could not see each other. The four precious carriers were in a square at the centre of the

squadron, surrounded by concentric screens of other ships. Yet within the fog, at a given time, he had to make an alteration of course towards Midway. There was only one way to do it: to signal the change by radio. So he did, with a low-powered transmission, hoping that nobody but his own ships would pick it up. To keep up schedule, he could not reduce his speed, and all that day and the next night, the Nagumo Force plunged blindly ahead through the fog.

At dawn it lifted at last. The relief of being able to see was doubled by the fact that there was nothing to see – no American ships or planes, nothing but the wide empty ocean. 600 miles (1,000 km) straight ahead of the Force was Midway – behind them, 600 miles of fog. They had survived it, and were dead on course and dead on time. Only another 350 miles (560 km) had to be covered before the first air strike was launched; Admiral Nagumo could congratulate himself. He had only one worry, the fear that his single brief transmission might have been picked up by the enemy. But nothing was heard from *Yamato*; the obvious conclusion was that all was safe. Admiral Nagumo ordered speed to be increased, and the Force moved on at twenty-four knots.

At the same time, 600 miles south-west of Nagumo, the Transport Group was also proceeding on schedule. At that moment they, Nagumo and Midway itself formed a near-perfect equilateral triangle; and at that moment, the men of the Transport Group suddenly saw, high above them, an American flying-boat, cooly circling and observing their movements. Their escorting destroyers sent up an anti-aircraft barrage; the plane

Rear-Admiral Raymond A. Spruance, commanding Task Force 16 at Midway.

which included two heavy aircraft carriers, the *Hornet* and *Enterprise*, six cruisers and nine destroyers; and on 1 June Task Force 17, of the carrier *Yorktown* (which the Japanese believed they had sunk), two cruisers and five destroyers. Task Force 16 was temporarily commanded by Rear-Admiral Raymond Spruance because its regular commander, Vice-Admiral William Halsey, was sick. Spruance, like his opponent Nagumo, was not a carrier expert, indeed he had never commanded one before, but he was to show much more ability than his opponent in instant decisions. Rear-Admiral Frank Fletcher, flying his flag in the *Yorktown*, was in tactical command of both groups. On 3 June these forces made rendezvous 325 miles (525 km) north-east of Midway. They had passed the position of Yamamoto's submarine screen before it was on station, and the Japanese had no suspicion they were there. Admiral Spruance told his crew: 'An attack for the purpose of capturing Midway is expected. The attacking force may be composed of all combat types, including four or five carriers, transports and train vessels. If the presence of Task Force 16 and 17 remains unknown to the enemy, we should be able to make surprise flank attacks on the enemy carriers ... The successful conclusion of the operation now commencing will be of great value to our country.'

At the same time, Midway's air defences were increased by thirty long-range Catalina flying-boats and a mixed collection of fighters, dive bombers and torpedo planes from the army and navy. It was one of these Catalinas that had sighted the Transport Group approaching the island 700 miles (1,100 km) away, and as soon as its reports came in, nine Flying Fortress high-level bombers took off from Midway. Late that afternoon, 3 June, they reached the enemy ships and dropped their bombs. They reported hitting two battleships or heavy cruisers and two transports. In fact, they hit nothing. After dark four Catalinas attacked with torpedoes with very slightly more success: they damaged one tanker.

This attack, of course, was reported to Yamamoto but again, for fear of disclosing his own position, he did not pass it on to Nagumo. The attack, after all, revealed only that his Transport Group was detected: it did not suggest to him the presence of the American fleet.

It was also reported to Admiral Nimitz, who relayed the news to Fletcher and Spruance, but with the warning that what had been found was not the enemy's main fleet. During that night, while Nagumo approached the island from the north-west, the American fleet approached to a position 200 miles (320 km) north of it.

At 4.30 next morning, 4 June, the Nagumo Force was exactly on schedule and ready to make its strike against the island. The Admiral had no reason to suspect that anything was wrong. The sea was calm, the air was clear, there was a light south-easterly breeze. Conditions were ideal, and the fly-off began. Within fifteen minutes, 108 aircraft were off from the four carriers and bound for Midway: thirty-six level-bombers, thirty-six dive-bombers and a fighter escort of thirty-six Zeros. At the same

was driven off, and a message flashed to Yamamoto in the Main Force. Now it was certain that a part of the fleet had been discovered – yet Yamamoto, confident that the Transport Group could defend itself, certain that the rest of the operation remained secret and determined to preserve that secrecy, did not relay the message to Nagumo. But the discovery had not been by chance. The Americans had known the secret of Yamamoto's plan before it started, and the Nagumo Force was steaming into a trap.

They knew because they had broken the salient point in the Japanese radio code. In Japan, of course, preparations for the great operation had been an open secret, though few people knew where it was bound. The Americans were alerted by a sudden increase in Japanese radio transmissions. The navy's chief cryptographer, an eccentric but brilliant lieutenant commander named Joseph Rochefort, studied the intercepted signals, and noticed that the group AF often occurred in them. From experience, he knew that two-letter groups beginning with A usually meant a location in the Pacific, and by a long process of reasoning he decided AF meant Midway. With the agreement of Admiral Chester Nimitz, Commander-in-Chief of the Pacific Fleet, he made a test. Midway was ordered to send out a bogus uncoded message that its distillation plant had broken down. Two days later a Japanese signal reported that AF was short of water. It was extremely careless of the Japanese signallers to fall into such an elementary trap, and that one mistake sealed the fate not only of the operation but also, in the long run, of their country.

On the day before Yamamoto left his base, Nimitz in Pearl Harbor ordered out Task Force 16, time, seven scout planes should have been launched to patrol the surrounding sea, but this was less successful. Only three took off on time. The others, from the attending cruisers and battleships, were delayed for half an hour by various engine troubles and faults in the launching catapults. For a while, the search of the sea was incomplete.

As the air strike homed in on Midway, an American flying-boat far above and undetected shadowed them. When they were 30 miles (48 km) from their goal, it dropped a parachute flare. Radar on the island also picked them up, and the job lot of aircraft on the runway began to take off.

The air battle over Midway lasted for twenty-five minutes, with the Zeros providing a furious defence for their bombers. Nearly 66,000 pounds (30,000 kg) of high explosive were dropped on the tiny islands. The hangars and the fuel storage tanks were destroyed; the airstrip was damaged and twenty-four people were killed; and that was about all. The Americans claimed fifty-three Japanese shot down; according to the Japanese they actually got six. The Japanese shot down seventeen and claimed forty-two; but even forty-two would have been nothing like the total obliteration that Yamamoto's plan had called for, because Midway that morning had held about a hundred and twenty planes.

Rear-Admiral Frank J. Fletcher, in tactical command at Midway, flew his flag in the Carrier *Yorktown*.

Torpedo bombers on the *USS Enterprise* before launching at Midway. Only four of these aircraft returned.

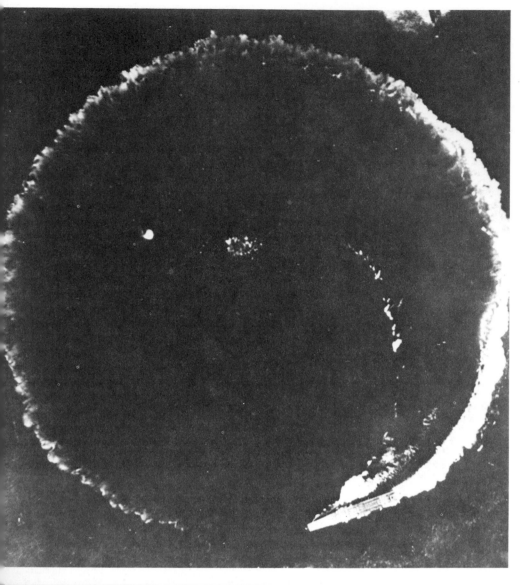

It was clear already to Nagumo that there were far more aircraft around than he had been led to expect. Less than half an hour after sunrise, the Nagumo Force had seen – and had been seen by – another American flying-boat. Nine fighters took off immediately, but the spy escaped in cloud; and over the next hour and a half, while the air battle over Midway was begun, fought and broken off, Nagumo had repeated sightings of enemy planes and his pilots made repeated, fruitless searches. Then, at seven o'clock, he received a signal from the commander of the first Air Strike: 'Second attack required.'

As Nagumo considered the message and pondered his next action, his mind was suddenly clarified. At 7.05 am the early morning calm was split by the raucous warning of an air raid. The Zeros, still circling, alert from the earlier sightings, pounced on six American torpedo bombers as they droned in to the attack, only 50 feet (15 m) above sea-level. Four were shot down; the fifth, also hit, nearly grazed *Akagi*'s bridge before exploding and plunging into the sea. Only the sixth escaped, limping back to Midway. Then, even as the ships' crews cheered, another four enemy aircraft appeared. Anti-aircraft shells exploded all around them, and once more the Zeros dived in as the torpedoes were released. But none struck the ships, and only two of the planes returned to Midway. The two attacks had taken ten minutes; seven American aircraft had been destroyed. It was totally unexpected that after being bombed, the island should still have the strength to counter-attack. Nagumo ordered preparations for a second strike at Midway.

This was a complex business. On the assumption that the First Air Strike would eradicate Midway's air power, the planes of the second wave had already been armed with torpedoes for the second part of the operation, the attack on whatever fleet the Americans sent to the islands' aid. Now the planes had to be rearmed with bombs – an arduous and lengthy task, for every plane had to be lowered from the flight-deck to the hangar-deck, rearmed and returned to the flight-deck.

Thirteen minutes after the order to rearm, Nagumo received a new message, this time from one of the scout planes. It read: 'Ten ships, apparently enemy, bearing 010°, distance 240 miles from Midway. Course 150°, speed over 20 knots.' For the first time, Nagumo knew that something more than an unprepared air force was lying in wait for him.

The scout plane was urgently asked for more detail. All that came back was that the enemy had changed course. Nagumo asked again – it was essential to know what warships were in the opposing force. This time the reply was more specific: 'Enemy ships are five cruisers and five destroyers.' On *Akagi*'s bridge there was a surge of relief. Then another message arrived: 'Enemy force accompanied by what appears to be an aircraft carrier.' And then minutes later: 'Two additional enemy ships, apparently cruisers, sighted.'

A force that size was bound to contain a carrier; and by that time, it was only 200 miles (320 km) away. It was almost within the striking range of the Nagumo Force – and they were almost within its range.

At precisely the same time one of the screening destroyers signalled that it had sighted enemy planes. More than a hundred were counted, and a frantic barrage was sent up – until someone realized the approaching aircraft were the first Air Strike, returning from Midway. Nagumo could feel all his nightmares coming true: the dilemma he had foreseen and dreaded was upon him, and he felt incompetent to cope. The enemy fleet was approaching and soon would be close enough to attack at any moment; the pre-invasion strike at Midway had failed; his carriers' decks were crowded with planes now armed with bombs for a land attack, not torpedoes for a ship attack; and the sky was full of his fighters and bombers, some in distress and all low on fuel, which had to be landed fast. The decks had to be cleared, but there were only two ways to do that: either the second wave

had to take off and attack the American fleet – but without fighter protection; or they had to go below while the first-wave fighters landed and prepared for an all-out strike – but then the entire Nagumo Force would be unprotected and vulnerable.

Nagumo decided on the all-out strike, believing that his total force was numerically superior to the enemy. Accordingly, the bombers on deck were taken back down to the hangars, their bombs removed again and replaced with torpedoes.

The planes returning from Midway began to land at 8.37 am. In their hurry, the men on the hangar-deck skimped their work and stacked the bombs they were removing anywhere; but by 8.55 am the first wave had landed safely, and their rearming and refuelling had started. Nagumo ordered his Force to head north for a while, to gain a breathing space, and simultaneously sent a message to Yamamoto, informing him of the American force's presence.

Admiral Spruance, very shortly before, had

Opposite: above A Japanese carrier at Midway circles to avoid attacks by American bombers.

Opposite: below 'Battle of Midway', by Robert Benny.

Below The Japanese heavy cruiser *Mukuma* collided with the *Mogami* and then was attacked and sunk by aircraft.

faced a similar problem and come to a similar conclusion: to attack at once. He had intercepted the first sighting signal that had been made to Midway about 5.30 am. At that moment, the *Yorktown* had a dawn patrol in the air, and she had to wait for its return; but Spruance with the *Hornet* and *Enterprise* made full speed towards the Nagumo Force. Within three hours, he reckoned, he would be within 100 miles (160 km), which was comfortable range for his fighters. By seven o'clock he had brought the range down to 170 miles (275 km), which was the absolute limit of their range – and he had decided that if he waited any longer he would probably lose his only real advantage, which was surprise. He was not a man to do things by halves, and at 7.02 am he began to fly off every aircraft he had: sixty-seven dive-bombers, twenty-nine tor-

pedo planes and twenty fighters.

The attack began disastrously. More than half the dive-bombers and exactly half the fighters failed to find the Nagumo Force because it had turned to the north. They turned the wrong way, towards the island. Two other squadrons also failed to find them, but turned to make a search in the open sea. A squadron of torpedo planes from the *Hornet* found the enemy but lost their fighter force. They attacked, but a swarm of Japanese Zero fighters dived on them and shot them all down; a few managed to fire their torpedoes, but all of them missed. Yet another squadron from the *Enterprise* found their target with their fighters, but the fighters were high up above the clouds while the bombers were below – and so were the Zeros. Ten of that squadron were shot down; four escaped, but

Sinking of a Japanese aircraft carrier, by Robert Benny.

without hitting anything. Then the *Yorktown*'s planes began to come in, and met an equally awful fate. A moment came when only fifty-four aircraft remained of the two hundred-odd the Americans possessed, and not a single hit had been scored.

Just as Nagumo made his turn to the north, there was a sudden surprise: an American submarine surfaced in the middle of his fleet. The submarine captain was as surprised as the Japanese and he hurriedly dived again, followed closely by depth-charges. However, none of them hit him, and at 9.20 am he came up again to periscope depth and fired a torpedo. The torpedo missed; the re-taliatory depth-charge missed; and the submarine escaped, pursued by a Japanese destroyer.

That incident gave the Americans the one bit of luck they needed. A squadron of dive-bombers,

flying high, observed the destroyer returning from its fruitless hunt for the submarine, and following its course they came upon the Japanese carrier fleet at a moment when the Zero fighters were far below pursuing the torpedo planes. At that very moment also – it was 10.20 am – the rearming of the Japanese bombers had been completed: they were ready and waiting for the signal to fly off for the all-out attack on the American fleet. Instead of the signal, they heard the klaxon warning.

For many of the Japanese sailors and airmen, that was the last thing they ever heard. One survivor remembered looking up and seeing, straight above him the dark silhouettes of the American bombers and then, as if in slow motion, the bombs floating gently through the air. There was a moment of ear-splitting, hellish noise – the

scream of the planes, the whistle of the bombs, the crashing explosions – and then silence. The bombers had vanished; and three of the four carriers had been mortally hit. The flagship *Akagi* had taken two bombs, one on the flight-deck, one on the midship's elevator, which drooped and twisted, the same survivor said, 'like molten glass'. The *Soryu* was hit by three bombs, the *Kaga* by four. In a few seconds, the Nagumo Force was crippled.

The bombs only started the devastation. It had happened at the moment when the carriers were most vulnerable, with planes, bombs, torpedoes, and fuel on deck and the ships headed into the wind for take-off. That wind blew on the creeping fires and raised them to a blaze which leaped from plane to plane and exploded their torpedoes. Down on the hangar-decks, flames raged through the careless random stacking of bombs; the induced explosions blew open watertight compartments; smoke, gas and fire filled the gangways; decks warped and buckled in the heat; iron ladders

The US Carrier *Yorktown* and supporting ships throw up an anti-aircraft barrage.

The Battle of Midway

4 June 1942

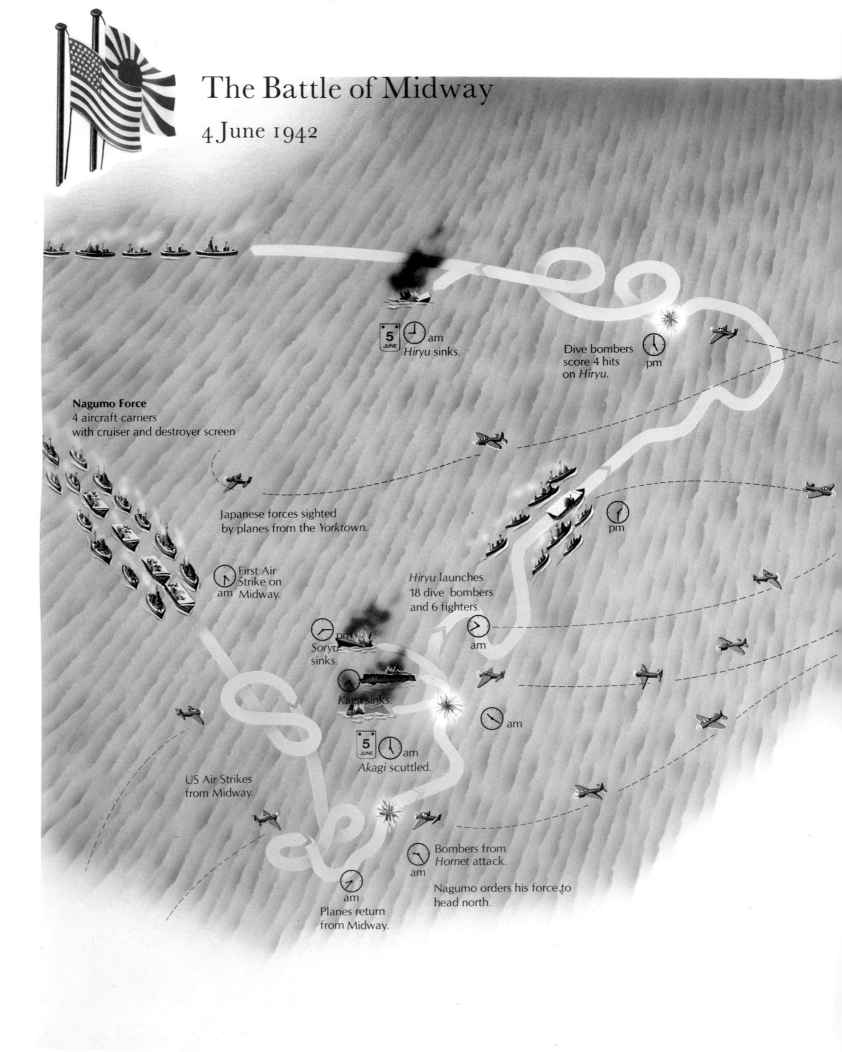

5 JUNE ⊙ am *Hiryu* sinks.

Dive bombers score 4 hits on *Hiryu*. ⊙ pm

Nagumo Force
4 aircraft carriers with cruiser and destroyer screen

⊙ pm

Japanese forces sighted by planes from the *Yorktown*.

⊙ am First Air Strike on Midway.

Hiryu launches 18 dive bombers and 6 fighters. ⊙ am

⊙ pm *Soryu* sinks.

Kaga sinks.

⊙ am

5 JUNE ⊙ am *Akagi* scuttled.

US Air Strikes from Midway.

⊙ am Bombers from *Hornet* attack.

Nagumo orders his force to head north.

⊙ am Planes return from Midway.

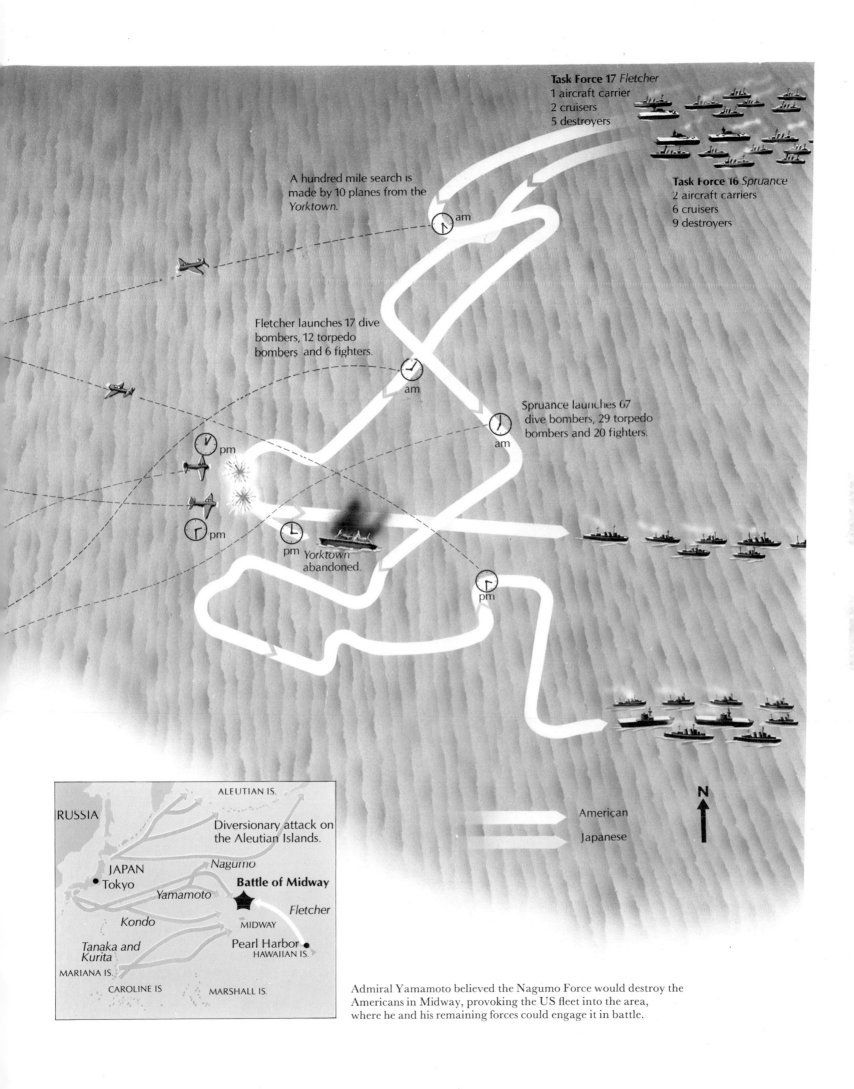

Task Force 17 *Fletcher*
1 aircraft carrier
2 cruisers
5 destroyers

Task Force 16 *Spruance*
2 aircraft carriers
6 cruisers
9 destroyers

A hundred mile search is made by 10 planes from the *Yorktown*.

Fletcher launches 17 dive bombers, 12 torpedo bombers and 6 fighters.

Spruance launches 67 dive bombers, 29 torpedo bombers and 20 fighters.

Yorktown abandoned.

ALEUTIAN IS.

RUSSIA

Diversionary attack on the Aleutian Islands.

JAPAN
Tokyo
Nagumo
Battle of Midway
Yamamoto
Fletcher
Kondo
MIDWAY
Tanaka and Kurita
Pearl Harbor
HAWAIIAN IS.
MARIANA IS.
CAROLINE IS
MARSHALL IS.

N

American

Japanese

Admiral Yamamoto believed the Nagumo Force would destroy the Americans in Midway, provoking the US fleet into the area, where he and his remaining forces could engage it in battle.

glowed red hot as men tried to climb them; in every part of the great ships men were suffocated, burnt or blown to pieces. For nine hours the vessels blazed, shuddering from time to time as new explosions tore them apart, and marking the position of the stricken fleet with vast columns of smoke. At 7.13 pm, the *Soryu* went down; twelve minutes later, the *Kaga*; and at 4.55 next morning, just before dawn, the flagship *Akagi* was scuttled. She was the first Japanese warship ever to suffer such a fate.

But Nagumo had not given up. While the *Akagi* burned, he had shifted his flag to a light cruiser, still determined to hit back if he could. He had already signalled the presence of the American fleet to Yamamoto, whose main force of thirty-eight ships was steaming through the fog that had beset Nagumo earlier. Yamamoto believed the Nagumo Force could cope with the opposition, which was still thought to include only one carrier. It was not until after his ships were hit that Nagumo learned, from a scout plane, that there were three American carriers. His next signal to Yamamoto reported not

victory but cataclysmic disaster. Yamamoto's response was to charge ahead to the rescue, increasing his speed to twenty knots through the fog. Nagumo's response was to order the biggest attack he could make from his one remaining carrier *Hiryu*.

It was a gallant effort, and it succeeded. At 10.40 am, twenty minutes after the other three carriers were hit, the *Hiryu* flew off eighteen dive-bombers and six fighters. They followed some American planes, which led them straight to the *Yorktown*. Ten of the bombers were shot down before they got there. The rest got through, and three bombs struck the *Yorktown*: the last of them went down her smokestack and put five of her six boilers out of action, bringing her to a stop. Only six of the twenty-four planes returned to their ship.

But by afternoon, the *Hiryu* had repaired and armed another sixteen planes. These were absolutely the last of the Japanese fleet. They took off, and hit the *Yorktown* again with two torpedoes. Her captain had to order his crew to abandon ship.

Meanwhile, the Americans had lost the *Hiryu*

Damage and fire control crews on the *Yorktown*. She had been hit by three bombs: one went down her funnel and put all but one of her boilers out of action.

and had been searching for her for three hours. While her last few planes were attacking the *Yorktown*, they found her. It was now for Admiral Spruance to scrape together the last of his own planes. He found twenty-four, including ten dive-bombers which had been in the air when the *Yorktown* was hit and had not been able to land on her. This final remnant found the *Hiryu* and peeled off to drop their bombs. The last few fighters of Nagumo's fleet followed them down, fighting now to save the last of their flight-decks. Three American bombers were shot to bits. The others between them dropped four bombs on the *Hiryu*, and she burst into flames.

That night, 5 June, therefore, these two great ships, the *Yorktown* and *Hiryu*, lay sinking, some 80 miles (130 km) apart. The *Yorktown* was already empty of men. In the *Hiryu* the senior officer was an admiral who had commanded two of the carriers. Ordering the men to leave her, he announced that he was solely responsible for the loss of both ships, and that he would stay on board to the end. He ordered a destroyer to torpedo and sink the wreck, and saying goodbye to his captain, the battle over, he was credited with a remark that expressed an admirably poetic approach to death: 'Let us now enjoy the beauty of the moon.'

It is not always easy to say exactly when a battle begins or ends. One might say the Battle of Midway lasted only a couple of minutes: certainly within that fraction of time when the three carriers were hit by bombs, the outcome was decided. Officially, the end was said to be two days later, 6 June, when Yamamoto signalled his fleet, 'The Midway operation is cancelled.' Yet even after that, there were further encounters. Submarines of both sides were prowling round the battle, and early one morning an American submarine sighted a column of Japanese ships retiring to the west. They sighted her too, and in taking evasive action two cruisers collided and damaged each other. Next day

Spruance's few remaining planes found them, sank one and so crippled the other that she was out of action for a year. On the same day, a Japanese submarine found the wreck of the *Yorktown*, being towed by a destroyer alongside her. She fired torpedoes which sank the destroyer and finally put an end to the *Yorktown*, which sank the next morning. These sightings by submarines were the only moments when enemy ships were in close contact. For the first time in history fleets had fought a decisive battle without ever seeing each other, at a range that began at 170 miles (275 km) and came down in the end to 80 (130 km).

Decisive it was. It had cost the Japanese four carriers, a cruiser, 250 aircraft and 3,500 lives, including those of hundreds of irreplaceable pilots. The Americans had lost one carrier, one destroyer, 150 aircraft and 307 lives. The Japanese navy never recovered. It was never able again to take the offensive, but only to defend a shrinking perimeter. Nor did Admiral Nagumo, who fought the battle, ever recover from it. Four months later he lost his command, and when at last it became very clear that his country could not win the war, he killed himself.

Yorktown crippled and burning after a second attack by torpedo bombers. Two days later a Japanese submarine sank her.

Leyte Gulf
1944

THE BATTLE of Leyte Gulf was the last of the great sea battles. Perhaps one should say the last so far; but whatever the future brings, it is hard to imagine that massed fleets of ships will ever meet again to fight at sea. It has also been called the greatest battle of all, but how does one measure greatness? In every age of fighting ships, the last battle has been the greatest. Unless one counts the motor torpedo boats at Leyte (PT boats), a larger number of ships was engaged at Jutland. But in the twenty-eight years between, ships had grown in size, and the tonnage of combat ships at Leyte Gulf was certainly bigger than ever before. So were the numbers of men, estimated overall at 280,000. Every known weapon of naval war was used, excepting mines, and in sheer destruction the battle had no rival in history. Further, it brought a new technique of war and a new word to western languages: Kamikaze.

Leyte Gulf is in the Philippine Islands – a link with the distant past, for the islands were named by Spanish explorers in honour of King Philip II who created the Armada. The Gulf is formed by three islands, Leyte in the middle, Samar in the north and Mindanao in the south. The Americans, advancing inexorably towards Japan, had assembled colossal fleets for the invasion of Leyte, more than 200 combat ships protecting some 600 transports, landing craft and supply vessels. To operate such fleets across the whole width of the Pacific needed all the American genius for large-scale organization, based on limitless industrial wealth.

Yet the fleets had one surprising weakness. Half of them were commanded by Admiral William F. Halsey, who was responsible to Admiral Nimitz, Commander-in-Chief, Pacific Fleet, based in Hawaii. The other half was commanded by Vice-Admiral Thomas C. Kinkaid, who was responsible to General Douglas MacArthur, Supreme Commander, Allied Forces, SW Pacific. The two halves had no commander in common except the Joint Chiefs of Staff thousands of miles away in Washington DC, and this lack of unity came close to losing them the battle.

Leyte Gulf is open to the east, the Pacific side of the chain of islands. Two navigable sounds give access to it from the west, the Surigao Straits in the southern corner of it, and the San Bernardino Strait on the northern side of the island of Samar. The Japanese guessed that this would be the scene of the next American landing, and almost all that was left of their navy was waiting in its bases, ready to defend it. Their strongest force, under an admiral named Kurita, was to approach by the San Bernardino Strait: it included both the super-battleships *Yamato* and *Musashi*, with three other battleships and no less than eleven heavy cruisers. Two separate weaker forces were appointed to pass through the southern strait, one close behind the other; they were commanded by two admirals named Nishimura and Shima, who oddly enough were said to have been rivals since their youth and no longer on speaking terms.

These forces were mighty in gunpower, but they

Previous pages F6Fs on the flight deck of *USS Cowpens* off the Marshall and Gilbert Islands in 1944.

Right: above Admiral William F. Halsey, commanding the Fifth Fleet.

Right: below A US carrier awaits its returning fighter planes after a Japanese air strike, by Lieutenant R. A. Genders.

had no carriers; for air protection, they depended on aircraft ashore. But there was a fourth force, which was to approach from the north beyond the islands, and this contained four carriers and two hybrid carriers, which had been converted from battleships by removing their after guns and building a short flight-deck instead. The Japanese called the whole operation 'Sho', which means victory; but it was a tragic name, for in fact they had almost despaired of victory.

The navy's Commander-in-Chief Yamamoto had been killed when the Americans ambushed an aircraft he was travelling in, by means of a broken code, and shot it down. When the new commander Toyoda was appointed in May 1944, he wrote: 'The war is drawing close to the lines vital to our national defence.' The lines he had in mind were mainly the oil-supply route from the fields the Japanese had captured early in the war. Already, American submarines had harried the tankers on that route, and in two strikes American carrier aircraft had sunk one third of the whole tanker fleet. Already, therefore, training of seamen and pilots had been drastically reduced for lack of fuel, and it was reckoned that if the whole fleet made one more sortie of 2,500 miles (4,000 km), it would be unable to move again for two months. If the Americans recaptured the Philippines, the tanker route would be gone, the Japanese war machine would collapse and her ships and planes would be useless. At all costs, Sho had to be a victory.

Above A photograph that gives some impression of the size of the American Fifth Fleet, assembled for the attack on Leyte. Almost every kind of major warship is visible.

Left Admiral Kurita, commanding the main Japanese fleet at Leyte Gulf.

A Kamikaze plane shown a split second before it crashed on the *USS Missouri*. This one did little damage, but the Kamikaze were a new and very formidable weapon, first seen at Leyte Gulf.

It was in these circumstances that the concept of Kamikaze was begun. Once before, in the year 1281, the Japanese Empire had been equally close to despair. At the command of the Mongol Emperor Kublai Khan, 3,500 ships bearing 100,000 warriors, the combined forces of China and Mongolia, had threatened the shores of Japan. The homeland had been saved when a great typhoon sank most of the enemy ships. The gods were thanked for the divine wind. Now, that story was remembered: Kamikaze means divine wind.

The name was given to a corps of pilots who were

trained to crash their aircraft into enemy ships. The concept of training men for suicide was one that many western people found hard to understand: they thought the pilots must be drugged or brainwashed in some sinister way. But they were not; on the contrary, they went to their death in a mood of ecstasy. It was really the final logical extension of the ancient idea of military glory. In every warring nation all through history, men had fought on when they had no hope of surviving, and had been admired for it. The Japanese merely took this tradition one stage further by organizing it.

Perhaps they were able to do it because their civilization was distinct from all others in the world. Few Japanese at that time had travelled outside it. It was the only world they knew, and its history was the only history. It had its own deep-rooted concepts of poetry and beauty. Moreover, its Emperor was divine; so the force of religion was added to patriotism. To many Japanese, it was unthinkable that their civilization might be destroyed by another they did not understand, and if it were destroyed they did not want to survive it. Kamikaze pilots were told before they flew off to their deaths, 'You are now as the gods, free from all earthly desires.' And evidently this was true to them. Many of the last letters they wrote home have been collected. Among them the most evocative phrases are perhaps, 'I think of springtime in Japan when I fly to crash against an enemy'; and, 'May our death be as sudden and

clean as the shattering of crystal.'

Kamikaze was the name given to the pilots, but the concept of willing death was shared by the navy for operation Sho. Indeed, the entire northern force of six carriers and their escorts was a deliberate suicide mission. Its carriers had less than half their normal complement of planes, its two hybrid carriers had none, and its pilots were so ill-trained that if they flew off they could not fly on again. There were no more naval aircraft or fully trained pilots left, so the carriers were useless and expendable. The only duty of that once-powerful

force was to sacrifice itself, to draw off one of the American fleets while the other Japanese forces fought their way into Leyte Gulf. Its commander, Rear-Admiral Ozawa, expected and intended his fleet to be sunk and himself and his men to die.

The American landing on Leyte began on 20 October. The defences crumpled under the monstrous weight of the attack, and by the afternoon of the 24th it was completed. The majority of the transports and supply ships had unloaded and gone, and the army was firmly ashore. The Japanese navy had not been able to start its approach until it was certain where the attack was coming, and the naval battle did not begin until the 23rd.

It began with a sighting by two US submarines, the *Darter* and *Dace*. What they saw in the half-light of dawn was the spectacle of Kurita's force of battleships and cruisers advancing towards them in two columns with, surprisingly, no screen of destroyers ahead. It was entering the western edge of the Philippine Islands. The submarines chose their positions with deliberate care. *Darter* fired her six forward tubes at very short range at the heavy cruiser *Atago*, which proved to be Admiral Kurita's flagship, then turned and fired her stern tubes at the next cruiser in line, the *Takao*. The *Atago* exploded and sank, the *Takao* had her rudder and two propellers blown off; Admiral Kurita and his staff had to swim for it, until a Japanese destroyer picked them up. *Dace* torpedoed a heavy cruiser in the other column, the *Maya*, which exploded, a Japanese admiral wrote, 'and when the spray and smoke had gone, nothing of her could be seen'. Thereafter, the *Darter* ran hard and fast on a coral reef, and the submarine *Dace* had to take off her crew and retire, with twice her usual complement, to Australia.

This astonishing success was reported to Admiral Halsey, who planned an air strike for the following dawn. But so did the Japanese air force based on shore. Three separate Japanese raids of fifty or sixty planes were made on a force of the light aircraft carriers east of the island of Luzon whose main job was escorting convoys. Fighters from the carriers put up a spirited defence, with general success – for the American planes were of the newest designs and the Japanese planes were old. Moreover the American pilots were fully trained. But one solitary glide-bomber got through and dropped its 550-pound (250-kg) bomb plumb on the flight-deck of the light carrier *Princeton*, which caught fire with a series of explosions. Destroyers and the cruiser *Birmingham* went alongside her to fight the fires and take off survivors. Most casualties were in the *Birmingham*, which was alongside when a final explosion blew off the *Princeton*'s stern and sprayed the hundreds of men on the cruiser's deck with steel debris. The *Princeton* had to be abandoned and torpedoed. This ignited her 100,000 gallons (450,000 lt) of aviation spirit, and she vanished in a mushroom cloud.

The Battle of Leyte Gulf

22–26 October 1944

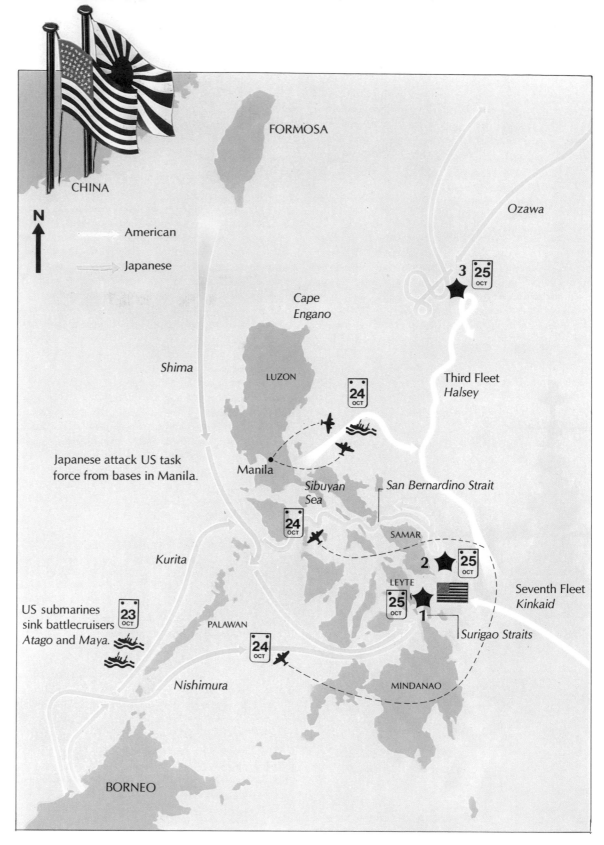

N

→ American

→ Japanese

FORMOSA

CHINA

Ozawa

Cape Engano

3 [25 OCT]

Shima

LUZON

[24 OCT]

Third Fleet
Halsey

Japanese attack US task
force from bases in Manila.

Manila

Sibuyan
Sea

San Bernardino Strait

[24 OCT]

SAMAR

2 [25 OCT]

Kurita

LEYTE

[25 OCT]

Seventh Fleet
Kinkaid

US submarines
sink battlecruisers
Atago and *Maya*.

[23 OCT]

1

PALAWAN

[24 OCT]

Surigao Straits

Nishimura

MINDANAO

BORNEO

Halsey's fleet included nine fast heavy carriers and seven light carriers, apart from the *Princeton*, and that same morning, 24 October, he launched 259 sorties against Kurita's force, which was almost 200 miles (320 km) away, approaching San Bernardino Strait. The Japanese had no air cover, because the land-based planes they depended on were busy attacking the American ships, but they had a remarkable anti-aircraft armament: there were 120 quick-firing anti-aircraft guns in each battle-ship, and a proportionate number in the cruisers; and the ships also used their big guns, with a kind of grape-shot, against aircraft 10 miles (16 km) away.

But they did not have the great advantage of American AA shells, the new electronic proximity fuse which did not need a direct hit but exploded when it passed near an aircraft. The great majority of the American planes passed through the barrage. They concentrated on the super-battleship *Musashi*, and that morning they hit her with no less than nineteen torpedoes and seventeen assorted bombs. She fell astern, and that evening she rolled over and sank, with the loss of more than half her crew of 2,300 men. The most powerful battleship ever built, excepting her sister ship *Yamato*, was overwhelmed by air attack alone. She had never sighted an enemy ship.

Other battleships were slightly damaged, and one cruiser was forced to return to base. In the evening, Kurita signalled to his commander-in-chief that he was retiring temporarily, and would 'resume the advance when the battle results of friendly units permit.' An hour or so later he received a signal which may have been made in reply: 'All forces will speed to the attack, trusting in divine guidance.'

The 'friendly units' Yamato had in mind may have been the land-based aircraft, but they had already shot their bolt in attacking the escort carriers. Or they may have been the much smaller forces that were approaching Leyte Gulf by the southern sound, the Surigao Straits. And that night in the southern sound the last traditional naval battle was fought, with no intervention from aircraft or submarines, the last time in history that a fleet advanced into battle in the traditional line ahead, and the last time its enemy used the tactic of 'crossing the T' which went back to the seventeenth century.

The first of the Japanese forces, which included two battleships, was commanded by Admiral Nishimura, the second, some distance behind, by

Admiral Shima. Nishimura entered the strait in line ahead, with four destroyers leading, apparently unaware that a vastly superior force was cruising back and forth across the far end of the sound, calmly waiting for him.

The battle began at midnight, when Nishimura was sighted by PT boats, which were lurking all along the strait under the darkness of the shores. Thirty of them attacked him with torpedoes as he passed, but all of them missed. However, they kept up almost a running commentary, reporting the enemy's progress to the big ships that were waiting.

Just before three o'clock, 25 October, Nishimura was coming to the end of the strait, beyond which were the open waters of Leyte Gulf. Picking their moment, five destroyers dashed into the strait. Within a minute and a quarter, they fired twenty-seven torpedoes. At the range they used, they had to wait eight minutes for the torpedoes to run their course. Then there was a series of explosions. The battleship *Fuso* was hit and broke in half. So were three destroyers. A few minutes later, the flagship *Yamashiro* was also hit. She slowed for a moment, but then came on again towards the waiting lines of cruisers and battleships, still hidden in the darkness, followed now by only one cruiser and one

1 The Battle of the Surigao Straits

25 October 1944
From about 3 am to 4.30 am

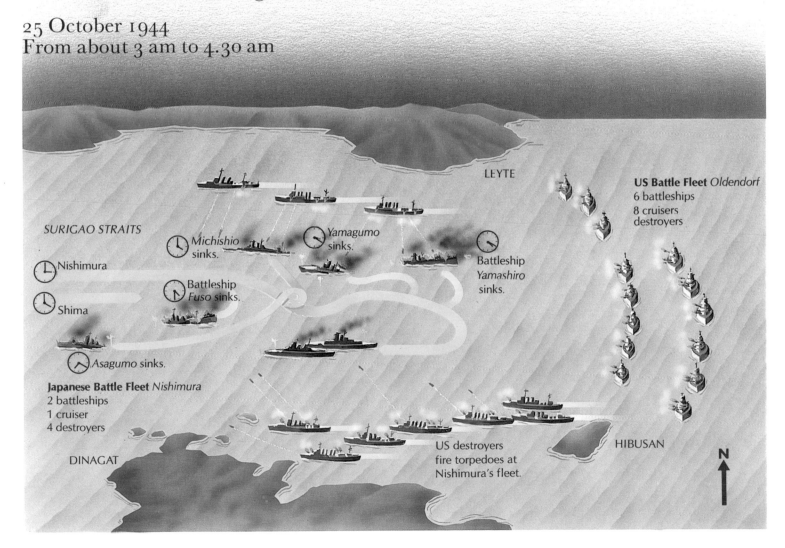

SURIGAO STRAITS

Michishio sinks.

Yamagumo sinks.

Nishimura

Battleship *Fuso* sinks.

LEYTE

Battleship *Yamashiro* sinks.

US Battle Fleet *Oldendorf*
6 battleships
8 cruisers
destroyers

Shima

Asagumo sinks.

Japanese Battle Fleet *Nishimura*
2 battleships
1 cruiser
4 destroyers

DINAGAT

US destroyers
fire torpedoes at
Nishimura's fleet.

HIBUSAN

N

destroyer. The Americans had sophisticated gunnery radar, the Japanese had only a primitive sort. So they steamed into the most shattering crossing of a T that had ever happened. At least four battleships and eight cruisers opened their broadsides.

The gunnery battle lasted little more than ten minutes. Its devastating accuracy, an American captain wrote, 'was the most beautiful sight I ever witnessed'. He had perhaps a specialized concept of beauty. 'The arched line of tracers in the darkness looked like a continual stream of lighted railroad cars going over a hill.' Then the Americans ceased fire, because their own destroyers were in the way: one, in fact, was hit by eight 'friendly' shells. But by then there was not much left to fire at. Admiral Nishimura turned back on his tracks in the end, with feelings of bewildering horror one can only imagine. Ten minutes later, his flagship *Yamashiro* turned over and sank, and he vanished with it. His cruiser *Mogami* had also turned, and was blazing in the middle of the strait. One destroyer limped away with its bow shot off.

The second southern force, under the rival Admiral Shima, entered a strait that was not only dark but black with smoke. The first thing that happened was that one of the cruisers was torpedoed by a PT boat. This was the PT boats' first success, and ironically the torpedo had been fired at a destroyer: it missed the destroyer and hit

Against the growing power of air attack, capital ships were fitted with anti-aircraft guns almost everywhere there was room for them. These are on the *USS Arkansas*.

the cruiser instead. And the first thing Shima saw was three burning wrecks. One, he correctly believed, was the cruiser *Mogami*. The others he thought must be the two battleships; but in fact the *Yamashiro* had already gone down, and what he saw was the two halves of the *Fuso*, which had broken apart and had not yet sunk. Next, on his second-rate radar, he picked up what he thought was two ships and fired sixteen torpedoes at them. But they were an island. Then he retreated, and by a strange miscalculation rammed the only thing that was plainly visible, the burning *Mogami*. He so damaged his own ship that her speed was cut to eighteen knots. He achieved nothing – but there was nothing much that he could possibly have achieved. Some American ships pursued him and passed many Japanese survivors swimming, who, to their amazement, refused to be rescued. So ended the last traditional naval battle, 'a funeral salute', the official American historian wrote, 'to a finished era of naval warfare. One can imagine the ghosts of all great admirals from Raleigh to Jellicoe standing at attention as Battle Line went into oblivion, along with the Greek phalanx, the Spanish wall of pikemen, the English longbow and the row-galley tactics of Salamis and Lepanto.'

Admiral Kinkaid, whose forces fought this battle in the south, believed all the time that the independent fleet under Admiral Halsey was watching the northern strait of San Bernardino and defending Leyte Gulf against Kurita's much more powerful force. But it was not. Halsey had gone off on a wild-goose chase of his own, and left not a single ship to guard San Bernardino.

Halsey was a heroic figure, who fought with outstanding skill and success before and after Leyte Gulf, but history has judged him very harshly for what he did that day. He would seem to have had two defects. One was an uncontrollable hatred of Japanese ('rats and barbarians') which went far beyond the normal enmity of war and was apt to warp his judgement. The other was a tendency to believe what it suited him to believe: in this case, the reports of the pilots who had attacked Kurita's force. It was common knowledge that reports of air successes were always exaggerated. Every air force in the world always claimed more than it had really achieved. Halsey, a man of long experience, must have known this as well as anyone, but he chose or pretended to believe the attack on Kurita's force had put it entirely out of action, and that he was therefore free to do what he personally wanted to do, to wipe out the Japanese carrier force that was reported in the north. He had ample force to do both. But he sent a thoroughly misleading signal to Kinkaid and tore off to the north with the whole of his colossal fleet of sixty-five powerful ships to demolish the seventeen ships of Admiral Ozawa. This was the weakened force the Japanese intended to sacrifice in order to draw the American fleet away from Leyte Gulf. Halsey fell for the bait and took it, hook, line and sinker, leaving the Strait of San Bernardino without a single ship to watch it.

Kurita, however, was very far from being out of action. The air attacks had cost him the *Musashi* and one cruiser, and that was all. He still had the *Yamato*, three other battleships and six heavy cruisers, with light cruisers and destroyer escorts. When the air attacks died away he resumed his

After the Kamikaze, dive bombers were the most effective air weapon. Here American bombers pull out of their dive after hitting a Mogami class cruiser at Leyte Gulf.

course on 25 October and passed through the San Bernardino Strait in the dark, astonished to find it unguarded. He turned south, and ahead of him Leyte Gulf was wide open.

The only ships in the way, in fact, were six escort carriers under Rear-Admiral Clifton Sprague. These small carriers, which Americans called baby flat-tops or jeep-carriers, were meant for anti-submarine patrols, guarding convoys and providing air cover for amphibious battles, and that is what they were doing by day. By night, they had nothing to do but lie well offshore, protected by destroyer screens. Apart from their aircraft, their only armament was a single 5-inch (127-mm) gun apiece.

At dawn on 25 October they had flown off fighters and torpedo planes to cover the ships in the

Gulf. Shortly after, to their amazement, they saw the pagoda-like masts of Japanese battleships on the northern horizon. They could hardly believe it – Kurita's force was not only still intact but had been let through, undetected by radar, aircraft, ships or anything else. Within a minute, shell splashes were rising round them. The range was 16 miles (26 km).

Kurita was almost equally surprised. He could not tell at that distance that the ships he saw were only escort carriers. He thought they must be Halsey's fleet. His chief of staff even claimed to identify one or two battleships, four or five fleet carriers and at least four heavy cruisers. Whoever they were, they had aircraft and Kurita had not. Nevertheless, he signalled 'General Attack'. It was not a well-chosen signal. He should have formed his

Japanese ships approaching Leyte manoeuvre to avoid American air attack.

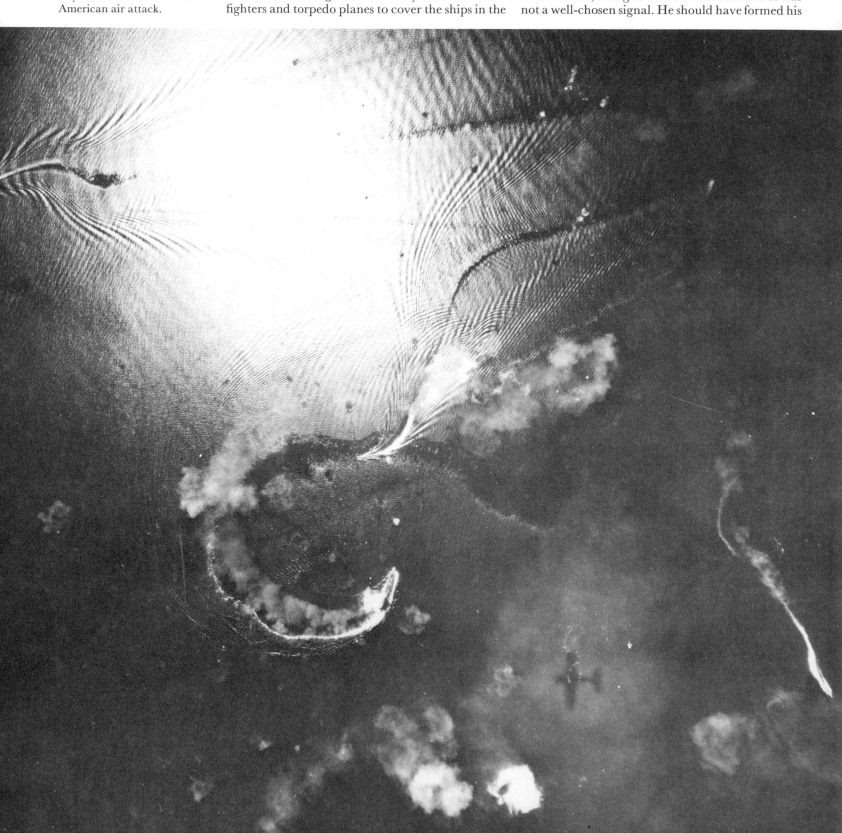

heavy ships into battle order and sent his light forces in at once for a torpedo attack. As it was, the order caused confusion in his fleet and it never got into any accepted battle formation.

Rear-Admiral Sprague's immediate reaction was to turn into the wind for launching, command his top speed which was only seventeen and a half knots, and order every operational plane to take off and every ship to make smoke. Also, within four minutes, he broadcast an urgent sighting report in plain language and an appeal for immediate help. Within another ten, every available plane had been launched from other carrier groups or diverted from other operations. The question was, would they arrive in time? All the carriers were being straddled by heavy shells and now that their planes were off they had no defence at all except their own solitary 5-inch guns, and their destroyer screen. Sprague at that moment expected none of them to last five minutes. But at 7.15 am a providential rain squall came across the sea and the carriers entered it. At the same time, he told his immediate screen of three destroyers to attack.

These three, the *Hoel*, *Heerman* and *Johnston*, each of 2,100 tons, charged out to challenge the enormous enemy fleet. (Each of *Yamato*'s three gun turrets weighed as much as a destroyer.) *Johnston*, closing at twenty-five knots to within 10,000 yards (9,000 m) of a heavy cruiser, fired all her torpedoes and hit it. It was the *Kumano*, flagship of one of the cruiser divisions, and it caught fire, lost speed and dropped out of the fight. Thereupon, *Johnston* was hit by 14-inch (356-mm) and 6-inch (152-mm) salvoes from a battleship and another cruiser. 'It was like a puppy being hit by a truck,' a survivor

2 The Battle of Samar Island

25 October 1944 From about 7 am to 9.30 am

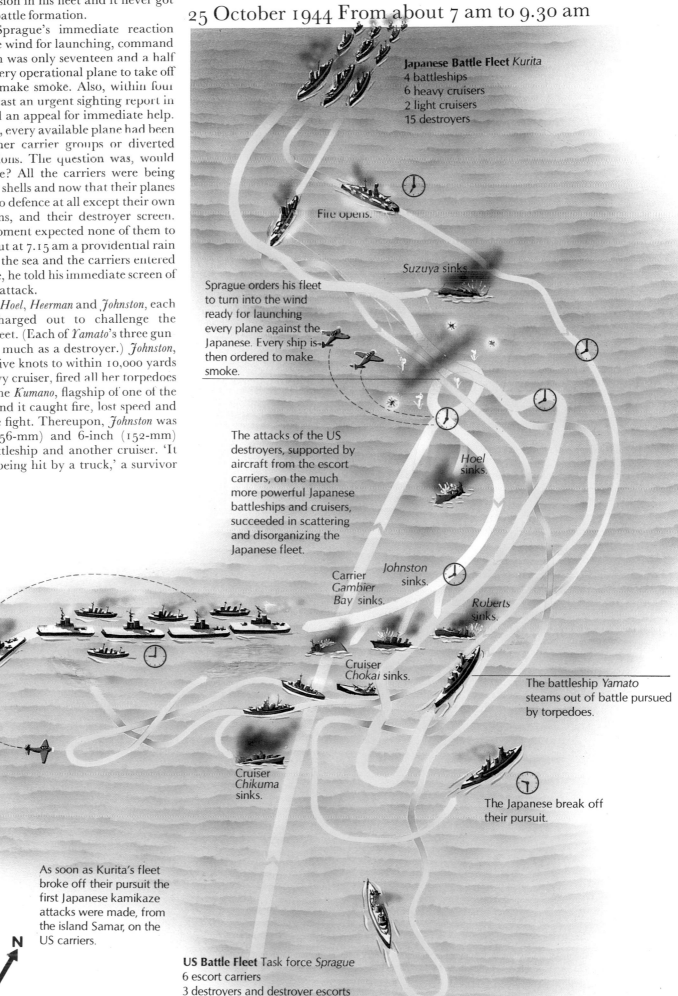

Japanese Battle Fleet *Kurita*
4 battleships
6 heavy cruisers
2 light cruisers
15 destroyers

Fire opens.

Suzuya sinks

Sprague orders his fleet to turn into the wind ready for launching every plane against the Japanese. Every ship is then ordered to make smoke.

The attacks of the US destroyers, supported by aircraft from the escort carriers, on the much more powerful Japanese battleships and cruisers, succeeded in scattering and disorganizing the Japanese fleet.

Hoel sinks.

Carrier *Gambier Bay* sinks.

Johnston sinks.

Roberts sinks.

Cruiser *Chokai* sinks.

The battleship *Yamato* steams out of battle pursued by torpedoes.

Cruiser *Chikuma* sinks.

The Japanese break off their pursuit.

As soon as Kurita's fleet broke off their pursuit the first Japanese kamikaze attacks were made, from the island Samar, on the US carriers.

N

US Battle Fleet Task force *Sprague*
6 escort carriers
3 destroyers and destroyer escorts

said. Yet she continued in action with her guns for another hour and a half before she sank.

Hoel did exactly the same, fired all her torpedoes and 500 rounds from her 5-inch (127 mm) guns and took over forty hits from everything up to 16-inch (406-mm): the big shells, being armour-piercing, went right through her without exploding but punched her full of holes. She fought for an hour with only one engine in action, but at last she also succumbed and sank.

One by one, all the other destroyers joined in this self-sacrificing defence of the carriers. Between them they damaged many ships much bigger than themselves, and above all they scattered and disorganized Kurita's fleet. The mighty *Yamato* herself, with Kurita on board, was engaged by destroyers and sighted their torpedo tracks approaching. She turned to evade them, and found herself caught between two separate spreads of torpedoes coming up astern of her, one on each side. She could not turn either way, and had to steam out of the battle, pursued by torpedoes, until they had run their course. By then she was so far away that she never caught up with the battle again, and Kurita could not command it.

All the time, of course, the Japanese were being attacked by aircraft. At any one moment, there were not very many of them, and coming in as they did from many different sources they never managed to organize a big concerted attack. But they harrassed the Japanese continually, and when they had dropped their torpedoes or bombs and even run out of machine-gun ammunition, many of them continued to make 'dry runs' merely to continue the harrassment and divert attention from the defenceless carriers.

Admiral Sprague sent out another plain-language appeal for help, saying his ships were 'in the ultimate of desperate circumstances'. Admiral Kinkaid relayed the appeal to Halsey, and learned for the first time that Halsey's force was not where it should have been and where he thought it was, but was much too far away to give any help. The light carriers were left to hide in their own smoke, dodge salvoes and shoot back with their single guns. Though most of them were hit by gunfire only one, the *Gambier Bay*, was sunk. Meanwhile, two of the Japanese cruisers went down, hit by destroyers or aircraft or both.

'At 09.25', Sprague wrote, 'my mind was occupied with dodging torpedoes when near the bridge I heard one of the signalmen yell, "Goddamit, boys, they're getting away!" I could not believe my eyes, but it looked as if the whole Japanese fleet was indeed retiring. However, it took a whole series of reports from circling planes to convince me. At best, I had expected to be swimming by this time.'

It was true. The gallant defence by nothing but destroyers and aircraft had convinced Kurita he was up against a much more powerful fleet than he really was. He was retiring to sort out his scattered ships and think things over. There was in fact nothing whatever to prevent him entering Leyte Gulf and causing havoc among the ships assembled there and the landing forces – though one must add that if he had, he would probably never have escaped again. But he had heard by radio that the attack through the southern strait had been a disaster, and oddly enough Sprague's desperate plain-language appeals for help from battleships and heavy carriers had convinced him that these ships were somewhere in the neighbourhood. He hovered around for three more hours, but then made up his mind he was heading into an ambush, and he retreated by the way he had come, through San Bernardino Strait.

A handful of destroyers, aided by aircraft, had turned back Japan's main fleet. It was a gallant action, but such self-sacrifice should never have been needed. Halsey's fleet, which should have done the job, was hundreds of miles to the north, pursuing the decoy fleet of Ozawa.

Ozawa had almost despaired of sacrificing his ships and his life, and to draw attention to himself he had launched all his aircraft to look for something to attack. Nearly all of them, being untrained for landing again on a carrier, had disappeared to airfields on the land. When Halsey found him at last he had only twenty-nine aircraft left in his six carriers, and most of them were

fighters. A carrier without its aircraft was a sitting duck. Against them Halsey took five fleet carriers, five light carriers, six battleships, eight cruisers and forty-one destroyers.

In the same dawn when Sprague sighted Kurita's battleships, Halsey's fleet was in contact with its pitiable enemy. During the night, several of his senior staff and Task Force commanders had been urging him to leave something to guard or at least to watch the Strait of San Bernardino. And most of the morning, he was deluged with signals which almost begged him to send some help to Sprague. But he could not bear to pull any ships out of the battle he had set his heart on. His only reaction was to order in a Task Force which was re-fuelling hundreds of miles away to the east. He did nothing else until ten o'clock, when he received a terse signal from Admiral Nimitz, the Commander-in-Chief, enquiring where he was. Then, or after another hour's delay, he detached a major force and sent it south. But it was fourteen hours' steaming away from Sprague, and much too late to be any help to him – too late even to intercept Kurita before he was back in the safety of the strait.

Yet the demolition of the Japanese decoy force off

Opposite: above Breech of a 16-inch gun: by Lieutenant Commander Shepler.

Opposite: below Boiler room of US battleship, by Lieutenant Commander Shepler.

Below Japanese carrier *Zuiho* under attack. She was part of Admiral Ozawa's decoy force and had entered battle almost empty of aircraft. These ships succeeded in their mission of drawing Halsey's fleet away from the main battle. *Zuiho* and three other carriers were sunk.

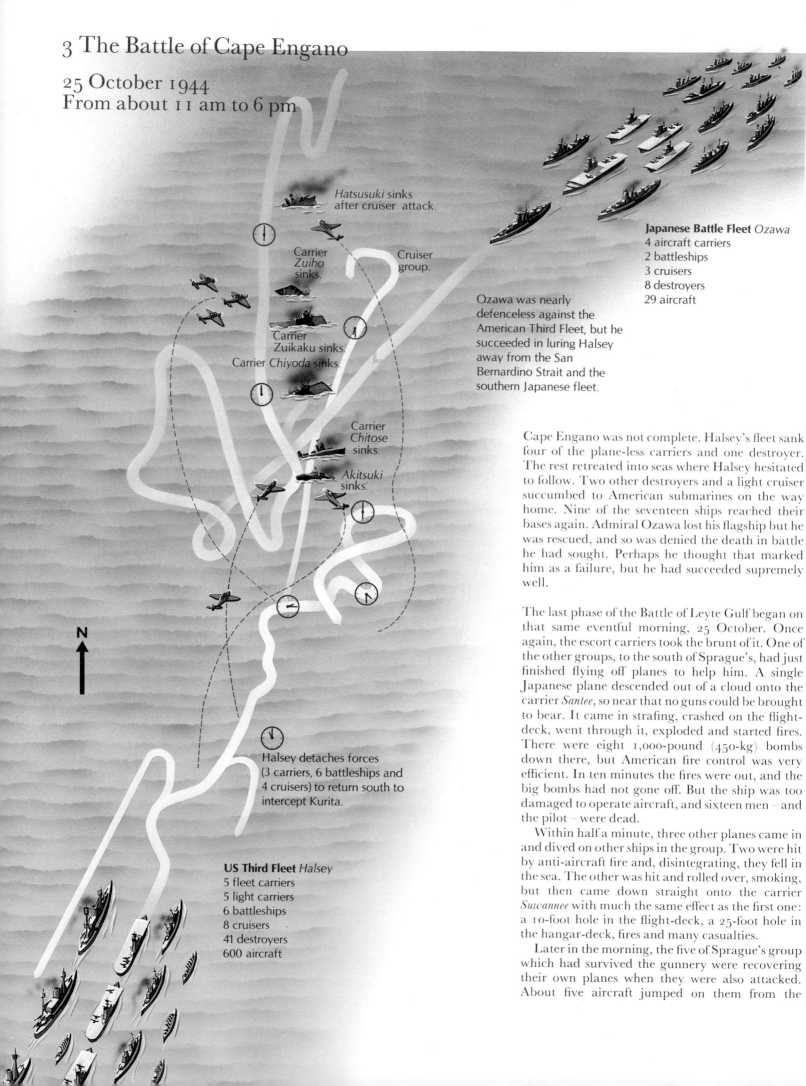

3 The Battle of Cape Engano

25 October 1944
From about 11 am to 6 pm

Hatsusuki sinks
after cruiser attack.

Carrier
Zuiho
sinks.

Cruiser
group.

Carrier
Zuikaku sinks.

Carrier *Chiyoda* sinks.

Carrier
Chitose
sinks.

Akitsuki
sinks.

Halsey detaches forces
(3 carriers, 6 battleships and
4 cruisers) to return south to
intercept Kurita.

Japanese Battle Fleet *Ozawa*
4 aircraft carriers
2 battleships
3 cruisers
8 destroyers
29 aircraft

Ozawa was nearly
defenceless against the
American Third Fleet, but he
succeeded in luring Halsey
away from the San
Bernardino Strait and the
southern Japanese fleet.

N

US Third Fleet *Halsey*
5 fleet carriers
5 light carriers
6 battleships
8 cruisers
41 destroyers
600 aircraft

Cape Engano was not complete. Halsey's fleet sank
four of the plane-less carriers and one destroyer.
The rest retreated into seas where Halsey hesitated
to follow. Two other destroyers and a light cruiser
succumbed to American submarines on the way
home. Nine of the seventeen ships reached their
bases again. Admiral Ozawa lost his flagship but he
was rescued, and so was denied the death in battle
he had sought. Perhaps he thought that marked
him as a failure, but he had succeeded supremely
well.

The last phase of the Battle of Leyte Gulf began on
that same eventful morning, 25 October. Once
again, the escort carriers took the brunt of it. One of
the other groups, to the south of Sprague's, had just
finished flying off planes to help him. A single
Japanese plane descended out of a cloud onto the
carrier *Santee*, so near that no guns could be brought
to bear. It came in strafing, crashed on the flight-
deck, went through it, exploded and started fires.
There were eight 1,000-pound (450-kg) bombs
down there, but American fire control was very
efficient. In ten minutes the fires were out, and the
big bombs had not gone off. But the ship was too
damaged to operate aircraft, and sixteen men – and
the pilot – were dead.

Within half a minute, three other planes came in
and dived on other ships in the group. Two were hit
by anti-aircraft fire and, disintegrating, they fell in
the sea. The other was hit and rolled over, smoking,
but then came down straight onto the carrier
Suwannee with much the same effect as the first one:
a 10-foot hole in the flight-deck, a 25-foot hole in
the hangar-deck, fires and many casualties.

Later in the morning, the five of Sprague's group
which had survived the gunnery were recovering
their own planes when they were also attacked.
About five aircraft jumped on them from the

clouds. Three were shot into the sea. One hit a carrier and bounced overboard, doing a lot of damage when it exploded. The last crashed through the flight-deck of the carrier *St Lo* and set off such massive explosions that great sections of the deck and elevators, and entire planes, were thrown hundreds of feet in the air. The ship blazed from stem to stern, and in half an hour she had foundered.

Naturally, it took the Americans a little time to realize that they were up against a new weapon of war, that these attacks were organized suicide. The attacks had come too late, and the Kamikaze were too few, to change the outcome of the battle. But in Japan there were endless eager volunteers. Potentially, they were a weapon of overwhelming power. These few attacks at Leyte Gulf had proved that an aircraft had ten or twenty times the chance of hitting a ship if its pilot had no thought of survival. In the later battle of Okinawa, 32 ships were sunk and 368 damaged, mostly by Kamikaze; nearly 5,000 sailors were killed and nearly 5,000 wounded. In one split second, the great fleet carrier *Bunker Hill* was made a blazing wreck by one plane that came down in a vertical dive, and 392 of her crew

were killed. No navy in the world could stand that rate of loss at the hands of a few men of ultimate determination. An official United States survey admitted that if the Kamikaze had acted 'in greater power and concentration, they might have been able to cause us to withdraw or revise our strategic plan'.

In fact, the threat of the Kamikaze did succeed in making the Americans change their strategy. The Battle of Leyte Gulf had irrevocably crippled the Japanese navy, not only by destroying so many ships, but also because possessing the Philippines gave the Americans a stranglehold on Japanese fuel supplies. Without enough oil, Japan could not continue to operate her remaining ships; nor could she keep her industrial power going.

Yet for fear of the immense casualties the Kamikaze might still have caused, the Americans hesitated to make a final sea-borne assault on Japan itself. Instead, they used their own secret weapon, the atomic bomb they dropped on Hiroshima. Air-power, in the form first used at Leyte Gulf, finally brought sea-power to a halt.

Above Last moment of a Japanese destroyer and her crew.

Epilogue

Opposite A3 Polaris missile being test-launched from a submerged submarine.

Left The Polaris submarine *HMS Resolution.*

ALF A LONG life-time has passed since Leyte Gulf, and brought the greatest changes since gunnery began at the time of the Spanish Armada. With guns, the striking range of ships was first a matter of yards, then of miles, and finally, after three centuries and a half, of tens of miles. Carrier aircraft increased it suddenly to hundreds of miles. Now guided missiles have probably made it thousands, and electronics can do all that the Kamikaze pilots did. Destructive power has increased even more abruptly. The most powerful missile at the Armada was the 50-pound iron shot. The biggest naval shell ever fired had little more than one ton of high explosive. Now warheads are measured in kilotons and megatons. Scientific destruction is evolving all the time, and nobody would dare to predict its future.

Yet navies still exist. The British, who were supreme at sea so long, were economically crippled by the Second World War, and can only afford a small but efficient navy. They have also lost the national will for power. As a world-wide force at sea, they have therefore followed their ancient rivals, the Spanish, the Dutch and the French, to oblivion; and supremacy at sea has passed to the new and perilous rivalry of Americans and Russians.

The capital ships of these new navies are aircraft carriers and nuclear submarines. Carriers have their uses in local areas of rivalry, if only because their presence is a statement of national interest in the area. So long as one of the rival navies has them, the other has to have them too. But all of them can be watched from above, wherever they are, by the satellites of the other side, and it seems unlikely they will ever fight the battle they were designed for. Like the Dreadnoughts in their era, the only practical use of the carriers in the future will be in simply existing, not in fighting; because if they were ever allowed to fight, their battle would probably trigger an all-out nuclear war, which no warship on the surface of the sea could expect to survive.

At present, the nuclear submarine is the only warship which might survive for a while in an all-out war. Perhaps Leyte Gulf was the last great sea-battle: one can only hope so. But it is possible to imagine another, fought between nuclear submarines hunting each other far down in the blackness of the ocean depths, long after their own bases and everything on the surface has been destroyed.

Acknowledgments

Photographs were supplied or reproduced by kind permission of the following (page numbers in italics indicate colour pictures):

BBC Hulton Picture Library 82 top, 83 bottom, 90 top, 99 top

Bibliothèque Nationale, Paris *11, 12*, 68 bottom

Bildarchiv Preussicher Kulturbesitz *114 top*

British Library 14–15

British Museum *1, 10 top, 14 top, 25 bottom*

City Museum, Plymouth *24 bottom* (photo Tom Molland)

Cooper-Bridgeman Library *28, 38–9*

The Master and Fellows of Corpus Christi College, Cambridge *16* (cccc Ms 16 f. 52r)

Crown Copyright *181* (photo MARS)

e.t. archive *78 bottom, 114 bottom*

Fitzwilliam Museum, Cambridge *6–7* (Ms Marlay Add. I f. 86)

Giraudon *80–1*

John Hamilton *128–9, 144 top and bottom, 145*

Hamlyn Picture Library *75 top, 92–3* (photo Graham Portlock)

Robert Harding Associates *58 bottom, 70 bottom left*

Cecil Higgins Art Gallery, Bedford *59 bottom* (photo Hawkley Studios)

Michael Holford *9 bottom, 10 bottom*

Richard Hough *93*

Robert Hunt *91 top*, 98 left, *100–1, 116 bottom, 118*, 119 bottom, *122, 179*

Imperial War Museum 103, 111 bottom, 115 bottom, 116 top, *117 top* (photo e.t. archive) 117 bottom, 123, 126 (photo MARS), *127* (photo Cooper-Bridgeman Library), 136–7 (photo MARS), 140, *endpapers*

ISEI *94* (photo Memorial Picture Gallery Meiji Shrine)

Erich Lessing, Magnum *112–3*

Lady Lever Art Gallery *31 bottom* (photo Cooper-Bridgeman Library)

Mansell Collection *71, 90 bottom* (photo Hamlyn Picture Library) 111 top, 146 top, 159 right

Ministry of Defence *124–5* (photo Michael Holford)

Morison History Project 152, 167 bottom

Musée de Versailles *84–5* (photo Musées Nationaux)

National Army Museum *49*

National Maritime Museum 13 bottom, *17, 21, 25*

top, 27, 29, 30, 31 top, 32–3, 34–5, 37 top and bottom, 39 right, *40–1, 42–3, 44–5*, 46, 47, *48 top left and top right*, 50 bottom, *51 top and bottom, 54, 55, 56–7, 58 top, 59 top, 60 top*, 62 top (photo Robert Hunt) and bottom, *64, 65, 66–7, 68 top, 69 top and bottom left*, bottom right, *70 top, 74–5* (photo e.t. archive), *77 bottom* (photo A. C. Cooper), *79, 85 top*, 86, *87, 98–9* (photo Derek Bayes), *104–5* (photo Derek Bayes), *106, 107 bottom* (photo Picturepoint) *110, 131, 132, 146–7*, 150–51

National Portrait Gallery *36 top, 48 bottom, 50 top, 83 top*, 102, *115 top*

Niedersächsisches Landesmuseum, Landesgalerie, Hannover *36 bottom* (photo Hans Nolter)

Nelson Museum *77 top*

Peter Newark Western Americana *82 bottom, 105 right, 156 bottom, 158–9*

Picturepoint *18–19*

Popperfoto 130, 133, 135, 136 top, 148, 153, *169, 172*

Prado, Madrid *18 left*

Private Collection *2–3* (photo Cooper-Bridgeman Library)

Roger-Viollet 92 bottom

Scheepvaart Museum, Amsterdam *40 bottom*

Science Museum *9 top* (photo Cooper-Bridgeman Library)

Siena, Archivio di Stato *20* (photo Scala)

Syndication International 149

Tiroler Landesmuseum Ferdinandeum, Innsbruck *22–3*

US Navy *141* (photo Robert Hunt), 154, 155 top and bottom (photo MARS), 156 top (MARS), 157 (MARS), 162 (MARS), 163, *164–5* (MARS), 166 top, and *bottom*, 167 top, 168, *172–3* (MARS), 174 (MARS), *176 top and bottom, 177, 180* (MARS)

Vaticano, Musei Vaticani *8* (photo Scala)

Victoria and Albert Museum *88–9* (photo A. C. Cooper), *91 bottom* (photo A. C. Cooper)

Victory Collection, Portsmouth Royal Naval Museum *78 above*

Weidenfeld and Nicolson Archives 13 top, *24 top*, 26, *76 top, centre and bottom, 138–9*

Worshipful Society of Apothecaries *32 top*

Picture research by Caroline Lucas

Index